Frommer's

# Amsterdam day BY day®

5th Edition

by Donald Strachan

# Contents

Published by:

**Frommer Media LLC**



ISBN: 978-1-62887-659-8 (print); 978-1-62887-660-4 (ebk)

Editorial Director: Pauline Frommer
Editor: Alexis Lipsitz Flippin
Production Editor: Erin Geile
Photo Editor: Meaghan Lamb
Compositor: Lissa Auciello-Brogan
Photo Research Interns: Henry Lin-David & Jill Sakowitz
Cartographer: Andy Dolan

Front cover photos, left to right: Bicycle with yellow flowers © Summer loveee / Shutterstock; Tour in the Rijksmuseum © Salvador Maniquiz / Shutterstock.com; Typical Dutch row houses © Adisa / Shutterstock.

Back cover photo: A lovely day on a bridge in Amsterdam overlooking a canal © Anton Havelaar / Shutterstock.

For information on our other products and services, please go to Frommers.com/contactus.

Frommer's also publishes its books in a variety of electronic formats. Some content that appears in print may not be available in electronic formats.

Manufactured in China

5 4 3 2 1

## About This Guide

Organizing your time. That's what this guide is all about.

Other guides give you long lists of things to see and do and then expect you to fit the pieces together. The Day by Day guides are different. These guides tell you the best of everything, and then they show you how to see it *in the smartest, most time-efficient way*. Our authors have designed detailed itineraries organized by time, neighborhood, or special interest. And each tour comes with a bulleted map that takes you from stop to stop.

Hoping to admire some van Goghs, or buy some tulip bulbs to take back home? Planning to pedal a canal or two or take a whirlwind tour of the very best that Amsterdam has to offer? Whatever your interest or schedule, the day by Days give you the smartest routes to follow. Not only do we take you to the top attractions, hotels, and restaurants, but we also help you access those special moments that locals get to experience—those "finds" that turn tourists into travelers.

The Day by Days are also your top choice if you're looking for one complete guide for all your travel needs. The best hotels and restaurants for every budget, the greatest shopping values, the wildest nightlife—it's all here.

Why should you trust our judgment? Because our authors personally visit each place they write about. They're an independent lot who say what they think and would never include places they wouldn't recommend to their best friends. They're also open to suggestions from readers. If you'd like to contact them, please send your comments our way at feedback@frommers.com, and we'll pass them on.

Enjoy your Day by Day guide—the most helpful travel companion you can buy. And have the trip of a lifetime.

## About the Author

**Donald Strachan** is a travel journalist who has written for publications worldwide, including *National Geographic Traveler, The Guardian, Sunday Telegraph,* CNN.com, and many others. He has also written several Frommer's guidebooks, including *London Day by Day* and *Frommer's Rome, Florence & Venice.* He lives in London, England.

## An Additional Note

Please be advised that travel information is subject to change at any time—and this is especially true of prices. We therefore suggest that you write or call ahead for confirmation when making your travel plans. The authors, editors, and publisher cannot be held responsible for the experiences of readers while traveling. Your safety is important to us, however, so we encourage you to stay alert and be aware of your surroundings.

## Heart Ratings, Icons & Abbreviations

Every hotel, restaurant, and attraction listing in this guide has been ranked for quality, value, service, amenities, and special features using a **heart-rating system.** Hotels, restaurants, attractions, shopping, and nightlife are rated on a scale of zero hearts (recommended) to three hearts (exceptional). In addition to the heart-rating system, we also use a kids **icon** to point out the best bets for families. Within each tour, we recommend cafes, bars, or restaurants where you can take a break. Each of these stops appears in a shaded box marked with a coffee-cup-shaped bullet.

## Frommers.com

Frommer's travel resources don't end with this guide. Frommer's website, **www.frommers.com,** has travel information on more than 4,000 destinations. We update features regularly, giving you access to the most current trip-planning information and the best airfare, lodging, and car-rental bargains. You can also listen to podcasts, connect with other Frommers.com members through our active-reader forums, share your travel photos, read blogs from guidebook editors and fellow travelers, and much more.

## A Note on Prices

In the "Take a Break" and "Best Bets" sections of this book, we have used a system of dollar signs to show a range of costs for 1 night in a hotel (the price of a double-occupancy room) or the cost of an entree at a restaurant. Use the following table to decipher the dollar signs:

| Cost | Hotels | Restaurants |
|---|---|---|
| $ | under $130 | under $15 |
| $$ | $130–$200 | $15–$30 |
| $$$ | $200–$300 | $30–$40 |
| $$$$ | $300–$395 | $40–$50 |
| $$$$$ | over $395 | over $50 |

## How to Contact Us

In researching this book, we discovered many wonderful places—hotels, restaurants, shops, and more. We're sure you'll find others. Please tell us about them, so we can share the information with your fellow travelers in upcoming editions. If you were disappointed with a recommendation, we'd love to know that, too. Please write to: Support@FrommerMedia.com.

# 15 Favorite **Moments**

# 15 Favorite Moments

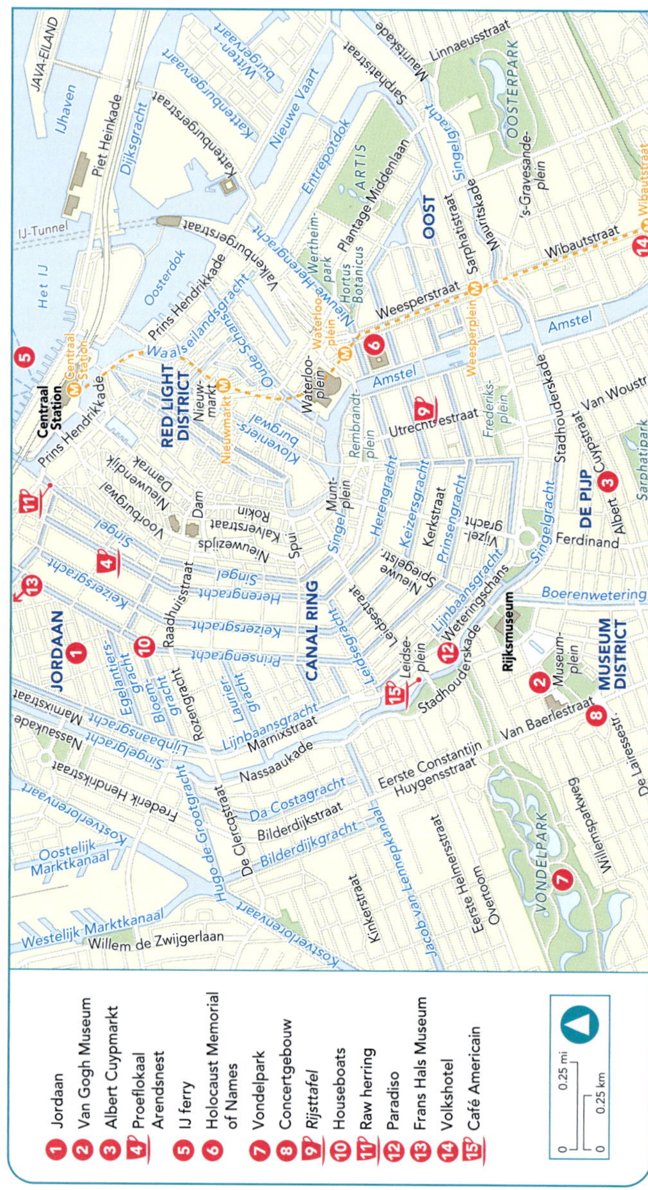


Previous page: Colorful homes and houseboats line an Amsterdam canal.

**Amsterdam is a special place.** It has some of the most beautiful architecture in the world, a history of triumph and tragedy, and in the 21st century, a vibrant multiethnic community. Despite its pride in its roots, this is not a city that lives in the past. Innovative new buildings go up at a rapid rate, the restaurant and nightlife scene is ever-changing, and culturally it's open to (almost) anything. Here are a few of our favorite Amsterdam moments. Experience some of these and you'll begin to know this wonderful city.

*Houseboats along a canal in the Jordaan district.*

1 **Strolling in the Jordaan,** no matter the weather, to discover tree-fringed canals, narrow cobbled streets, gabled houses, and houseboats. Then stop for a coffee and some of the famous apple cake at **Winkel 43.** *See p 55.*

2 **Admiring brushstrokes at the Van Gogh Museum** late in the afternoon just before the museum closes. That's when the usually crowded galleries are a little emptier, and you get the chance to admire Vincent's unique technique without being jostled. *See p 15.*

*Albert Cuypmarkt street-market stalls.*

3 **Heading down to the Albert Cuypmarkt** early in the morning as the stalls on this long street are being laid out for a day of frantic shopping and street food. Grab an outdoor table at one of the many cafes and take it all in. *See p 78.*

4 **Working your way through the biggest range of Dutch beers you'll ever encounter** at Proeflokaal Arendsnest. More than 50 are on tap, and that's before we start counting the bottled beers in its well-stocked fridge. *See p 111.*

5 **Drinking in the view of the IJ waterway and its gleaming 21st-century architecture** from one of the free ferries that ply between Centraal Station and Amsterdam-Noord, all day and for most of the night. Sunset is the ideal crossing time, and while you're over in Noord, discover some of Amsterdam's hottest places to eat. *See p 166.*

6 **Pausing in solemn horror at the Holocaust Memorial of Names,** taking in the enormity of the Holocaust's impact in the Netherlands. *See p 66.*

*Frans Hals Museum in Haarlem.*

7 **Picnicking in Vondelpark** on a sunny afternoon feels like being a million miles from the city. The English-style park is an echo of Amsterdam's surrounding countryside. You'll hear (and maybe see) the bright-green parakeets that have made the park their home, but do watch out for cyclists. *See p 83.*

8 **Dressing up for a concert at the Concertgebouw,** the majestic neoclassical concert hall on Museumplein. The acoustics and classical repertoire are among the best in Northern Europe. *See p 120.*

9 **Tucking into a rijsttafel,** the iconic sharing menu of Amsterdam's Dutch-Indonesian restaurants, where chefs show off their mastery of 20 or more traditional dishes. Among our favorites are **Blauw** (p 98) and **Tujuh Maret** (p 103).

10 **Peeking at the houseboats,** at eye level as you pedal a canal bike around the Canal Ring, shows you Amsterdam from a different perspective. *See p 87.*

11 **Eating raw herring with pickles and chopped onions** at Stubbe's Haring is all about sampling a delicacy held dear to Dutch hearts. Don't dangle the fish by its tail over your mouth—it's considered bad manners. Chop it up and eat it with a fork instead. *See p 103.*

12 **Catching a gig at Paradiso,** a legendary Amsterdam live music venue for almost 60 years, and enjoying the vibe of the contemporary city at play. *See p 121.*

13 **Discovering an unparalleled Frans Hals collection** along the pretty lanes of Haarlem. It's only a short hop by train from central Amsterdam to one of Europe's great art collections, which is displayed inside a Golden Age building. *See p 142.*

14 **Soaking weary muscles in a rooftop hot tub with a view,** at the Volkshotel, then popping down one floor for a cocktail on the terrace of the hotel's buzzy bar-restaurant, **Canvas.** *See p 138.*

15 **Living the Americain Dream** over coffee amid the Art Nouveau and Art Deco ambience of the Amsterdam American hotel's Café Americain. Guests will be relieved to learn that service has improved considerably since one postwar Dutch wag dubbed the waiters here "unemployed knife throwers." *See p 89.*

*Canvas restaurant at the Volkshotel.*

# 1 The Best Full-Day Tours

# The Best in One Day

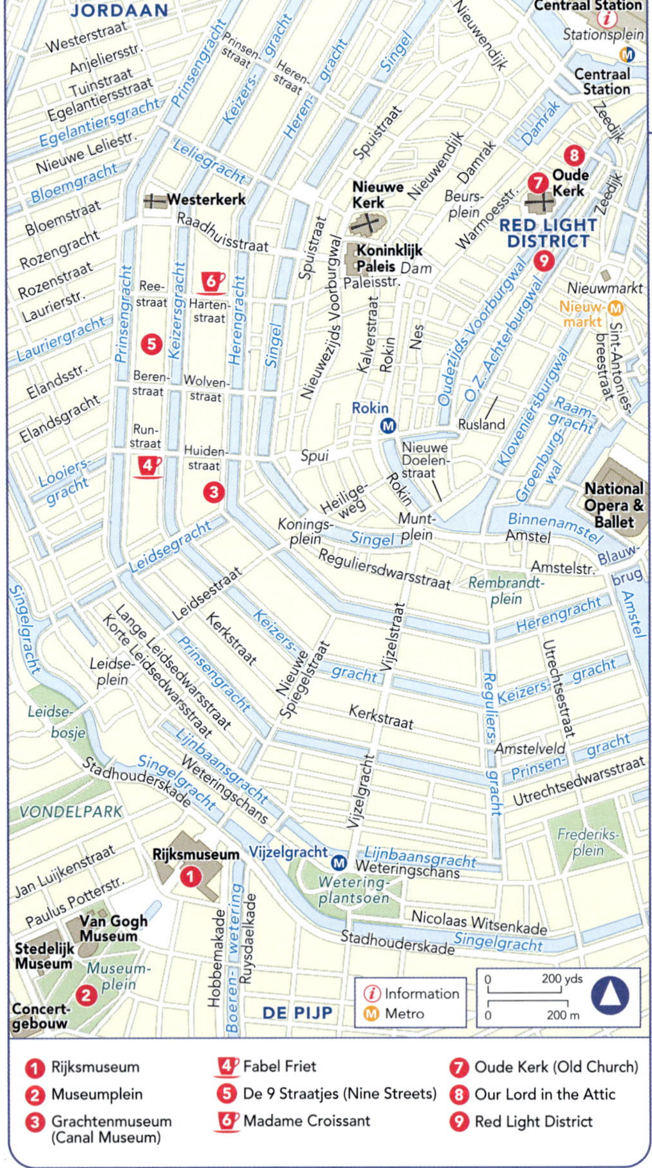


1 Rijksmuseum
2 Museumplein
3 Grachtenmuseum (Canal Museum)
4 Fabel Friet
5 De 9 Straatjes (Nine Streets)
6 Madame Croissant
7 Oude Kerk (Old Church)
8 Our Lord in the Attic
9 Red Light District

*Previous page: Rembrandt's* The Night Watch *at the Rijksmuseum.*

**In the 17th century, Amsterdam was one of the most powerful cities** in the world, when it experienced a period of great wealth and worldwide expansion. Understanding this history, the Dutch Golden Age, is vital to capturing the essence of the city, so today's the day for seeing the very best—and having plenty of memorable experiences along the way. START: **Tram 1, 2, 7, 12, 17, or 19 to Rijksmuseum.**

*Nighttime view of the Rijksmuseum.*

1 ♥♥♥ **Rijksmuseum.** Opened in 1855, this is the world's biggest repository of Dutch Golden Age treasures, four sprawling floors in a redbrick monolith designed by architect Pierre Cuypers (who also designed **Centraal Station;** p 30). A 21st-century refurb spectacularly spruced up the stained glass and neo-Gothic wall art in the central **Voorhal (Great Hall)** ♥♥, but the layout remains a little confusing. All the famous **Dutch Old Masters** ♥♥♥ hang together in the Gallery of Honour on the second floor, which inevitably gets crowded; our advice is to arrive early and begin here, before moving on to quieter parts of the collection. Around 2.7 million people visit this museum annually, and they all want to see Rembrandts galore, especially *The Night Watch*, and the wonderful works by Jan Vermeer and Jan Steen, so patience is key. Vermeer's *The Milkmaid* (1660) and Steen's *The Merry Family* (1668) are mesmerizing, as is Gerard van Honthorst's *The Merry Fiddler* (1623), so bear with the crowds.

There's much variety in the rest of the museum. Of particular note are the galleries on Floor 2, which contextualize Dutch art within the national struggle for independence from Spain, which was also an important root of later Dutch colonialism. Tucked away on Floor 3, and always quiet, **1900–1950 Galleries** ♥ showcase the

## The I amsterdam City Card

This might be one of Europe's best-value sightseeing cards. Amsterdam museums can be pricey—admission fees of 15€ to 20€ per person are not unusual. The **I amsterdam** card provides free entry into almost every major one, including the **Rijksmuseum** (which you'll need to prebook), as well as free travel on public trams, metro, and buses, but not NS trains (p 163). It entitles cardholders to a free canal cruise; free 24-hour bike rental; discounts on last-minute theater tickets and some experiences; and free admission to attractions outside Amsterdam, including museums in **Haarlem** (p 141). The only "major" sights not currently included are the **Anne Frank Huis** (p 13) and the **Van Gogh Museum** (p 15). The card really comes into its own for culture-packed, multiday stays. It costs 65€ for 24 hours, 90€ for 48 hours, 108€ for 72 hours, and 123€ for 96 hours. For more details or to buy online—choose a physical card to be collected from the I amsterdam store in Central Station (p 31) or use the app—go to www.iamsterdam.com.

optimism of De Stijl and 1930s Neorealism, and the subsequent despair of 1940s Fascism.

Lines are usually long, so reserve a ticket online before your visit or turn up promptly at opening. And—like everywhere else in Amsterdam—watch out for the bicyclists who stream through the museum's underpass. 🕓 *2½ hr. Museumstraat 1. www.rijksmuseum.nl/en.* ☎ *020/674-7000. Admission 25€ adults, free for kids 18 and under. Daily 9am–5pm. Tram: 1, 2, 7, 12, 17, or 19 to Rijksmuseum.*

**2** ♥ **Museumplein.** After the intensity of the Rijksmuseum, take a breather in the open space of Museumplein, home to the others in Amsterdam's triumvirate of great art museums, the **Van Gogh** (p 15) and the **Stedelijk** (p 21). The elaborate facade of the **Royal Concertgebouw** (p 120) faces the Rijksmuseum across the piazza, which buzzes with buskers, food vendors, cafes, and public artworks. In winter, the area in front of the Rijksmuseum is transformed into an ice rink. 🕓 *30 min. Museumplein. Tram: 2, 5, or 12 to Museumplein.*

**3** ♥♥♥ **Grachtenmuseum (Canal Museum).** Take the tram to the Grachtengordel (Canal Ring) to an elegant mansion housing the Canal Museum. This excellent place helps you understand why Amsterdam looks the way it does (spoiler: It's all built on wooden piles driven deep into the subsoil) and how it got here—and it does so by means of a genuinely creative self-guided audio-visual tour. "Tours" depart every 10 minutes to prevent crowding. First, a sound-and-light show centers on a large model of the city as it was 400 years ago: booming, grim, and overcrowded, with a

*An audio tour in the Grachtenmuseum.*

serious hygiene problem. Growth became imperative but seemed almost impossible because of the surrounding waters. The planning and engineering challenges of building a handsome ring of three canals are described in lively detail via short films, immersive wall visuals, and interactive models. It's a very entertaining introduction to the city. *45 min. Herengracht 386. grachten.museum/en. 020/ 421-1656. Admission 17.50€ adults, 9.50€ ages 6–17. Mon noon–5pm, Tues–Sun 10am–5pm. Tram: 2, 12, or 17 to Koningsplein.*

4 ♥ **Fabel Friet.** Double-cooked, chunky Dutch fries are an Amsterdam art form. This is one of the best, with a menu of toppings that includes mayo (the classic), curry, and peanut sauce. Lines are often long around lunchtime, so arrive just after the peak. *Runstraat 1. www.fabelfriet.nl. 020/303-1422. $.*

5 ♥♥ **De 9 Straatjes (Nine Streets).** One of the joys of Amsterdam is just to roam, so try not to succumb to the temptation to get through your travel checklist

*Shoppers on De 9 Straatjes (Nine Streets).*

*Interior of Our Lord in the Attic museum.*

at breakneck speed. This compact block of streets, just north of the Canal Museum (3), runs alongside and crosses the city's prettiest canals, Herengracht, Keizersgracht, and Prinsengracht. With boutiques and bars everywhere, it can get busy; but even here, a little peace is only ever just around the corner. *1 hr. de9straatjes.nl/en.*

6 ♥ **Madame Croissant.** Let's hope you haven't overdone the fries: Croissants with savory (brie cheese, Serrano ham) and sweet or fruit fillings are made fresh and beautifully presented. *Hartenstraat 29H. www.madame-croissant.de/en. No phone. $.*

## Amsterdam Facts & Figures

Amsterdam has 930,000 permanent residents and receives almost a million visitors each month, who can choose between more than 70 museums. Much of the city is under sea level; its inhabitants own more than 1.2 million bicycles and encompass 179 different nationalities or ethnicities. Amsterdam has 165 canals spanned by about 1,200 bridges—the Grachtengordel (Canal Ring) was listed as a World Heritage Site by UNESCO in 2010. The city has eight functioning windmills and owns 22 paintings by Rembrandt.

## The Dutch Royal Family

The Kingdom of the Netherlands is a constitutional monarchy recognized in 1815 at the Congress of Vienna, after the first defeat of Napoleon, whose forces had contributed to ending two centuries of the Dutch Republic (1579–1795). Willem-Alexander was invested as King of the Netherlands on April 30, 2013—on what was Queen's Day—when his mother Queen Beatrix abdicated in his favor. He is married to Spanish Queen Máxima, and they have three daughters, Catharina-Amalia (heir and Princess of Orange), Alexia, and Ariane. The Dutch Royal Family is the principal branch of the European House of Orange-Nassau, which is why the Dutch always wear orange for national celebrations (and sports). You can visit the King's official home, the **Koninklijk Paleis** (p 29, 3), when it is not being used for state events and ceremonies. To learn more about the family and its modern-day role, see www.royal-house.nl.

7 ♥♥ **Oude Kerk (Old Church).** Now put to both religious and secular use, this late-Gothic, triple-nave church is Amsterdam's oldest building. It was begun in 1250 and completed with the extension of the bell tower in 1566. The exterior is encrusted with 17th- and 18th-century houses, and its barnlike interior was stripped of all its adornment in the Alteration of 1578, when Catholicism was suppressed. Rembrandt's beloved first wife was buried below tombstone 29K, in the transept chapel, which bears the simple inscription: SASKIA 19 JUNI 1642. Of particular interest in a typically spartan interior are the magnificent 1742 organ, regularly used for recitals; 16th-century stained glass windows, restored in 2025; and an intricate handpainted "wallpaper" decorating the **Mirror Room** ♥. *30 min. Oudekerksplein 23. oudekerk.nl/en. ☎ 020/625-8284. Admission 13.50€ adults, 7€ students and ages 13–17, 3.50€ kids 6–12. Mon–Sat 10am–6pm; Sun 1–5:30pm. Closed Jan 1 , Dec 25, and when exhibitions rotate. Tram: 4 or 14 to Dam.*

8 ♥♥♥ **Our Lord in the Attic.** After the Alteration (p 38), Protestants were allowed to worship in public, but Amsterdam's Catholics had to attend services in semi-secret, including here, in one of the last surviving "attic churches" (which are exactly as they sound). It's an extraordinary piece of history. *45 min. See p 39,* 4.

9 ♥ **Red Light District.** A step away from these two churches and you're immersed in the seedy underbelly of Amsterdam's Red Light District. For more, see p. 44. *20 min. Dusk is the best time to visit; although it's technically "open" 24/7, the neighborhood's bars must close by 2am. Metro: Nieuwmarkt.*

# The Best in Two Days

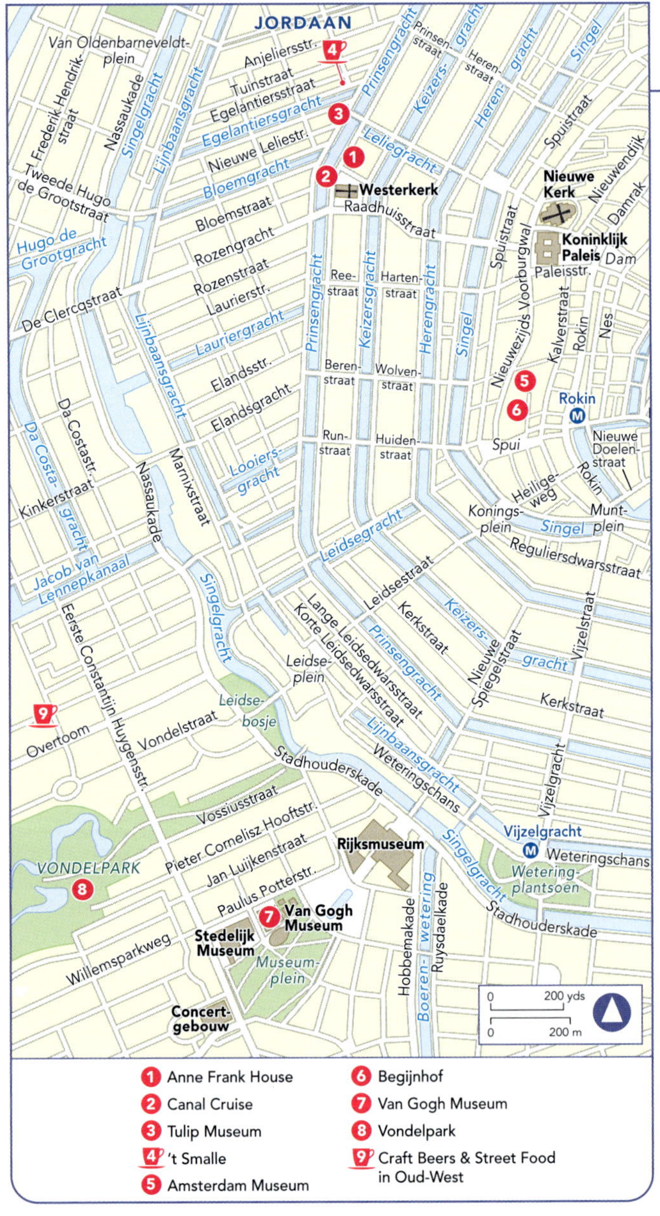

**Amsterdam is famous for many things** apart from canals and churches, including Anne Frank and Van Gogh, who bookend this busy second day in the city center. A boat ride, tulips, and Amsterdam's prettiest green space will help you dig further into the city and its residents' psyche. START: **Tram 13 or 17 to Westermarkt.**

*The Secret Annex to-scale model in the Anne Frank House museum.*

**1 ♥♥♥ Anne Frank House.** You must buy tickets online before your trip; you will not get in otherwise. Every Tuesday, time slots are issued for visits 6 weeks later. This is one of Amsterdam's most popular sights, and (obviously) space is very limited. Tragically, the incarceration of 13-year-old Anne Frank and her Jewish family during the Nazi occupation of Amsterdam would have gone largely unmarked had she not written of her time in the so-called Secret Annex, in a diary that was published by her father after her death. Otto Frank took his family and four other Jewish refugees into hiding behind his jam-making factory on July 6, 1942; they remained there for 761 days until they were betrayed to the Nazis and deported, Anne ultimately to Bergen-Belsen in Germany, and her parents to Auschwitz-Birkenau in Poland. Along with her sister Margot, Anne died of typhus a few months before Liberation. Only their father survived the war.

The claustrophobic secret rooms behind the bookcase where the family hid carry sad reminders of their life there: the posters Anne put up to decorate her bedroom; the height marks against the wall; the steep, creaking stairs. Narrated soundbites from her diary and heartrending words from her father augment the somber atmosphere. Despite the crowds, this haunting museum has the power to silence everyone. If you are unsure how to introduce children to this upsetting story, check the museum's YouTube channel, which includes a vlog-style serialization of her diary. *90 min. Prinsengracht 263–267 (entrance in Westermarkt). www.annefrank.org/en. ☎ 020/556-7105. Admission 16€ adults, 7€ kids 10–17; no children ages 9 and under. Daily 9am–10pm (closes 5pm on national holidays). Closed Yom Kippur. Tram: 13 or 17 to Westermarkt.*

**2 ♥♥ Canal Cruise.** Admittedly, it's all a bit cheesy, but a canal cruise is still the best way to see corners of the city you'll easily miss from dry land. Many cruises loop northwards from the Canal Ring into the IJ, past the gleaming contemporary architecture of **Eye Filmmuseum** (p 21) and **NEMO** (p 35), head down the Amstel River, giving sight of the **Magere Brug**

*A canal cruise is one of the best ways to see the city.*

**(Skinny Bridge)** ♥♥, and take in Herengracht's mighty mansions and its **Seven Bridges Viewpoint** ♥♥ at the junction with Reguliersgracht. There's a recorded commentary in English. Both **Circle Line** (amsterdamcircleline.nl/en) and **Lovers** (www.lovers.nl/en) depart from docks beside the Anne Frank House; you can ride for free, once, with an **I amsterdam City Card** (p 8). *1¼ hr. Ticket typically 16€–20€ adults, 8€ ages 4–13. Tram: 13 or 17 to Westermarkt.*

**3** ♥♥ **Tulip Museum.** The Tulip Museum across the Prinsengracht tells a cheery and informative story of Amsterdam's obsession with tulips, which arrived from the Himalayas and nearly brought the country down when trade in the bulbs collapsed in 1637 (p 17). It's all showcased in a well-designed six-room exhibition with displays on the tulip's connection with the Ottoman court and its use in Golden Age art. Upstairs is a souvenir store selling seasonal bulbs: Only buy tulip bulbs in the second half of the year, or else they are last year's. *45 min. Prinsengracht 116. amsterdamtulipmuseum.com. 020/421-0095. Admission 7€ adults, 4€ students. Daily 10am–6pm. Closed Apr 27 and Dec 25. Tram: 13 or 17 to Westermarkt.*

**4** ♥♥♥ **'t Smalle.** On the edge of the Jordaan, 't Smalle is a traditional "brown cafe" decked out in wood and glass and offering a menu of traditional lunchtime snacks like Dutch cheese or sausage buns. Of course, there's beer to wash it down. Order at the bar and sit outside by the canal. *Egelantiersgracht 12H. t-smalle.nl/en. 020/786-7748. $.*

**5** ♥♥ **Amsterdam Museum.** It's a lively walk through the edge of the Old Center (p 47) to the city's historical museum—or at least, it will be when the museum's complete restructuring project is finished in 2028. The collection is housed in an interconnected space at the heart

*The Amsterdam Museum.*

of the oldest part of the center, spanning a medieval convent and a 17th-century orphanage. Telling the story of Amsterdam's progression from simple fishing village to world power, the displays take a whistle-stop tour through the main stages of the city's history via Old Masters' paintings, diverse life stories, maps, tools, armor, and sculptures. Until the modernized museum opens, there is a scaled-down offering in the same building as **H'ART** (p 25, ❷), at Amstel 51. ⏱ *1½ hr. Kalverstraat. www.amsterdammuseum.nl/en. ☎ 020/523-1822. Admission 20€ adults, 7.50€ students, free kids 17 and under. Daily 10am–5pm. Closed Apr 27 and Dec 25. Tram: 2 or 12 to Koningsplein.*

❻ ♥♥ **Begijnhof.** Take a short detour into one of Amsterdam's truly ancient corners: an almshouse established in medieval times as a home for religious women who had taken a vow of chastity. ⏱ *15 min. See p 38,* ❶.

❼ ♥♥♥ **Van Gogh Museum** Jump on tram 2 or 12 at Koningsplein and alight at Museumplein. Right out of the gate, let's say the

*An 1889 version of* Sunflowers *at the Van Gogh Museum.*

Van Gogh is expensive, especially when a temporary exhibition is on and ticket prices rise by 8€ or more. But you will not be short-changed: More than 200 of the master's portraits, landscapes, and still lifes, plus 500 drawings, are held here, forming the biggest Van Gogh collection in the world. The museum opened in 1973, designed by Gerrit Rietveld, leading exponent of the De Stijl movement; it has three floors of white, airy space in which to show off the tortured artist's ethereal works over three separate periods and artistic influences. Vincent van Gogh was born in 1853 in Groot-Zundert in the south of Holland, and in his short life produced over 800 paintings.

Works displayed are contextualized alongside contemporary pieces by Pissarro, Gauguin, and Monet. Explanatory exhibits help visitors understand Van Gogh's experimentation with color and brushes, his love of the outdoors and relationship with nature, work, and the land. You'll see seminal paintings as his career is tracked from early still lifes through his Japanese stage to his untimely death at Arles in 1890. Van Gogh was prolific in his last years, and famous examples of his brilliance on display include the gloomy *Potato Eaters* (1885), *Bedroom at Arles* (1888), and an 1889 version of *Sunflowers*. Book a timed admission ticket a couple of weeks ahead to be sure of availability; if you forget, a few extra tickets for the following day are issued online at 5pm. *1¾ hr. Museumplein 6. www.vangoghmuseum.nl/en. ☎ 020/570-5200. Admission 24€ adults, free for kids 17 and under; Mon–Fri student tickets half-price. Daily 9am–6pm (Oct–Mar usually closes 5pm); Fri open until 9pm year-round. Tram: 2, 5, or 12 to Museumplein.*

8 ♥♥ **Vondelpark.** A 5-minute stroll from the Van Gogh (wander down **P.C. Hooftstraat** to gawk at the expensive stores) brings you to

*Sumptuous flower beds in full bloom at Keukenhof Gardens in Lisse.*

## Tulip Madness at Keukenhof

The biggest, brightest tulip show of all is found in Keukenhof Gardens (www.keukenhof.nl) near Lisse, where 7 million daffodils, hyacinths, crocuses, and tulips burst into bloom in April, forming psychedelic swaths among the trees and pathways. The gardens are open only from late March to mid-May for guided tours and trips through the surrounding bulb fields by electric boat. Tulips first arrived in Amsterdam around 1600, and their popularity reached manic heights in the 1630s, when the prized bulbs imported from Ottoman Türkiye were changing hands for astronomical amounts of money—as much as an Amsterdam canal house at their peak. The market abruptly collapsed in 1637, but the tulip is still critical to Holland today, with the country producing 75% of the world's tulip bulbs. Tourists fly in every spring to view the Bollenstreek (bulb region) southwest of Amsterdam between Leiden and Haarlem, where the bulbs thrive on fertile sandy soil backed by the North Sea dunes. ***Tip:*** If you buy any bulbs to take home, make sure they are officially certified for export on the packet.

Amsterdam's biggest, greenest public park, 44 hectares (109 acres) of peace and picnicking grounds. This cherished open space is crammed with trees, lawns, lakes, and bridges crisscrossed with walking, biking, and jogging tracks, although as usual cyclists take precedence, so watch your step. Summer sees the lakeside cafe-bars full and weekend open-air concerts at the **Openluchttheater** (p 122). ***50 min. Enter through the gate on Van Eeghenlaan, at the corner of Jacob Obrechtstraat. Open 24 hr. Tram: 3 to Van Baerlestraat.***

9 ♥♥ **Craft Beers & Street Food in Oud-West.** If it's off-season or just a bit cold, you may wish to move on quickly from the park. Thankfully, the Oud-West neighborhood has excellent bars within walking distance, including Craft & Draft (p 110), as well as Foodhallen (p 100), former tram sheds whose indoor and outdoor spaces are now crammed with bars and street food vendors. ***$$–$$$.***

# The Best in Three Days

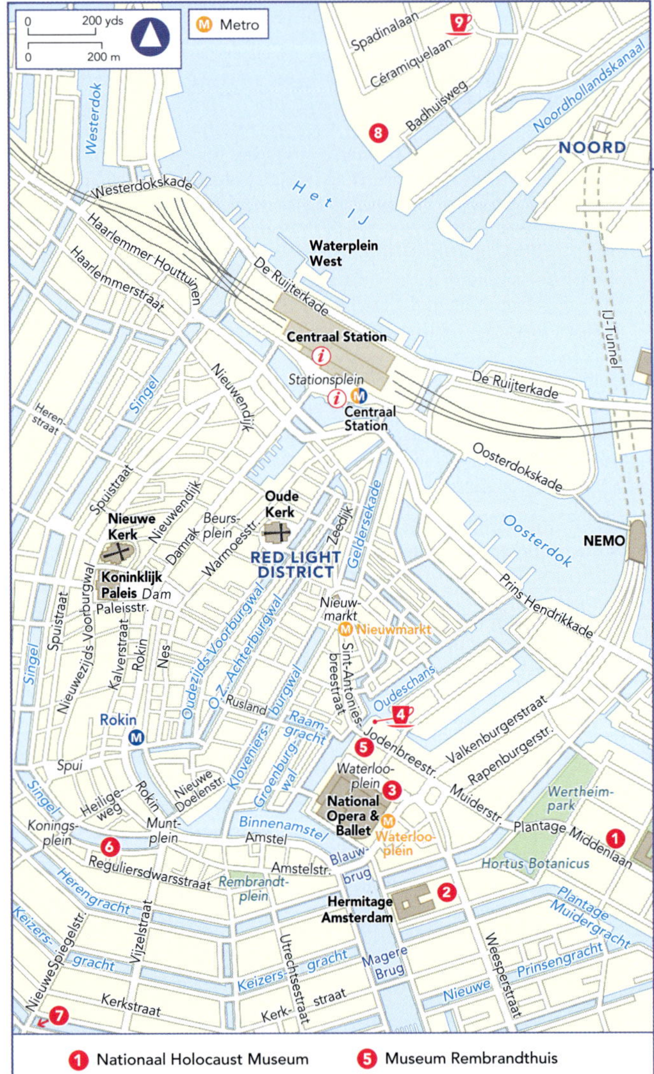


1 Nationaal Holocaust Museum
2 Holocaust Memorial of Names
3 Waterlooplein Flea Market
4 Café de Sluyswacht
5 Museum Rembrandthuis
6 Bloemenmarkt (Flower Market)
7 Stedelijk
8 Eye Filmmuseum
9 Dining in Amsterdam-Noord

**Today you will explore highs and lows of Amsterdam history.** Begin at this century's most important new museum—the National Holocaust Museum—before returning to the Golden Age through the home of its best-known chronicler in paint, Rembrandt. After that, mooch around markets and encounter more great art before rewarding yourself at the end of the day with drinks and dinner in Amsterdam's most exciting neighborhood. The first six stops of the tour are comfortable on foot. START: **Tram 14 to Artis/Holocaustmuseum.**

❶ ♥♥♥ **Nationaal Holocaust Museum.** A warning: Quite obviously there are some *very* unsettling—yet completely necessary—images here from the start. It is a relatively small museum but manages to chronicle expertly and engagingly the creeping social and cultural isolation, violent intimidation, and finally mass deportation and murder of the Dutch Jewish community during the years of Nazi occupation from 1940. Around 140,000 Jews lived in the Netherlands at the start of World War II; just over 30,000 survived the Holocaust. Among many affecting exhibits is a long wall plastered in drily worded executive ordinances that day by day stripped the freedoms of, and increased the pressure on, Amsterdam's Jews and ultimately, from 1942 onward, led tens of thousands through the Westerbork transit camp to the "industrial murder machine" of Auschwitz. Not a fun stop on your itinerary, to be sure, but an essential one. 🕓 *1½ hr. Plantage Middenlaan 27. jck.nl/en. No phone. Admission 20€ adults (30€ including other Jewish Quarter locations; p 65), 10€ students, 8€ ages 13–17, 6€ kids 6–12. Daily 10am–5pm. Closed Apr 27. Tram: 14 to Artis/Holocaustmuseum.*

❷ ♥♥♥ **Holocaust Memorial of Names.** It's impossible to represent the scale and the horror of Amsterdam's experience of the Holocaust. This moving memorial at least attempts to communicate the former, by way of 102,000 bricks each inscribed with the name of a Dutch victim. 🕓 *20 min. www.holocaustnamenmonument.nl/en.* *See p 66, ❷.*

❸ ♥ **Waterlooplein Flea Market.** Two canals were filled in 1882 to form a market square that by 1893 lay at the heart of the Jewish Quarter. Before World War II, it was a daily market central to Jewish life, but when Amsterdam's Jews were deported, it fell into disrepair. During the 1960s, the market was reborn when dazed hippies floated in from all over Europe in the haze of their summer of love to sell bongs and water pipes. Today the market has

*Display of Holocaust artifacts in the Nationaal Holocaust Museum.*

around 300 stalls flogging anything from piles of vintage clothes and secondhand jewelry to flying jackets and dental instruments. If you take time to scrabble deeply around the stalls, you may find something decent. Thrift stores populate the streets beside the market. *30 min. Waterlooplein 2. waterlooplein.amsterdam/en. Mon–Sat 9:30am–6pm. Tram: 14 to Waterlooplein.*

4 ♥ **Café de Sluyswacht.** Tilting at a precarious angle, this former lock-keeper's cottage dates to 1695, making it one of the oldest and therefore most famous pubs in Amsterdam. Inside all is crooked, with wooden bars and uneven stone floors. Sample the tap *witbier* and a plate of mature Dutch cheese and enjoy the terrace with views over Oudeschans canal or the Rembrandthuis. *Jodenbreestraat 1. sluyswacht.nl. 020/625-7611. $.*

5 ♥♥♥ **Museum Rembrandthuis.** Just opposite Cafe de Sluyswacht is the former home of Rembrandt van Rijn, Dutch painter of Amsterdam's Golden Age. He bought this elegant townhouse in 1639 when his career as the city's premier portraitist was flying, yet overstretched himself with a mortgage and such extravagances as his own etching studio—and financial woes plagued his life for years. The house brought him little personal happiness as his adored first wife Saskia died here in 1642 and he was declared bankrupt in 1656. Rembrandt's belongings were all sold off—ironically, the room-by-room inventory for sale is what enabled his home to be so meticulously reassembled. He moved to a smaller house on Rozengracht, where he died in 1669. The house reopened as a museum in 1911 and was extended in 2023 while preserving the layout of a typical 17th-century home, with servants' quarters in the basement and three floors atop this. Rembrandt's hallway served as his gallery, and the family's living quarters are hung with his oil paintings, all explained with the excellent audioguide. Upstairs is his personal museum of prints and objects and the studio where he painted *The Night Watch*. *1 hr. Jodenbreestraat 4. www.rembrandthuis.nl/en. 020/520-0400. Admission 21.50 € adults, 15€ ages 18–25, 8€ kids 6–17. Daily 10am–6pm. Closed Jan 1, Apr 27, and Dec 25. Metro: 51, 53, or 54 to Waterlooplein.*

6 ♥ **Bloemenmarkt (Flower Market).** Catch tram 14 from Waterlooplein or walk along the River Amstel to the world's only floating flower market. This explosion of color is now a permanent fixture housed on a row of platforms and

*Painting studio in the Museum Rembrandthuis (Rembrandt House Museum).*

moored barges. Yes, these days it's touristy, but the seasonal displays are always a pleasure to look at, especially over Christmas and during the spring when the stalls are a riot of bright blooms. *30 min. Singel. Daily. Tram: 4 or 14 to Muntplein.*

**7 ♥♥♥ Stedelijk.** When you have walked the length of the market, jump on tram 2 or 12 from Koningsplein; devotees of modern art and design will fall in love with this museum, which houses 500-plus works from around 1870. The original 1895 building by A. W. Weissman was enhanced with a curious bathtub-like extension appended to its flank. The interior is bright, white, and airy, all the better to show off its stellar collection of works by the most famous names of the 19th to 21st centuries. After a vibrant mural by CoBrA founder Karel Appel in the first gallery, the roster of artists exhibited include Mondriaan, Chagall, Van Gogh, Spencer, Pollock, Picasso, Kandinsky, and pop artists Warhol and Lichtenstein. Interspersed with the fine art, the museum's design collection is organized into three sections: up to 1950; 1950–80; and 1980 to the present. Standouts include Bauhaus, De Stijl, and Functionalist items, including Gerrit Rietveld's 1927 painted *Chair*. The bookshop stocks a range of art and cultural criticism titles. *1½ hr.*

*The floating Bloemenmarkt (Flower Market).*

*Museumplein 10. www.stedelijk.nl/en. ☎ 020/573-2911. Daily 10am–7pm (Fri until 9pm). Admission 22.50€ adults, 10€ students, free for ages 18 and under. Tram: 2, 5, or 12 to Museumplein.*

**8 ♥♥ Eye Filmmuseum.** It would be a shame to leave Amsterdam without heading across the IJ to the Amsterdam-Noord neighborhood—easily reached by the frequent, free 4-minute ferry ride from Centraal Station. In total contrast to the quaint canals of the center, the Noord waterfront is an industrial zone transformed by daring contemporary architecture, notably this spacecraft-like home of Dutch film and the **A'DAM Tower** (p 35, 1) beside it. Inside is a small permanent

*Stedelijk Museum.*

collection on the technology of film, but the real draw for movie nerds are rotating temporary exhibitions: Subjects of recent shows have included Martin Scorsese, Tilda Swinton, and Werner Herzog. There are always screenings to accompany the exhibits, as well as niche indie movies, festival prizewinners, and the latest releases playing all day, every day. *1 hr. IJpromenade 1. www.eyefilm.nl/en. 020/589-1400. Admission 15€ adults, free ages 17 and under. Daily 10am–7pm. Closed Apr 26. Ferry: F3 to Buiksloterweg.*

9 ♥♥♥ **Dining in Amsterdam-Noord.** To cap off your day, two of our favorite dining spots in the city are within walking distance of the Eye Filmmuseum: Pelusa (p 102) and Café De Ceuvel (p 98). Or have a glass of wine at Wijnbar Vindict (p 113), then check out what music and cultural events are scheduled at Tolhuistuin (p 122). The free ferry service from Buiksloterweg back to Centraal Station runs until very late (and you can even take a bike aboard). *$$–$$$$.*

## Photography Galleries

Amsterdam's art scene is not just about Old Masters, paint, and De Stijl; there are options for photography lovers as well. The **FOAM Photography Museum** (p 26) runs hard-hitting exhibitions in a modern gallery behind a traditional townhouse facade at Keizersgracht 609. Images are all beautifully displayed against pristine white walls, and exhibits change regularly. Check online to see what's on when you are in town. Also on Keizersgracht at 401 is the **Huis Marseille Museum voor Fotografie** (p 27), another gallery largely specializing in contemporary photography, based in a former merchant's house. It's named for the stone plaque on the front of the building, which depicts the harbor in Marseille, France.

*Inside the FOAM Photography Museum.*

# 2 The Best Special-Interest Tours

# Amsterdam for Art Lovers

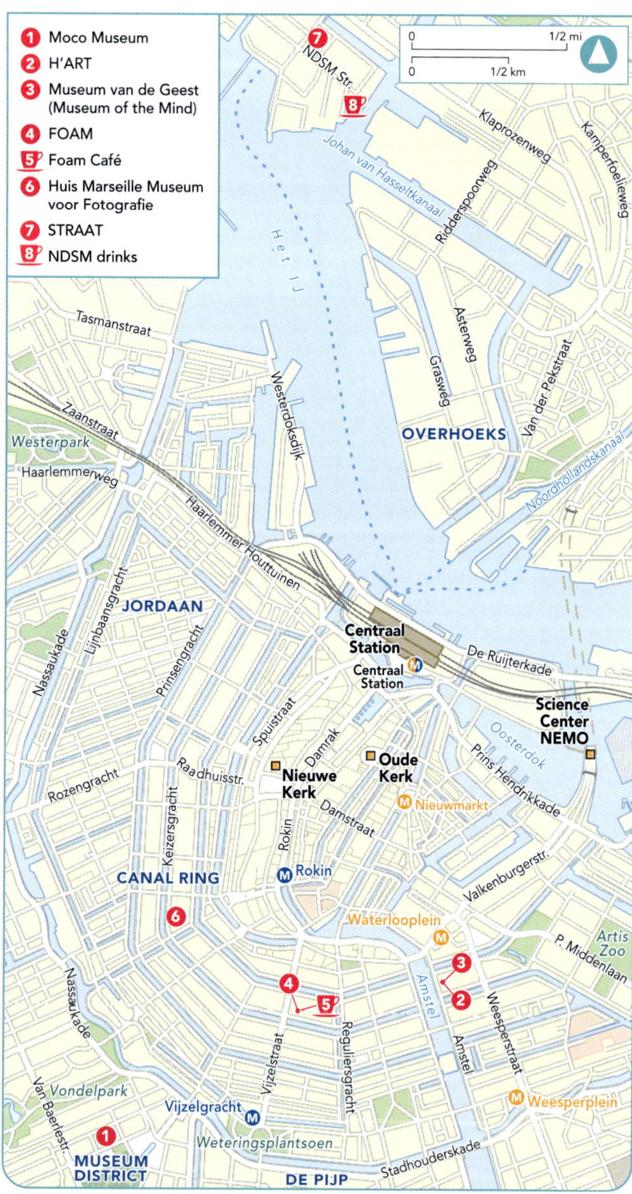


*Previous page: STRAAT showcases street art and graffiti on an industrial scale.*

**Amsterdam serves up a feast of visual arts.** With more than 20 Rembrandts, 200 Van Goghs, numerous Vermeers, a well-earned rep for street art, and a plethora of Impressionist and post-Impressionist paintings, art lovers will be in heaven. This tour is for those who have already made a beeline to the top museums and are ready to dig deeper into the city's artistic riches. You'll catch a blockbuster one-off show, contemporary photography, and monumental street art inside an abandoned shipbuilding warehouse. ***Note:*** If you complete this full-day tour, an **I amsterdam City Card** (p 8) will already have paid for itself. START: **Tram: 2, 5, or 12 to Museumplein.**

1 ♥ kids **Moco Museum.** The Old Masters make way for new ones at this collection dedicated mostly to internationally known modern and contemporary artists who create in a broad brush of styles, from Banksy's radical street art and video installations by Yayoi Kusama to a brilliantly immersive, disorienting combo of mirrors and digital screens in the basement. At almost 50 years of age, a couple of Warhols feel "classical" by comparison. The space isn't ideal given Moco's popularity with Gen Z—it's mazelike and can feel cramped. It's usually best to arrive early while most are still sleeping off last night. *45 min. Honthorststraat 20. mocomuseum.com/locations/amsterdam. No phone. Admission 20€ adults, 18€ students and ages 7–17, free for kids 6 and under. Daily 9am–8pm. Tram: 2, 5, or 12 to Museumplein.*

2 ♥♥ **H'ART.** Ranged around a giant courtyard, the Amstelhof is a grand former almshouse almost surrounded by the Amstel and canals. It's been transformed into the leading Amsterdam space for major temporary and touring exhibitions. Art from all over the world pops up here; recent hits have

*Tour guide at Moco Museum.*

included a Kandinsky retrospective and, with origins closer to home, 2025's "The Leiden Collection," a unique gathering of works by Rembrandt and Vermeer. Unusually, tickets to the city's marquee temporary exhibition space are included with the **I amsterdam City Card** (p 8). ⏱ *1½ hr. Amstel 51. www.hartmuseum.nl/en. ☎ 020/530-8755. Admission varies by exhibition, typically 25€–27.50€ adults, 15€–17.50€ students, free for kids 17 and under. Daily 10am–5pm. Closed Apr 27. Tram: 14 to Waterlooplein.*

**3 ♥ Museum van de Geest (Museum of the Mind).** Smaller but no less interesting, exhibits here draw on a Haarlem sister museum's collection of Outsider Art: works created by folk and self-taught painters, visual artists of every stripe who operate beyond the mainstream "art world," or artists from marginalized communities. A recurring theme of the rotating exhibitions is the mysterious workings of the human mind: emotion, well-being, obsession, mental disturbances, and care. ⏱ *45 min. Amstel 51. www.museumvandegeest.nl/amsterdam. ☎ 020/541-0670. Admission varies by exhibition, typically 17.50€ adults, 13€ ages 13–21, free for kids 12 and under. Daily 10am–5pm. Closed Apr 26. Metro: 51, 53, or 54 to Waterlooplein.*

**4 ♥♥♥ FOAM.** Cross the Skinny Bridge and follow Keizersgracht across Reguliersgracht with its renowned "Seven Bridges" view to find, facing the **Museum Van Loon** (p 30), this gallery dedicated to photography. On the outside, it's a traditional canal-house; inside is a partly stripped-out warren of rooms that form the backdrop to the work of established names, such as the New York School photographer and color pioneer Saul Leiter, or new Dutch talent. At least two exhibitions run concurrently. The address itself has its own place in Amsterdam history: This was a regular meeting point during World War II for the Dutch anti-Nazi resistance. ⏱ *1 hr. Keizersgracht 609. www.foam.org. ☎ 020/551-6500. Admission 16€ adults, 7€ students and ages 13–17, free for kids 12 and under. Sat–Wed 10am–6pm, Thurs–Fri 10am–9pm. Closed Apr 27. Tram: 4 to Keizersgracht.*

*Photo exhibition room at the Huis Marseille Museum voor Fotografie.*

*The colorful sprawl of STRAAT, a museum of street art inside a former NDSM wharf warehouse.*

**5 ♥ Foam Café.** Decorated with old exhibition posters, this is a calm space for coffee and cake, or a light lunch—toasted sandwiches, soup, and the like. *Keizersgracht 609. www.foam.org. No phone. $.*

**6 ♥♥ Huis Marseille Museum voor Fotografie.** Keep following Keizersgracht for 4 blocks to Amsterdam's original photography museum, housed in an aristocratic merchant's house. Here, exhibitions on historic and contemporary themes rotate around four times a year. Space created by moving into the adjacent house now allows it to show some of the permanent collection, too. *40 min. Keizersgracht 399–401. huismarseille.nl/en. 020/531-8989. Admission 12.50€ adults, 6.50€ seniors and students, free for kids 17 and under. Daily 10am–6pm (Thurs until 9pm). Closed Jan 1, Apr 27, and Dec 25. Tram: 2, 12, or 17 to Keizersgracht.*

**7 ♥♥♥ kids STRAAT.** Take any tram to Centraal Station, then catch the free ferry F4 to NDSM from directly behind the building. It's a 2-minute walk from the dock to this cavernous former shipbuilding warehouse, which showcases street art and graffiti on an industrial scale. The sheer size and urban streetlike layout is impressive on its own, but works in a mix of global styles are also treated with the artistic seriousness they deserve. The collection is constantly growing: Everything here is site-specific except for a regular roster of temporary exhibitions. Neighborhood walls are also smothered in accomplished graffiti art. *1 hr. NDSM-plein 1. straatmuseum.com/en. No phone. Admission 19.50€ adults, 13.50€ students, 9.50€ ages 13–18, free for kids 12 and under. Mon noon–5pm, Tues–Sun 10am–5pm (hours can vary during holidays and off-season, so check website before you go). Ferry: F4 to NDSM.*

**8 ♥♥ NDSM Drinks or Casual Dining.** Before hopping on a ferry back to Centraal Station, pause for a drink or a casual dinner at one of our favorite NDSM bar-restaurants: IJver (p 100) or Noorderlicht (p 111). In summer, the party here continues 'til late. *NDSM-werf. $$.*

# Architectural Amsterdam

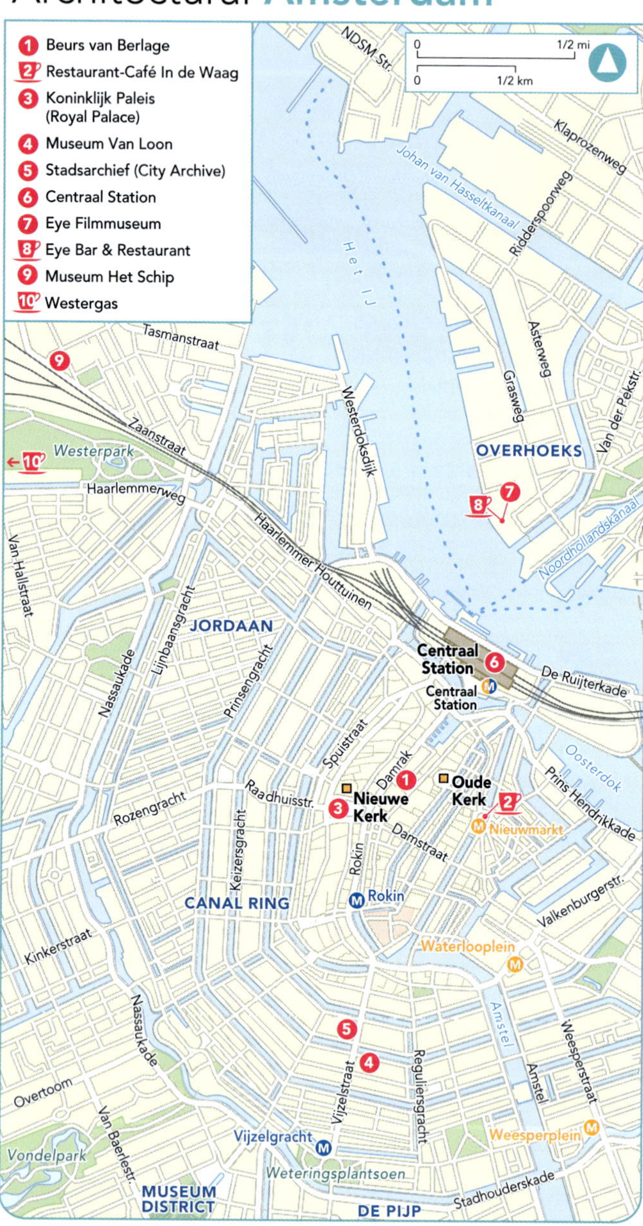

**Amsterdam has so many architectural styles** that the city seems to adopt multiple personalities depending on which direction you're looking. Architecture buffs can entertain themselves just by walking the streets or taking a tram ride, especially in the UNESCO-listed Grachtengordel (Canal Ring). On this tour, you'll see buildings that encapsulate the city's major phases of architecture, from a medieval relic through the heyday of Amsterdam School design to photogenic postmodernism. START: **Tram 4 or 14 to Dam.**

*Beurs van Berlage.*

1 ♥ **Beurs van Berlage.** Amsterdam's former stock exchange was built in 1903 by Hendrik Berlage and is now an occasional events and concert venue (p 120). This monumental building was one of the precursors of the Amsterdam School architectural style and is exceptional for its use of patterned brickwork and clean lines, which broke away from the fancy Dutch Renaissance Revival styles of the time as seen at the **Stedelijk Museum** (p 21). A frieze decorating the facade of the building shows man's (questionable) evolution from Adam to stockbroker. *10 min. Damrak 243. beursvanberlage.com. 020/531-3355. Tram: 4 or 14 to Dam.*

2 ♥ **Restaurant-Café In de Waag.** Walk through the Red Light District, which has some fine gabled architecture, to the fringe of Amsterdam's Chinatown and the city's only surviving medieval gate. Built in the 14th century, it became a public weigh house and then a guild house. One of the guilds lodged here was the Surgeon's Guild, immortalized in Rembrandt's The Anatomy Lesson (1632), which depicts a dissection underway in the upper-floor Theatrum Anatomicum. That part of the building is rarely open, but you can refuel from 11am (9am weekends) in the historic surrounds of its first-floor rooms—with eggs Benedict or just a coffee. *Nieuwmarkt 4. indewaag.nl/en. 020/422-7772. $$.*

3 ♥♥ **Koninklijk Paleis (Royal Palace).** Back at Dam Square, the huge building that dominates this monumental space is the official residence of the reigning Dutch House of Orange, although these days the royals prefer to live in The Hague. The palace was designed by Jacob van Campen in 1655 as the City Hall and has a solid, neoclassical facade; it was repurposed into a royal palace by Louis, brother of Napoleon Bonaparte, when he became king in 1808. Its grand interior, including the **Burgerzaal (Citizens' Hall)** ♥♥, is often open to view, except during periods of royal residence and state receptions. *1 hr. Dam. www.paleisamsterdam.nl/en. 020/522-6161. Admission 13.50€ adults, 9€ students, free ages 17 and under. Daily 10am–5pm (check the website as changes and closures are frequent). Tram: 2, 4, 12, 14, or 17 to Dam.*

*Citizens' Hall at the Royal Palace.*

❹ ♥♥ **Museum Van Loon.** Catch tram 4 to Keizersgracht and stroll to this elegant double-fronted mansion first owned by Ferdinand Bol, a student of Rembrandt. Between 1884 and 1945, it was the property of the Van Loons, who were founders of the Dutch East India Company and one of the richest families in Amsterdam. Although this is a beautiful house as befits the family's wealth, its grand rooms have an air of benign neglect, almost inviting visitors to grow accustomed to the idea that such times have now passed—further enhanced via rotating exhibits that confront Dutch colonial history. It's also worth a visit to see how the Dutch aristocracy lived, among scores of family portraits, photos of notable visitors (including royalty and President Obama, who held his foundation dinner here), Louis XV furniture, and a marble-lined staircase with an ornately curlicued brass balustrade. Out back is a formal knot garden and coach house modeled on a Greek temple. 🕓 *45 min. Keizersgracht 672. www.museumvanloon.nl.* ☎ *020/624-5255. Admission 16€ adults, 12.75€ students, 9€ kids 6–18. Daily 10am–5pm. Closed Jan 1, Apr 27, and Dec 25. Tram: 4 to Keizersgracht.*

*Knot garden at the Museum Van Loon.*

❺ ♥♥ **Stadsarchief (City Archive).** An Amsterdam icon so renowned that it's informally named after its designer: "De Bazel." He worked as an apprentice to Cuypers (see ❻, below) in the 1880s but De Bazel's own influence can be seen in later Expressionist, Rationalist, and Art Nouveau styles that permeated design in Amsterdam. You need not linger long, but take time to admire it inside and out. 🕓 *15 min. Vijzelstraat 32.* ☎ *020/251-1511. Free admission. Tues–Fri 10am–5pm, Sat–Sun noon–5pm. Tram: 4 or 14 to Rembrandtplein.*

❻ ♥♥ **Centraal Station.** Jump on any of the trams heading north to Centraal Station, which is an architectural masterpiece in its own right. Designed by architect Pierre Cuypers, who also had the **Rijksmuseum** (p 7) on his resumé, it was built between 1884 and 1889 on three artificial islands in the IJ channel. Amsterdammers thoroughly disliked it at the time, but now it is

## The City & the Sea

Amsterdam lies below sea level. That it does not lie beneath the sea itself is due to Dutch engineering skill, which has kept the city above water for 800 years. Solid buildings stand 5.5m (18 ft.) below sea level and 900,000 people live where waves should be lapping. This in part explains why Amsterdammers take sustainability, especially water preservation, so seriously. Tap water here is so good that there's no need to buy any single-use plastic bottles. If seacoast defenses—a complicated system of dams, polders, dykes, and walls—should ever be breached, most of the city would vanish like Atlantis. A cross-section of topography between here and the North Sea shows that the Vondelpark would become a lake, Metro tunnels would be flooded, and the trams would float away. On the plus side, if you were standing on top of the Oude Kerk tower, you wouldn't even get your feet wet.

loved for its extravagant Renaissance Revival facade. The left-hand central tower has a gilded weathervane; the right one has a clock. Several canal cruises leave from here, and many trams start or terminate out front. *10 min.*

**7 ♥♥ Eye Filmmuseum.** Take the free ferry (F3), or just stand and stare from the panoramic quay behind at Centraal Station. The pristine white shape of Amsterdam's film museum hovers over the north bank of the River IJ like a mantis. Built in 2012 by Austrian firm Delugan Meissl Associated Architects, the Eye was the first major public building to be constructed north of the river in the 21st century—but very much not the last. The gleaming complex houses several movie theaters, an exhibition space, a store, and a restaurant with a terrace looking back to Centraal Station. *1 hr. IJpromenade 1.* *See p 21, 8.* *Ferry: F3 to Buiksloterweg.*

**8 ♥ Eye Bar & Restaurant.** If you do hop across on the ferry, make for the building's suntrap terrace (a glass-walled interior) or outdoor patio. Drinks and snacks are served all day. *IJpromenade 1. www.eyefilm.nl/en/restaurant. No phone. $$.*

*Inside the Stadsarchief.*

## Spouts, Necks & Bells: Amsterdam's Gables

The townhouses and warehouses of Amsterdam's old center all have gables, and it's easy to judge their age by their shape. Simple triangular wooden gables came first, followed by spout gables (Keizersgracht 403) with a little point on top, mostly on warehouses, in the 14th century. These simply followed the pitch of the roof, but over time, more ornate designs crept in. Step gables were popular in the 17th century (Brouwersgracht 2 in the Jordaan), and elegant, straight neck gables (Herengracht 168) adorned with ornamental shoulders appeared between 1640 and 1780. Rounded bell-shaped gables (Prinsengracht 359) were introduced in the late 17th century and remained popular until the end of the 18th century.

The hook sitting central on most of these gables is called a *hijsbalk* and was used with a rope and pulley system for hauling cumbersome items in and out of houses, bypassing steep, narrow interior staircases. Most of the canalside houses lean a tad forward to prevent loads crashing into the facades.

**9 ♥♥ Museum Het Schip.** From the elevated section above the Centraal Station concourse, take bus no. 22 west to the city's most famous example of Amsterdam School architecture, a housing development known as "The Ship," which also has a didactic-style museum—an essential stop for anyone interested in architecture. The Amsterdam School ethos was influenced by modernism and the socialist-democratic concept of beauty held by Hendrik Berlage. Its popularity in the early 1900s reflected a desire among the next generation of young Amsterdam architects to make life better for the Dutch working classes. As a result, social housing was a particular interest, which the School and city planners hoped could gradually replace slum dwellings. Inspired by European Art Nouveau, Expressionism, and British Arts and Crafts, their buildings are epitomized by heavy brickwork, elaborate masonry, painted glass, and wrought-iron. Michel de Klerk (1884–1923) was one leading exponent: He designed Het Schip to resemble an ocean liner; the brick complex incorporated social housing, a school, and a post office. The

*Historic gable styles of townhouses along Amsterdam's canals.*

*Het Schip, a housing block by Michel de Klerk, is a highlight of Amsterdam School architecture.*

latter is the only one of De Klerk's interiors open to the public, via guided visit only; tours are included in the ticket price and depart hourly from noon (3pm only in English). Other notable Amsterdam School buildings include the **City Archive** (5, above) and **Grand Hotel Amrâth** (p 134). *1 hr. Oostzaanstraat 45. www.hetschip.nl/en. 020/686-8595. Admission 16.50€ adults, 8€ students, 5€ kids 5–12. Tues–Sun 11am–5pm. Closed Jan 1, Easter, Apr 27, and Dec 25. Bus: 22 0r 48 to Spaarndammerstraat.*

10 ♥♥ **Westergas.** Walk back through Westerpark to an enormous construction built in the early 19th century. Once a gas factory supplying the rail tracks nearby, the site has been transformed into western Amsterdam's party central. Its industrial redbrick buildings host several bars, including one operated by local brewery Troost (p 112); an indie cinema, Het Ketelhuis (www.ketelhuis.nl); nightclubs, restaurants, and a theater; the vast drum-shaped Gashouder (gashouder.nl/en), erected in 1903 to store coal gas to power the city and now a concert venue; and one of our favorite Amsterdam hotels, Conscious Westerpark (p 132). You could spend hours around here. *www.westergas.nl/en. $–$$.*

## Amsterdam's Addresses

The gables on Amsterdam houses were there for decoration and to hide the pitch of the roof but also had another function, which was to help identify the building before postal addresses were invented. To help this, *gevelstenen* (gable stones) of ornamental tiles, sculptures, or reliefs that played on the original owner's name or profession were added to the facades to make identification easier. Walls in the Begijnhof and on Sint-Luciënsteeg have pretty gable stones, including the oldest known, dating from 1603 and showing a milkmaid carrying her buckets. Then the French annexed the Netherlands in 1806, introducing a system of house numbers to Amsterdam and spoiling all the fun.

# Amsterdam with Kids

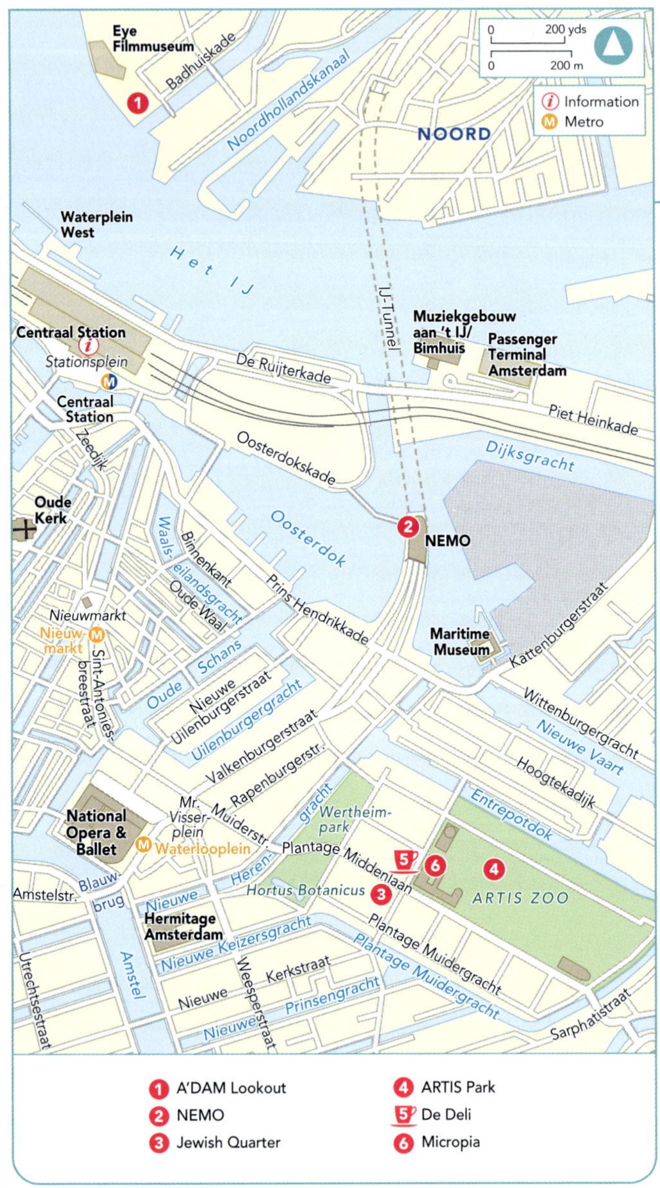


1. A'DAM Lookout
2. NEMO
3. Jewish Quarter
4. ARTIS Park
5. De Deli
6. Micropia

**Despite some obvious considerations, Amsterdam caters brilliantly for children.** The city has interactive museums designed to appeal to youngsters; canal boats and trams to ride; and bikes to hire. With playgrounds in all the parks, kids' shows in several theaters, and pancakes on almost every menu, there's always something to do, even if it's pouring rain outside. But as anyone with toddlers will tell you, pushing baby strollers across all those cobbles ain't much fun. START: **Ferry F3 from Centraal Station to Buiksloterweg.**

**1 ♥♥♥ A'DAM Lookout.** Kids love swings, but how about Europe's highest, 100m (318 ft.) up? Accessed from the A'DAM Tower's panoramic deck on an additional ticket, the self-explanatory **Swing Over the Edge** offers quite a view—360° across the city and beyond. Thankfully, you can also enjoy the same view without the sensation of dangling from a metal crane 21 stories above the IJ. Note, you must be 1.2m (47 in.) tall to ride the swing. Revamped as a culture, dining, and general fun hub, the tower itself dates to the 1970s, when it was designed by Arthur Staal for oil company Shell. *1 hr. IJpromenade 4. www.adamlookout.com. ☎ 020/242-0100. Admission to Lookout 18.50€, 12.50€ ages 4–12 (2€ cheaper if you prebook online); Swing 7.50€; various combo tickets (with drink, with burger, with VR experience) available online. Daily 10am–10pm. Ferry: F3 to Buiksloterweg.*

*Swing Over the Edge at A'DAM Lookout.*

**2 ♥♥ NEMO.** From back at Centraal, walk along Oosterdokskade to the regenerated eastern docks and the unmistakable pale green, ship-shaped building designed by Renzo Piano. Inside, it's more play station than museum, a great place to head with younger kids on a rainy day. Its mission is to introduce science and technology to kids in an understandable format, through games, experiments, and demonstrations. There's even a lab for supervised experiments. Renovated in 2025 and open to everyone, NEMO's broad, stepped **living roof ♥♥** is an attraction in itself, a public space to hang out, catch the sun, and take in sweeping views over the docks and **Muziekgebouw aan 't IJ** concert hall (p 121). *1½ hr. Oosterdok 2. www.nemosciencemuseum.nl. ☎ 020/531-3233. Admission 21.50€, free for kids 3 and under. Tues–Sun*

*The science educational museum NEMO.*

*10am–5:30pm (Apr–Sept also open Mon on public holidays and during school break). Closed Jan 1, Apr 27, and Dec 25. Bus: 22 to Kadijksplein.*

**3 ♥♥♥ Jewish Quarter.** Depending on your children's ages, you may wish to introduce them to some of the monuments or history of Amsterdam's Jewish Quarter, a 15-minute walk from NEMO. It can be upsetting, of course, but it's also important—if they are old enough to understand. There's inevitable sadness, but less in the way of graphic imagery, at the **Hollandsche Schouwburg** (p 68, 10) and the **Nationaal Holocaust Namenmonument** (p 19, 2). *1 hr. Tram: 14 to Artis/Holocaustmuseum.* *See "The Jewish Quarter," p 65.*

**4 ♥♥ ARTIS Park.** Amsterdam's zoo opened in 1838 and covers more than 14 hectares (35 acres) of tree-lined pathways and landscaped gardens ringing with the calls of birds, lemurs, and monkeys. More than 900 animal species live here, where a 19th-century ambience combines harmoniously with a 21st-century emphasis on conservation and nature. The free ARTIS app helps you navigate to see lions, jaguars, gorillas, elephants,

*Two elephants and their calf at ARTIS.*

and giraffes; feeding-time favorites, the penguins and sea lions; and regular zookeeper talks. Admission includes the zoo's 3D Planetarium. *3 hr. Plantage Kerklaan 38–40. www.artis.nl/en. 020/523-3670. Admission 29.50€, 25.50€ kids 3–12. Daily 9am–6pm. Tram: 14 to Artis/ Holocaustmuseum.*

5 ♥ **De Deli.** Casual eating options abound at the zoo, but you may prefer to load up on something more inspiring like a fresh filled focaccia or salad. Kids of every age love the cheesy fries. *Plantage Kerklaan 41. 020/354-2669. $–$$.*

6 ♥♥♥ **Micropia.** The world's first museum dedicated to microbes zooms in—all the way in—to show curious minds much more than meets the eye. We each carry more than 100 trillion tiny organisms in us, and this ingenious multimedia space shows their importance to every living thing on the planet, by way of bubbling tubes, video walls, magnifiers, and even a digital body scanner. *1 hr. Plantage Kerklaan 38–40. www.artis.nl/en/artis-micropia. 020/523-3670. Admission 17.50€ (6€ add-on to a zoo ticket), free for kids 12 and under. Daily 9am–6pm. Tram: 14 to Artis/ Holocaustmuseum.*

*Science demonstration at Micropia.*

# Alteration Amsterdam

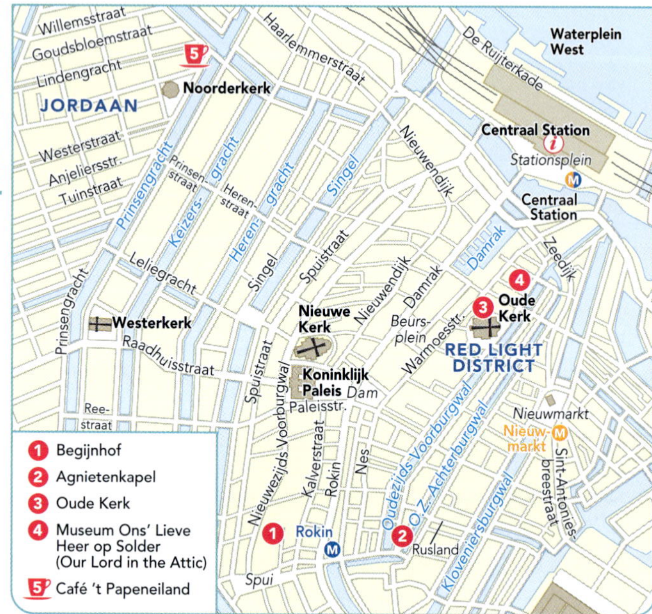


**The Alteration was one of the great upheavals in Dutch history.** On May 26, 1578, Amsterdam's Catholic government fell, heralding a Protestant Reformation. Sermons in Latin and veneration of the saints became a thing of the past—at least officially. To stave off the bloodshed and destruction that plagued the Reformation in so much of Europe, the Dutch found what has, in various scenarios since, become a traditional solution to any problem: a muddle of semi-official tolerance, a 17th-century "don't ask, don't tell" policy, if you like. This relaxed half-day walk takes you to some of the locations where this Alteration story—a tale of tolerance (mostly) and good business over fanaticism—can still be detected. START: **Tram 4 or 14 to Rokin.**

**1** ♥♥ **Begijnhof.** Founded in the Middle Ages, this *hofje* (almshouse) remained in operation for centuries after the changeover from Catholicism to Protestantism. The **Engelse Kerk (English Protestant Church)** dates to 1607 and is used today by British expats. Opposite the church, at no. 30, is the **Begijnhofkapel,** a clandestine Catholic chapel dating from 1671 that's also still in use today: Sunday Mass is conducted in French and Dutch. ⏱ *30 min. Spui and Gedempte Begijnensloot. See also p 15, 6.*

**2** ♥ **Agnietenkapel.** Head back to Rokin, follow Grimburgwal, then make a left after crossing Oudezijds Voorburgwal as far as no. 229–231, where you'll spot an elaborately

*Altar inside Begijnhofkapel.*

ornamental gateway from 1571. This leads to the chapel (1470) of what was the St. Agnes Convent until the Protestant takeover in 1578. It later became part of the Athenaeum Illustre, the city's first university, which was formed in 1632, and today is still a University of Amsterdam building. *5 min. Oudezijds Voorburgwal 229–231.*

3 ♥ **Oude Kerk.** The church owes its stark interior in part to a 1566 *Beeldenstorm,* an outburst of destructive iconoclasm. Radical Protestants sacked the church, smashing many of the accoutrements of Catholic worship in the process. Twelve years later, it became a Protestant church. *20 min.* *See also p 11,* 7.

4 ♥♥♥ **Museum Ons' Lieve Heer op Solder (Our Lord in the Attic).** Still one of the city's best-kept historical secrets. Following the Alteration and the conversion of all churches in 1578, practicing Roman Catholicism was suppressed. If you chose not to follow the Protestant Reformed Church, you had to worship at home, even communally, which led to a proliferation of "house churches." Between 1661 and 1663, wealthy Catholic merchant Jan Hartman bought this house and two others behind it and converted all three attics into a clandestine but richly decorated Catholic chapel—quite a feat of engineering. Worshippers entered from a side street and climbed the narrow stairs to the hidden third-floor church, which could accommodate a congregation of 150. Incredibly well-preserved, the chapel has splendid baroque flourishes, an organ and double-deck wooden gallery, and altar paintings shining like new. *1 hr. Oudezijds Voorburgwal 38–40. www.opsolder.nl/en. 020/624-6604. Admission 17€ adults, 7.50€ kids ages 5–17. Daily 10am–6pm (1st Sun of month opens 11am). Mass held in the attic chapel on the first Sun of each month (except July–Aug) from 9:30am; free admission. Closed Apr 27 and Dec 25. Metro: Nieuwmarkt.*

5 ♥ **Café 't Papeneiland.** Relax over coffee or a beer beside the "Brewers' Canal" (Brouwersgracht). This brown cafe has Alteration heritage: Its basement had a tunnel entrance through which Catholics would secretly make their way to chapel. It's a 15-minute walk away—on the edge of the Jordaan—but feels like the appropriate spot to cap your history tour. The cafe also serves a mean apple pie. *Prinsengracht 2. www.papeneiland.nl. 020/624-1989. $.*

*Oude Kerk.*

# Alt-Amsterdam

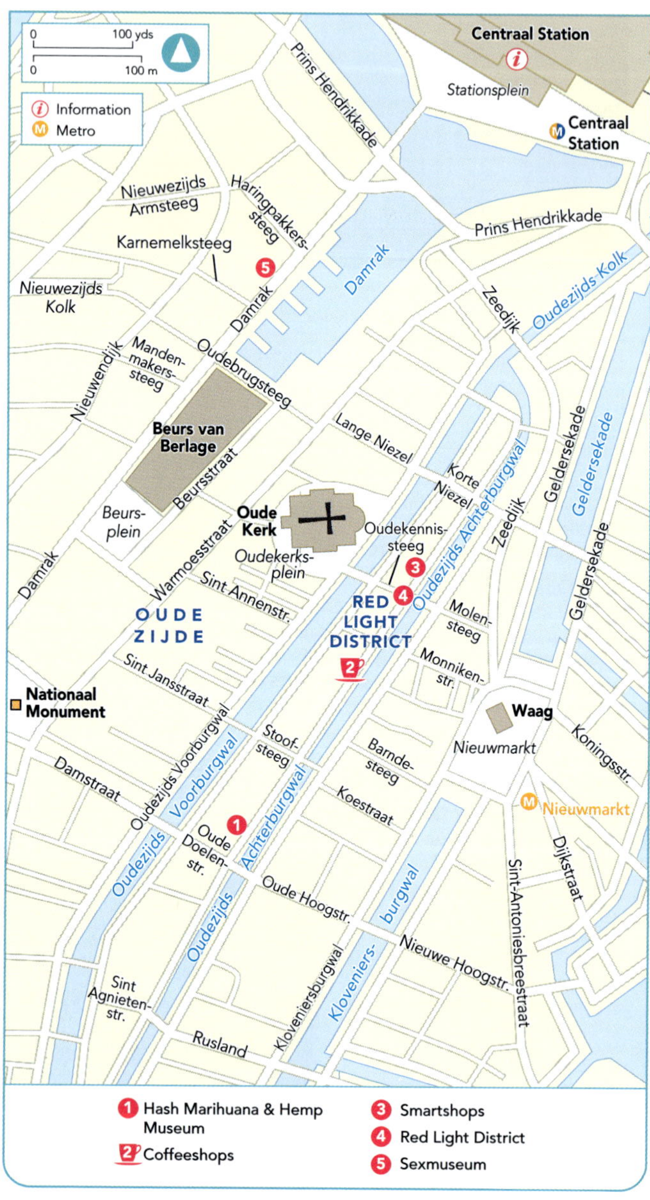

**Amsterdam deservedly has a reputation as a party town.** Sex work is legal, soft drugs are tolerated, and Amsterdammers generally hold "live-and-let-live" attitudes toward every aspect of life. Pretty much anything goes, apart from intolerance. But Amsterdam has always had its gritty substrata, born long before 17th-century sailors scrambled off ships into its Red Light District. The walking tour explores this seedier side and offers a few tips on navigating it safely. The area's crowds tell you this side to the city is not as "alternative" as perhaps it once was. START: **Tram 4 or 14 to Dam.**

*Paintings in the Hash Marihuana & Hemp Museum.*

❶ ♥♥ **Hash Marihuana & Hemp Museum.** On the cusp of the Red Light District, this twin-site museum is not a bad place to start for anyone genuinely curious about the history of soft drugs and medicinal applications of hemp. There's the predictable display of pipes—many beautifully carved—and some lovely old paintings depicting 16th-century farmers smoking dope. *1 hr. Oudezijds Achterburgwal 148. hashmuseum.com/en. ☎ 020/624-8926. Admission 11.50€ adults,*

## Cleaning Up the Red Lights

Amsterdam's Red Light District is notorious for an "anything goes" vibe, but recently the warren of streets, also called *Rosse Buurt, De Wallen,* or *De Walletjes,* has been undergoing some mild gentrification. Several coffeeshops and around half the brothel windows have closed. "To let" signs are common sights in empty windows. But the area is still packed every evening.

*Smokey Coffeeshop.*

*free for kids 12 and under (must be accompanied by an adult). Mon–Fri 10am–8pm, Sat–Sun 10am–10pm. Closed Apr 27. Tram: 4 or 14 to Dam.*

2 ♥ **Coffeeshops.** Amsterdam's coffeeshops are not known for their flat whites—although most do have tables and sell drinks and snacks—but for selling marijuana and hashish. Collectively they have brought millions of euros into the city via cannabis tourism since the decriminalizing of soft drugs in 1976. Today, despite many closures, more than 150 remain, mostly around the Red Light District but also in every city neighborhood. Operating in a legal gray area, they cannot advertise, sell alcohol, or sell drugs to anyone under age 18. It's illegal to buy drugs on the street in Amsterdam, so if you want a smoke, drop by a coffeeshop where, just like everywhere else in the city, nicotine is banned indoors.

## Amsterdam's Alternative Red Light Districts

Although Amsterdam's most famous Red Light District is around the Oude Kerk, there are two others. Singelgebied is bounded by the Nieuwezijds Voorburgwal and Singel canal; a few of the prostitutes here are trans, and there are gay sex shops and cinemas. The city's smallest Red Light District is south of the city center in De Pijp, on Ruysdaelkade along the Boerenwetering canal.

## Soft Drugs Tolerance

Amsterdam's reputation as a party town is due in part to its *tolerance* toward soft drugs. The practice is technically illegal, but tolerated: Whereas it's fine to carry 5 grams (⅙ oz.) of marijuana for personal use, it's not fine to buy it anywhere other than in a **coffeeshop** (p 42). This is a licensed venue where you can purchase and often sit and smoke all day if you wish. Coffeeshops are not permitted to sell alcohol. Although around 160 coffeeshops still operate in Amsterdam—down from 350 in 1999, according to city hall data—many have been closed down as civic leaders clean up the city's act (p 41). There has been intermittent talk of introducing an I.D. or membership system that would prevent overseas tourists from utilizing their services, but this has so far been vetoed as both impractical and financially unviable. Hallucinogenic psilocybin mushrooms and other "legal highs" are sold at **Smartshops** (below), not coffeeshops. Note that it is still illegal to smoke dope in the street all over the center (a fine of 100€ will follow), to buy drugs on the street, and to buy drugs at all if you are under 18. Don't be tempted to take any drugs out of the country with you: As any dog owner will tell you, they will be sniffed out at the airport.

3 ♥ **Smartshops.** If you want to get high without smoking a joint or eating a space cake, you may wish to explore Amsterdam's smartshops, which sell natural psychoactives and supposed aphrodisiacs, as well as magic mushrooms. One popular and long-running retailer is the

*Magic Mushroom Gallery smartshop.*

*Red Light District.*

**Magic Mushroom Gallery** (Spuistraat 249; magicmushroom.com).

❹ ♥♥ **Red Light District.** In Amsterdam's infamous *Rosse Buurt* (Red Light District), barely-clad sex workers advertise themselves behind glass windows along the canals and alleyways. There are also live sex shows (p 122) that leave nothing to the imagination. Early evening is the best time to visit, before it gets crowded with drunks but late enough that you can see the red reflections in the canals. Although the area is generally safe, **a word of warning:** Don't photograph the sex workers; it is not appreciated and may be rewarded with a 240€ fine. 🕒 *30 min. Along Oudezijds Achterburgwal and the alleyways that intersect it. Metro: Nieuwmarkt.*

❺ **Sexmuseum.** Amsterdam's "Venustempel" opened in 1985, which makes it the oldest sex museum in the world. Obviously, the collection is pretty explicit: There's erotic ephemera and objects, photographs, waxwork figures in various states of undress, and a model Marilyn Monroe fashioned after her *Playboy* nude calendar appearance in 1955. 🕒 *40 min. Damrak 18. sexmuseumamsterdam.nl.* ☎ *020/622-8376. Admission 10€; ages under 16 not admitted. Daily 10am–6pm. Closed Dec 25. Take any tram to Centraal Station.*

# 3 The Best Neighborhood Walks

# The Old Center

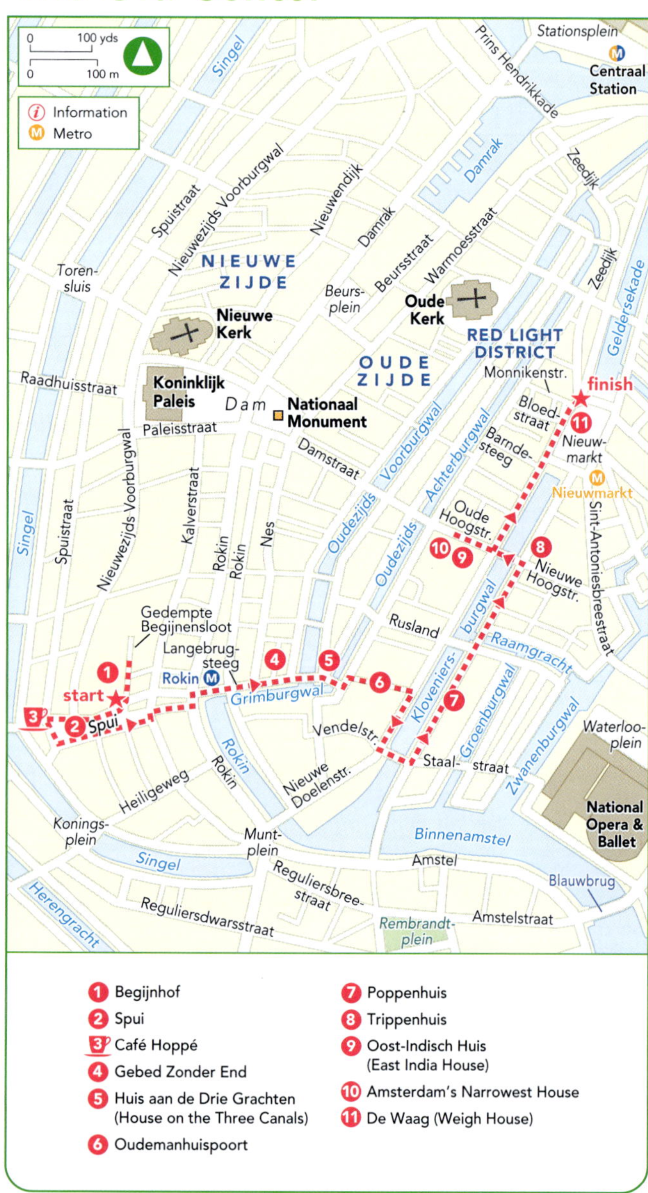


1. Begijnhof
2. Spui
3. Café Hoppé
4. Gebed Zonder End
5. Huis aan de Drie Grachten (House on the Three Canals)
6. Oudemanhuispoort
7. Poppenhuis
8. Trippenhuis
9. Oost-Indisch Huis (East India House)
10. Amsterdam's Narrowest House
11. De Waag (Weigh House)

*Previous page: Walking through Kalverstraat.*

**Take a stroll through the medieval core of old Amsterdam,** the epicenter from which the city expanded outwards in the 1660s. Here you'll find the oldest and narrowest houses, ornately decorated facades, and one or two surprises in a confounding tangle of narrow streets that's a real contrast with the gridlike regularity of the Grachtengordel (Canal Ring). START: **Metro M52 to Rokin.**

*Gabled houses surround the courtyard at Begijnhof.*

1 ♥♥ **Begijnhof.** Just off Spui, but seemingly in another world, this cluster of photogenic gabled houses around a leafy garden courtyard is the perfect place to feel the ambience of old Amsterdam. Black-painted no. 34 is the city's oldest standing house, built around 1455, and one of only two timber houses remaining in the city. Amsterdam was a destination for religious pilgrims and an important Catholic center before the Calvinist rebellion and Alteration in 1578 (p 38). The Begijnhof was a *hofje* (almshouse, see p 48) built to offer devout women (*beguines*) the option to live independently of husband and children (and without becoming a nun) at a time when such a thing was unheard of. The Begijnhof is now a residence for seniors, and as such, you're requested to keep fairly quiet as you walk around. *30 min. Gedempte Begijnensloot. begijnhofkapelamsterdam.nl. Free admission. Daily 9:30am–6pm.*

2 ♥ **Spui.** Back into noisy reality, this square (pronounced *spow*) is both elegant and animated. At its south end is a statue of a small boy, ***Het Lieverdje (The Little Darling),*** who is supposed to represent a typically mischievous Amsterdam child. At no. 21 is the **Maagdenhuis,** the main downtown building of the University of Amsterdam.

3 ♥ **Café Hoppe.** Going strong since 1670, Hoppe serves coffee, beer, jenever, snacks, and more with a substantial side of history. *Spui 18–20. www.cafehoppe.com/en. 020/420-4420. $$.*

4 ♥ **Gebed Zonder End.** Go to the east end of Spui, cross Rokin and Nes, and walk along Langebrugsteeg to Grimburgwal. The tiny, flower-filled alleyway of Gebed Zonder End is located in an area between Nes and Oudezijds Voorburgwal that in medieval times boasted more than 20 monasteries and convents. Legend has it that you could always hear the murmur of prayers from behind the walls. Today, however, you're much more likely to hear laughter

## Amsterdam's Hofjes

Amsterdam has many secret courtyards surrounded by almshouses—they could be considered an early form of care communities where the poor, elderly, or disadvantaged of the parish could be housed and supported. The best known is the **Begijnhof** (p 15), where a community of pious women lived for several centuries. **H'ART** (p 25) also occupies a former *hofje*, where homes were provided for elderly women of slender means. Zon's Hofje at Prinsengracht 159–171 is another example. A walk around the pretty streets of the Jordaan will reveal several *hofjes*, such as the **Raepenhofje** (p 57) and the **Suykerhofje** (p 56).

and chatter coming from the restaurant **Kapitein Zeppos** (p 101).

**5 ♥ Huis aan de Drie Grachten (House on the Three Canals).** Continue along Grimburgwal, then cross Oudezijds Voorburgwal and Oudezijds Achterburgwal. Between these two waterways and abutting Grimburgwal canal, you'll spot the handsomely restored, red-brick and step-gabled Dutch Renaissance mansion built in 1609, with red-painted wooden shutters. In the first half of the 20th century, this was a bookstore that used to print clandestine literature during World War II. *Oudezijds Voorburgwal 249.*

**6 ♥♥ Oudemanhuispoort.** Cross the bridge to the far side of Oudezijds Achterburgwal. Pass the Gasthuis, once a hospital and now part of the university campus, and turn right into a dimly lit arcade, the Oudemanhuispoort, which hosts a secondhand book and prints market Monday through Saturday. Farther down the passageway on the left you'll see a doorway leading to a courtyard garden featuring a bust of Minerva, placed there in 1881. It's a lovely spot for a few minutes of solitude. *Off Grimburgwal.*

**7 ♥ Poppenhuis.** Turn right on Kloveniersburgwal and cross over the canal on Staalstraat; turn left until you reach this handsome neoclassical mansion built in 1642 by the highly successful architect Philips Vingboons for Joan Poppen, the dissolute son and heir to Jacob Poppen, a rich merchant who was a three-time mayor of Amsterdam. *Kloveniersburgwal 95.*

**8 ♥ Trippenhuis.** Farther along you'll see a double-fronted neoclassical house built between 1660 and 1664 by Jacob Vingboons, the sibling of Philips, for the Trip brothers, who were arms dealers. This explains the

*Book market in the arcade at Oudemanhuispoort.*

martial images and emblems dotted about the facade, all of which could use a good scrub. Originally there were two buildings behind a single facade, but they have since been joined and now house the Royal Netherlands Academy of Arts and Sciences. The building is not open for visitors. *Kloveniersburgwal 29.*

**9 ♥♥ Oost-Indisch Huis (East India House).** Walk back to the Bushuissluis canal bridge and cross over to Oude Hoogstraat, where this impressive 1606 building occupies the left side of the street. This was once the warehouses and headquarters of the Vereenigde Oostindische Compagnie, or VOC (Dutch East India Company), a trading giant across Asia in the 1600s and 1700s; forerunner of Dutch colonialism, notably in Indonesia; and a substantial profiteer from both slavery and the spice trade. Here, ship crews were recruited and the company's invaluable collections of early maps were stored. The building now belongs to Amsterdam's university. It's not officially open for visits, but you can sometimes stroll into the courtyard and maybe even peek at hallways hung with paintings of the 17th-century Dutch trading settlement of Batavia (now Jakarta, Indonesia). *Oude Hoogstraat 24.*

**10 ♥ Amsterdam's Narrowest House.** In stark contrast to the gigantic facade of East India House, next door is the city's teeniest house. Squashed in next to Hendrik de Keyser's ornate church gate, Oude Hoogstraat 22 is just 2m (6½ ft.) wide and was built around 1733 as a single story; this miniscule abode was rented out to a watchmaker, and by 1787, etchings show that it had gained two more floors and a bell gable. Blink and you'll miss it. Head back to Kloveniersburgwal and go left. At nos. 10–12 is the drugstore Jacob Hooy & Co., which has been dispensing medicinal relief since 1743. *Oude Hoogstraat 22.*

**11 ♥♥ De Waag (Weigh House).** Kloveniersburgwal ends at Nieuwmarkt, a large and buzzing piazza dominated by the massive edifice that was once one of the city's medieval gates. The Waag later became the city's weigh house for goods coming in off the ships, and now it's a popular place to loiter over a cocktail to watch Amsterdam at play. Nieuwmarkt is the gateway to both the Red Light District and Chinatown. *Nieuwmarkt,* *See also p 29, 2.*

*The De Waag.*

# Amsterdam's Canal Ring

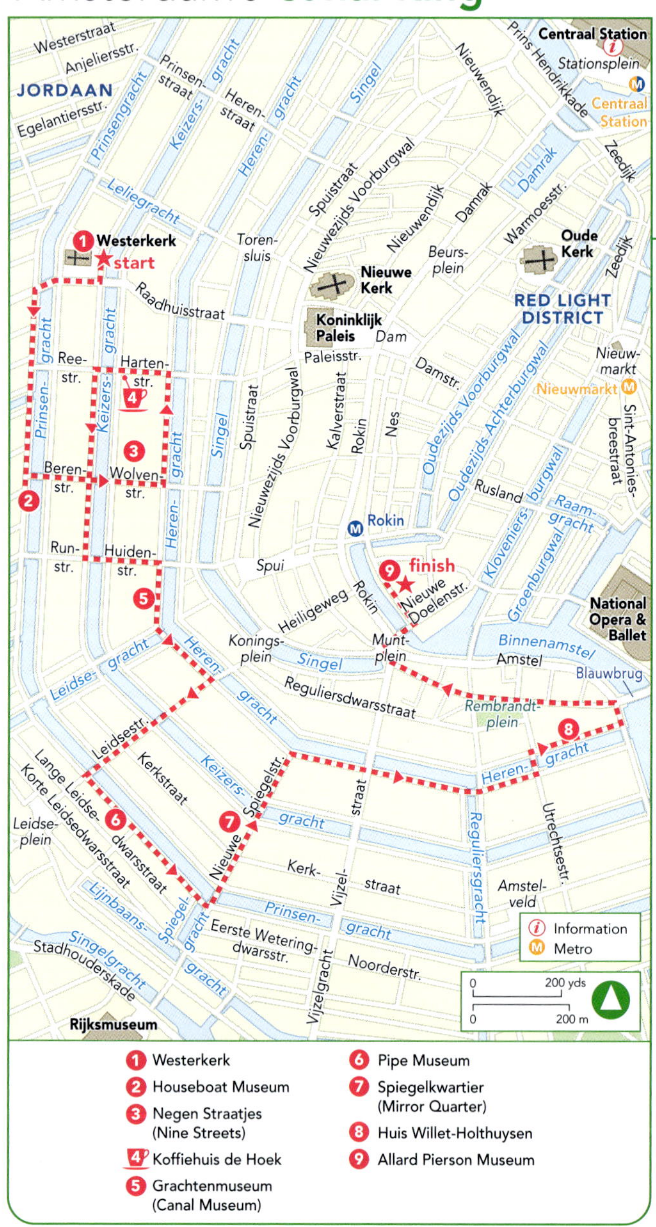


1 Westerkerk
2 Houseboat Museum
3 Negen Straatjes (Nine Streets)
4 Koffiehuis de Hoek
5 Grachtenmuseum (Canal Museum)
6 Pipe Museum
7 Spiegelkwartier (Mirror Quarter)
8 Huis Willet-Holthuysen
9 Allard Pierson Museum

**Amsterdam's glory days were in the 17th century,** an era known as the Golden Age, and there's nowhere better to see the awesome architecture of that time than on the UNESCO-listed Grachtengordel (Canal Ring), which was built to enable the city to expand outwards in a grid pattern, adding three extra canals: Herengracht (Gentlemen's Canal), Keizersgracht (Emperor's Canal), and Prinsengracht (Princes' Canal). The area owes its diversity of styles to wealthy buyers designing their houses to individual tastes; today discover majestic mansions strung along tranquil canals. START: **Tram 13 or 17 to Westermarkt.**

*Crown of Maximilian at the top of Westerkerk church.*

**1 ♥ Westerkerk.** Just around the corner from the Anne Frank Huis, the Protestant Westerkerk is yet another ecclesiastical masterpiece by the celeb architect of the time, Hendrick de Keyser, who designed the Noorderkerk and the Zuiderkerk as part of the new development of the Grachtengordel (Canal Ring). The foundation stone was laid in 1620 (De Keyser died a year later), and the tower was finally completed in 1638; it is more than 85m (279 ft.) tall and is topped with the Crown of Maximilian. Every 15 minutes, its tinkly carillon bells ring out across the city. The church itself is austere; in line with the Calvinist beliefs of the time, there is no altar. But the gold and silver pipes and baroque sculpture adorning the organ make up for the lack of ornamentation. It is the burial place of Rembrandt—although no one knows where his grave is on the unmarked stone floor—and has been the venue for several royal weddings. On Wednesdays at 1pm there's usually a 30-minute organ recital, which is free to attend. *20 min. Prinsengracht 279. westerkerk.nl. 020/624-7766. Free admission. Mon–Fri 11am–3pm.*

**2 ♥ Houseboat Museum.** Two blocks down Prinsengracht to the left you have a chance to glimpse into the lives of Amsterdam's 2,500 houseboat residents. The Houseboat Museum is on board the *Hendrika Maria*, a former cargo barge built in 1914. It was domesticated in 1967, becoming first an artist's studio, then 12 years later, a home. It retains the unique red, yellow, and brown color scheme that typified European 1970s home decor. Walking around reveals a surprisingly roomy timber-roofed living space with box beds, a kitchen, and living room with a couple of armchairs. *25 min. Prinsengracht 296K. houseboatmuseum.nl. 020/427-0750. Admission 9.50€ adults, 5€ kids 5–12. Daily 10am–5pm. Closed Jan 1, Apr 27, Aug 1, and Dec 25.*

**3 ♥♥ Negen Straatjes (Nine Streets).** Turn down Berenstraat or Huidenstraat into one of Amsterdam's best-known shopping areas,

*Strolling the Nine Streets shopping area.*

consisting of nine side streets between Herengracht and Prinsengracht, a one-stop shopping destination with chic stores selling clothing from independent designers, artisan jewelry, organic soaps, and vintage fashions, all interspersed with steadily encroaching high-end chain stores, plenty of bars and restaurants, and a few boutique hotels. The smart **Pulitzer Hotel** (p 136) is just a step away. *1 hr. Between Herengracht and Prinsengracht. de9straatjes.nl/en. Most stores open daily.*

4 ♥ **Koffiehuis de Hoek.** An old-style Amsterdam cafe on the corner overlooking the canal, this place bursts at the seams at lunchtime. Grab a table for an all-day breakfast, or sandwiches piled high with salami and salad. *Prinsengracht 341. koffiehuisdehoek.nl. 020/625-3872. $–$$.*

5 ♥♥♥ kids **Grachtenmuseum (Canal Museum).** Pretty much everywhere you have walked so far today ought to be underwater. This unexpectedly creative little museum helps you understand why it isn't, thanks to the miracle of the canals, around 9 feet deep, and their Golden Age builders. *1 hr. Herengracht 386. See p 8, 3.*

6 ♥ **Pipe Museum.** Walk 1 block farther and turn right down Leidsestraat, crossing over Prinsengracht, and turning left along its south side to the Pipe Museum. Although this may appear to be of niche appeal, in fact the display of pipes is quite entrancing. An accompanied visit shows you the world's largest collection of Dutch clay pipes, intricately carved and bejeweled Meerschaum pipes, and bronze cast pipes from Cameroon. The basement **shop** (p 75) also sells pipes. *30 min. Prinsengracht 488. pipemuseum.nl/en. 020/421-1779. Admission 15€ adults, 7.50€ kids 6–16. Mon–Sat noon–6pm. Closed Jan 1, Apr 27, and Dec 25.*

7 ♥ **Spiegelkwartier (Mirror Quarter).** Continue along Prinsengracht and turn left up Nieuwe Spiegelstraat to Kerkstraat on the canal bend; this has been Amsterdam's main antiques-dealing center for nearly 100 years. This posh little 'hood has multiple stores selling paintings, antiques, Russian icons,

silver, gold jewelry, and, of course, plenty of genuine blue-and-white Delftware. From here it's an easy hop over the Singel to the **Rijksmuseum** (p 7), or turn right along Vijzelstraat until you hit Herengracht once more and take a right. *30 min. Spiegelgracht. spiegelkwartier.nl.*

**8 ♥♥ Huis Willet-Holthuysen.** On the left side of the Herengracht is a magical museum with a pristine interior dating from the 19th century, when it was home to an art-collecting couple with a taste for the French 18th century. Bequeathed to the city in 1895, it's redolent of the sybaritic lifestyle of Amsterdam's prosperous merchant classes, and every curtain, every piece of furniture displayed, and every choice of wallpaper, down to the deep-blue fabric in the gentleman's parlor, is in keeping with the period. Displays include an introduction to the aristocratic family who lived here and a collection of Meissen porcelain. An exquisite formal knot garden at the rear of the house was laid out in 1972, in French 18th-century style, after a fire destroyed the original coach house. *1 hr. Herengracht 605. www.amsterdammuseum.nl/en. No phone. Admission 15€ adults, 7.50€ students, free for kids 17 and under. Daily 10am–5pm. Closed Apr 27 and Dec 25.*

**9 ♥♥ Allard Pierson Museum.** Loop back around towards the center, following the Amstel—a river, not a canal—to a building beside one of Amsterdam's oldest stretches of canal, Rokin. In what is nominally the University of Amsterdam's archaeology museum, thoughtful curation has created the sense of a journey, tracing "culture" from Ancient Egypt to the banks of the Amstel, via Greece, Rome, Etruria, Byzantium, and the Holy Roman Empire. A fascinating historiographic section built around the museum's cast collection asks why these were made, and questions what this may tell us about art, history, and our enduring interest in them. It's a museum for museum lovers. *1 hr. Oude Turfmarkt 127–129. www.allardpierson.nl/en. 020/525-7300. Admission 15.50€ adults, 7.50€ students, 3.50€ kids 5–18. Tues–Sun 10am–5pm. Closed Jan 1, Apr 27, and Dec 25.*

*Interior of the Willet-Holthuysen museum.*

# The Jordaan

Haarlemmer-plein
Haarlemmer Houttuinen
Haarlemmerdijk
Vinkenstraat
Binnen Oranjestraat
De Wittenkade
De Wittenkade
De Wittenstraat
Nassaukade
Singelgracht
Marnixstraat
Brouwers-gracht
Drie-hoek-str.
Palm-gracht
Palm-dwarsstr.
Palm-str.
Brouwersgracht
Jacob Catskade
Kattensloot
Eerste Marnix-plantsoen
Lijnbaansgracht
Tweede Goudsbloem-dwarsstr.
Willemsstr.
Goudsbloem-str.
Lindengracht
Derde Goudsbloemdwarsstr.
Tweede Lindendwarsstr.
Eerste Linden-dwarsstr.
Noorder-kerk
Frederik Hendrik-plantsoen
Lindenstr.
Tichel-straat
Karthuizers-straat
Gieters-straat
Tweede Boomdwarsstr.
finish
Westerstraat
Anjeliersstr.
Marnixstraat
Nassaukade
Tweede Anjeliersdwarsstr.
JORDAAN
Prinsengracht
Keizers-gracht
Tweede Tuindwarsstr.
Tuinstraat
Egelantiersstr.
start
Tweede Egelantiersdwarsstr.
Singelgracht
Keizersgracht
Egelantiersgracht
Eerste Lelie-dwarsstr.
Tweede Lelie-dwarsstr.
Leliegracht
Lijnbaansgracht
Nieuwe Lelie-str.
Prinsengracht
Herengracht
Wester-kerk
Eerste Bloem-dwarsstr.
Bloemgracht
Wester-markt
Bloemstraat
Rozengracht
Rozenstraat
0
200 yds
0
200 m
1 Prinsengracht
2 Bloemgracht
3 Egelantiersgracht
4 Karthuizersplantsoen
5 Lindengracht
6 Jordaanmuseum
7 Palmgracht
8 Brouwersgracht
9 Winkel 43

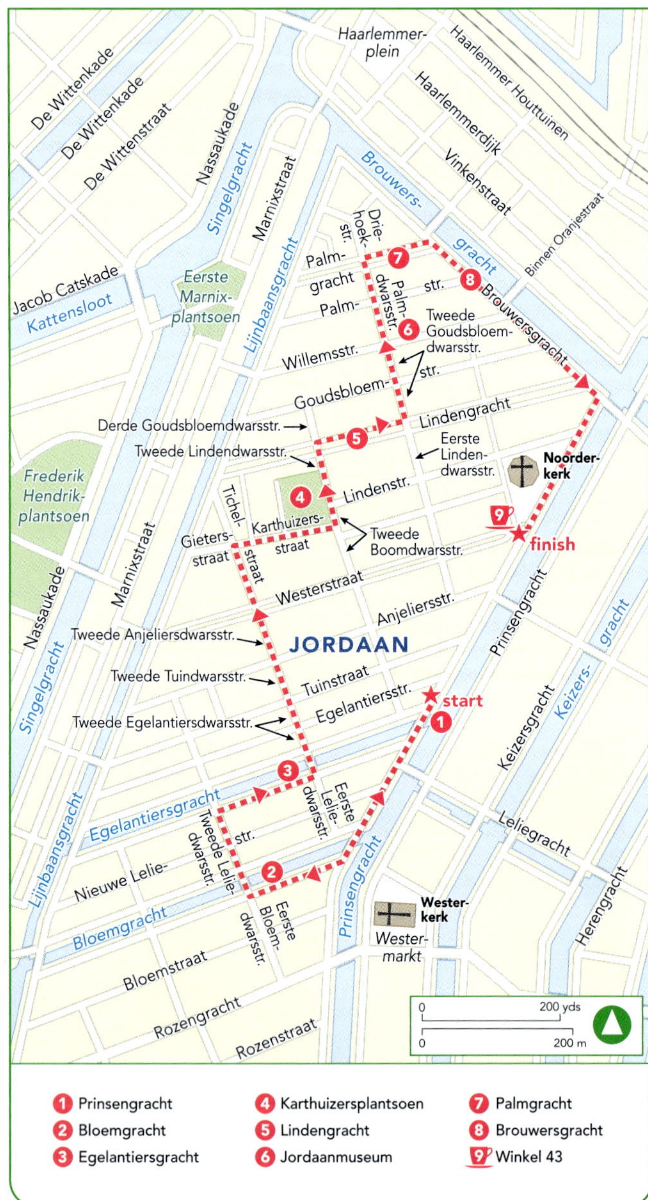

**The Jordaan is one of Amsterdam's loveliest and most distinctive neighborhoods,** once inhabited by Amsterdam's working classes but now thoroughly gentrified. Among the district's charms are narrow streets, tiny canals crossed with humpbacked bridges, and several delightful, centuries-old almshouses, or *hofjes* (p 48), as well as galleries, traditional brown cafes (p 110), and cafes. Aim to start this walk after lunch, and you'll spend a couple of hours gradually working your way to an appetite for some iconic Dutch apple cake. START: **Tram 13 or 17 to Westermarkt.**

❶ ♥ **Prinsengracht.** Start your walk outside the hardware store **Gunters & Meuser** at nos. 2–6, on the corner of Egelantiersgracht, for a fine example of Amsterdam School architecture, circa 1917. Its intricate brickwork and cast-iron ornaments were influenced by the Art Nouveau style. To the left of the store, at no. 8, a step-gabled house dating from 1649 is decorated with sandstone ornaments that depict the English monk St. Willibrord (the first bishop of Utrecht, in 695) and a brewer. *Prinsengracht 2–6.*

❷ ♥ **Bloemgracht.** Turn right and walk along Prinsengracht before taking a right onto Bloemgracht, the grandest of the Jordaan canals and originally home to workers who produced dyes and paints. Nos. 77 and 81 are former sugar refineries from 1752 and 1763, respectively. The three fine step-gabled houses at nos. 87–91 date from 1642, and are now owned by the Hendrick de Keyser Foundation, an organization that preserves buildings of architectural and historic importance throughout the Netherlands. Their carved gable stones represent a townsman, a countryman, and a seaman. *Bloemgracht 87–91.*

❸ ♥♥ **Egelantiersgracht.** Turn right on to Derde Leliedwarsstraat to reach Egelantiersgracht and bear right along the canal. Named for the eglantine rose or sweetbriar, Egelantiersgracht is one of the city's most picturesque and tranquil small canals and is lined with 17th- and 18th-century houses. If the door is open, take a peek into the **Sint Andrieshofje** at nos. 105–141. Cattle farmer Ivo Gerritszoon financed this almshouse of 36 houses, which was completed in 1617 and remodeled in 1884. A corridor decorated with Delft blue tiles leads up to a small courtyard with a manicured garden. *Egelantiersgracht 105–141.*

*The Egelantiersgracht canal.*

**4 ♥♥ Karthuizersplantsoen.** From Egelantiersgracht, turn left onto Derde Egelantiersdwarsstraat, walk 2 blocks and take a right down Tuinstraat before turning onto Tweede Tuindwarsstraat. Carry on across Westerstraat and walk along Tichelstraat until you hit Karthuizersstraat. On this street at nos. 11–19 is a row of neck-gabled houses from 1737, named after the four seasons. At nos. 69–191, you'll find the Huiszittenweduwenhof, which dates from 1650 and used to shelter poor widows. Nothing is left of the Carthusian monastery (1394) that once stretched from Karthuizersplantsoen to Lijnbaansgracht and was destroyed in the 1570s during the Alteration (p 38). A playground marks the spot where its cemetery stood. *Karthuizersstraat 13–19.*

**5 ♥♥ Lindengracht.** Turn left onto Tweede Lindendwarsstraat to reach Lindengracht, and take a right down this street, once the Jordaan's most important canal—since filled in. It is now the site of a lively Saturday street market. The 15 small houses (originally there were 19) of the pretty **Suykerhofje** at Lindengracht 149–163 were built in 1667 as a refuge for Protestant widows of a "tranquil character," who had been abandoned by their husbands. Make a left onto Eerste Lindendwarsstraat, then the second right into Willemsstraat. *Lindengracht 149–163.*

**6 ♥ Jordaanmuseum.** Not exactly a museum, more a work-in-progress to preserve the pre-gentrification history of the Jordaan, both here and online. Signage, maps, and old photos fixed to the wall and sidewalk illustrate the former site of *gangen*, alleyways where poor residents of the Jordaan lived in cramped and unsanitary conditions until the early 20th century. The idealist architecture of the Amsterdam School was, in part, a response to the shame

*Saturday market along Lindengracht.*

*Brouwersgracht canal is lined with houseboats.*

many felt at the continued existence of these slums. (To dig deeper into this fascinating social history, make for **Het Schip,** p 32, ❾.) *Willemsstraat 22–110 (opposite the corner of Eerste Goudsbloemdwarsstraat). jordaanmuseum.nl.*

❼ ♥ **Palmgracht.** Return to Eerste Lindendwarsstraat, take a right and follow it for 2 blocks to Palmgracht. Turn right onto this tree-shaded street, which was also once a canal. The house at nos. 28–38 hides a small cobblestoned courtyard garden behind an orange door that's the entrance to the **Raepenhofje,** an almshouse from 1648. If you're lucky, the door will be open and you can peek into the courtyard. *Palmgracht 28–38.*

❽ ♥♥ **Brouwersgracht.** Continue along Palmgracht to the enchanting "Brewers' Canal" lined with houseboats and narrow, gabled facades that tilt discernibly forwards. Take a right, and when you reach Prinsengracht turn right again and follow the canal into Noordermarkt, a triangular "square" dominated by its church, **Noorderkerk,** another Hendrick de Keyser design dating to the 1620s. A farmers market is held here on Saturday mornings.

9 ♥♥♥ **Winkel 43.** Impressive though the church is, it plays second fiddle in Noordermarkt to perhaps Amsterdam's most famous apple cake: crumbly, infused with sweet warming spices, and flying out of the kitchen from morning 'til late at night. Don't be put off by a queue; it clips along pretty fast. Waitstaff will inquire whether you want whipped cream on top: That one is a no-brainer. *Noordermarkt 43. winkel43.nl/en.* ☎ *020/623-0223. $.*

# Amsterdam-Noord & **the IJ**

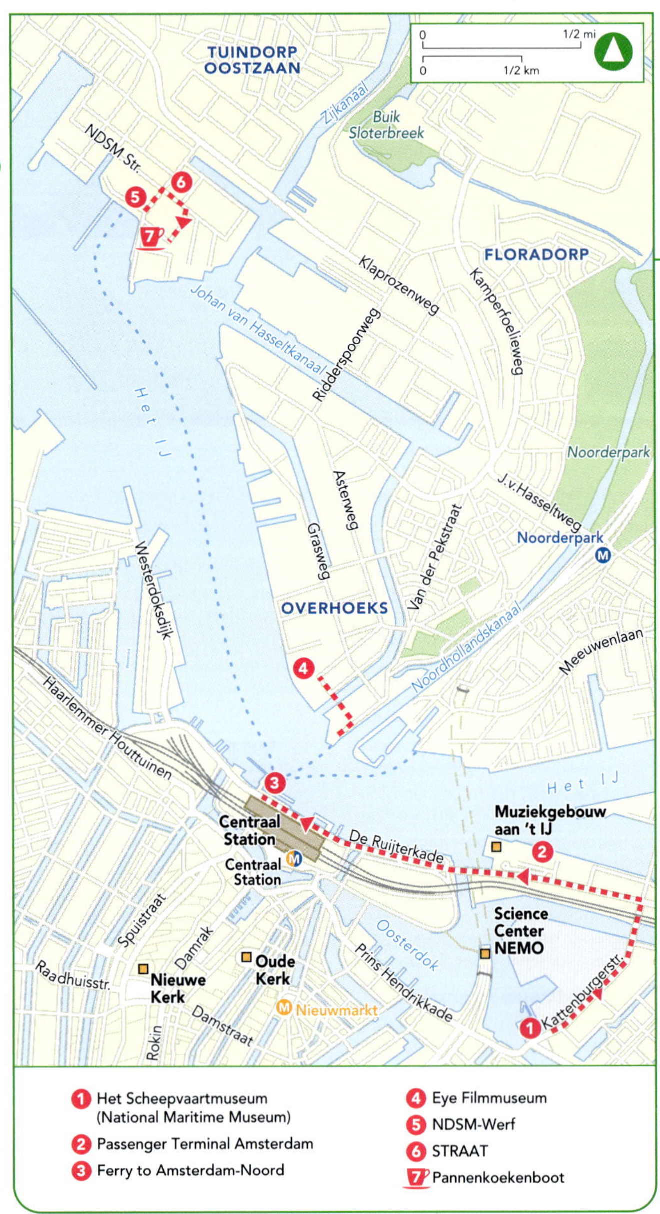


1 Het Scheepvaartmuseum (National Maritime Museum)
2 Passenger Terminal Amsterdam
3 Ferry to Amsterdam-Noord
4 Eye Filmmuseum
5 NDSM-Werf
6 STRAAT
7 Pannenkoekenboot

**Holland's history and culture are inextricably connected to the sea.** This family-friendly tour begins at an excellent maritime museum and sails you across Amsterdam's still-bustling shipping channel by ferry, twice. You'll see the daring new architecture of the docklands, including the Muziekgebouw aan 't IJ concert hall and Eye Filmmuseum, as well as other burgeoning cultural hubs across the IJ in Amsterdam-Noord. This walk is comfortable by foot and ferry, but also a good option in the saddle: Noord is flat, relatively traffic-free, and crisscrossed by cycle lanes; it's also free to take a bike on the ferry. Simply ride it on and off. START: **Bus 22 to Kadijksplein.**

1 ♥♥♥ kids **Het Scheepvaartmuseum (National Maritime Museum).** Housed in a mammoth naval arsenal built in 1656, Amsterdam's Maritime Museum is a gem, as befits one of the world's great seafaring nations. Displays include paintings and models of ships, seascapes, navigational instruments, and cannons and other weaponry and showcase the importance of the city's maritime history, including interconnections with colonialism, slavery, and European power politics, especially its constantly shifting relations with Britain and France. The well-organized displays are anything but dry, enlivened by the clever use of interactive light, sound, multimedia, and audiovisual aids throughout all three wings. For those with an interest in history, the best exhibits detail the growth of the Dutch East India Company (VOC) and don't shy away from its deep implication in the slave trade. Another gallery looks at our evolving relationship with the whale, from prey to protected species. Exhibits entertain kids with tales of naval derring-do, but the main event for youngsters is to board the gaily painted, full-size replica of the VOC merchant ship *Amsterdam*, moored on the quay outside. Everything on board is as it was in 1749 when the original "Eastindiaman" foundered on its maiden voyage to the Dutch East Indies (present-day Indonesia). It's hard to see how a museum on this theme could be any better. *2½ hr. Kattenburgerplein 1. www.hetscheepvaartmuseum.com. ☎ 020/523-2222. Admission 18.50€ adults, 8.50€ students and kids 13–17. Daily*

*VOC merchant ship Amsterdam, moored on the quay outside the National Maritime Museum.*

*10am–5pm. Closed Jan 1, Apr 27, and Dec 25. Bus: 22 to Kadijksplein.*

**2 Passenger Terminal Amsterdam (PTA).** Cross Jan Schaefer Bridge over the IJ for a peek at this ultramodern facility just east of Centraal Station. The PTA sees 200,000 passengers through its doors annually and is best visited when a giant oceangoing cruise liner is docked. The neighboring shiny glass concert hall is the **Muziekgebouw aan 't IJ** (p 121). 10 min. *Piet Heinkade 27. www.ptamsterdam.com. Tram: 26 to PTA.*

**3 ♥♥ kids Ferry to Amsterdam-Noord.** Walk or hop on tram no. 26 to Centraal Station and take the free 3-minute ride from the Waterplein West dock across to the north bank of the IJ. You'll get a sailor's-eye view of the city's busy harbor traffic and the chance to examine the innovative architecture of the Eye Filmmuseum and the A'DAM Tower beside it. *5 min. Ferry: F3 to Buiksloterweg.*

**4 ♥♥ Eye Filmmuseum.** As well as multiple screens, a cafe-bar, and headline temporary exhibitions, the Eye also has a small but engaging permanent museum collection. It aims to present the essence of film as a technology that captures light and movement, tracing innovations from the magic lantern to the smartphone. It also has booths where you can sit and watch classic movies. *40 min.* *See also p 21, 8.*

**5 ♥♥ kids NDSM-Werf.** Back behind Centraal Station, board another free ferry to the NDSM-Wharf. The journey takes around 10 minutes, with ferry departures approximately every 15 minutes; the countdown to the next departure is displayed on digital boards at the berth. The destination is a former shipyard that belonged to

*The colorful NDSM-Wharf.*

the Nederlandsche Dok en Scheepsbouw Maatschappij (Netherlands Dock and Shipyard Corporation) and was long derelict before being taken over by a community of artists who still inhabit several workshops and studios. One weekend each month, the vast space hosts one of Europe's biggest indoor/outdoor flea markets, **IJ-Hallen** (ijhallen.nl/en). Summer music festivals are another mainstay. *30 min. Ferry: F4 to NDSM-Werf.*

6 ♥♥♥ kids **STRAAT.** A ridiculously Instagrammable, monumental space laid out in a vague re-creation of a city grid. The global street art inside is in turn playful, political, and protesting; you can get up close and crane your neck for a detailed look, or climb a platform at one end for the widescreen view. Everything inside interacts subtly with the space (complete with rusting shipping cranes from the warehouse's previous life) as well as the place: You'll spot artworks that reference tulips and a remixed *Girl with a Pearl Earring.* *1½ hr. See p 27, 7.*

7 kids **Pannenkoekenboot.** Unless you're traveling with kids, you may wish to skip this and opt instead for a beer and a great burger at IJver (p 100). But the all-in-one boat trip and pancake dinner can also be a lot of fun. You have 1¼ hours to take in the IJ panoramas and as many pancakes as you like. The last trip usually departs at 7:30pm, earlier in winter. *MS van Riemsdijkweg 41. amsterdam.pannenkoekenboot.nl.* ☎ *020/636-8817. $$–$$$.*

# De Pijp

**On a sunny day "The Pipe" is a busy, happy morass** of street-market shoppers, brunching couples, and kids on scooters. The many outdoor terraces attached to bars and cafes are packed; dogs hurtle around Sarphatipark or leap into its pond. Although increasingly popular for dining and after-dark fun, De Pijp is at heart a locals' neighborhood. It's best to do this tour Monday through Saturday, when the market is on, preferably around lunchtime, when you'll have an appetite for the delicious street food hawked at the Albert Cuypmarkt. START: **Tram 3 to Tweede van der Helststraat.**

1 ♥ **Sarphatipark.** Named after Dutch-Jewish doctor and city planner Samuel Sarphati (1813–66), this pretty green space is the neighborhood's communal garden. It also has a dark history: In 1942, during the Nazi Occupation of the Netherlands, the park's name was changed because of Sarphati's heritage. It was later a gathering point for the June 1943 *razzia*, one of the last large-scale roundups of Amsterdam's Jews. Thousands from De Pijp were forcibly deported and later murdered in Auschwitz and Sobibor. *30 min. Sarphatipark. Tram: 3 to Tweede van der Helststraat.*

**2** ♥♥♥ **kids Graze around Albert Cuypmarkt.** From fried chicken to Surinamese salads, you can buy pretty much anything somewhere along the Cuypmarkt. The Dutch have a seriously sweet tooth, and their treats are unbeatable: You'll likely have to wait in line for one of Rudi's Stroopwafels (opposite no. 182; originalstroopwafels.com; Mon–Tues and Fri–Sat only), which come warm and oozing honey fresh off the griddle. Poffertjes Albert Cuyp (at no. 161) knocks out light little pancakes, best topped simply with butter and a dusting of icing sugar. *Albert Cuypstraat. Mon–Sat only. $. See also p 78.*

**3** ♥♥ **Heineken Experience.** The Heineken brewery once defined De Pijp. Now the redbrick brewhouse, which functioned from 1867 until 1988 before production was moved to The Hague and Den Bosch, hosts a rollicking journey through the brand's growth from microbrewery to a multimillion-euro global company. This is perennially one of the most popular draws in Amsterdam, so book your time slot at least a day or two in advance. The tour takes in the original copper brewing vats, malt silos, and vintage brewing equipment, plus a whole lot of other immersive, interactive experiences. The ultimate goal for many is to chug back a Heineken beer at the bar—it costs a little extra to complete the task on the panoramic rooftop, from where you can survey De Pijp and look north towards the Canal Ring and the church spires of the Old Center. Ages 18 and up only. *2 hr. Stadhouderskade 78. www.heinekenexperience.com/en. 020/205-0593. Admission 25€ adults (includes 2 beers), 30€ with rooftop (includes 3 beers); 25% discount with I amsterdam City Card (p 8). Daily 10:30am–7pm (last entry 5:15pm). Tram: 24 to Marie Heinekenplein.*

*Display of Heinekens through the years at the Heineken Experience.*

# Amsterdam's Jewish Quarter

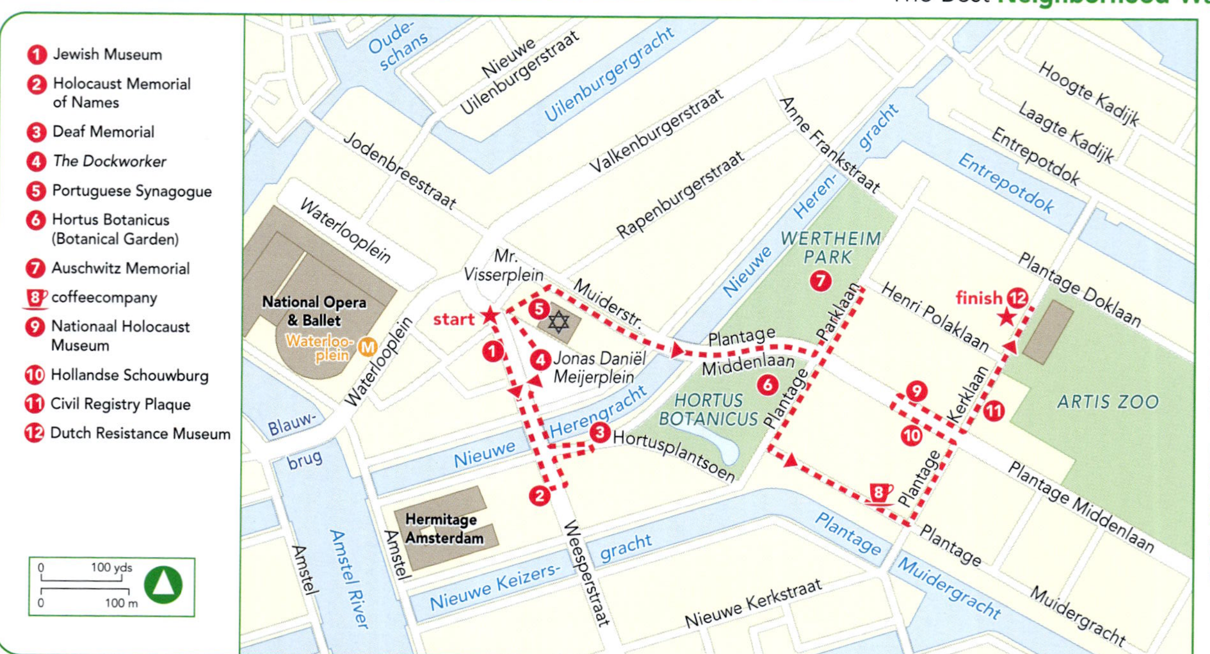

**Amsterdam's Jewish Quarter lies to the east of the old city center** around the Plantage. Before World War II, this was a bustling area crammed with shops and businesses. Waterlooplein market lay at the heart of the district; its synagogues and theaters were the soul of the community. The atrocities of World War II saw all this decimated: Mass deportations led to imprisonment and mass murder in Nazi extermination camps. Today the Jewish Cultural Quarter is full of memorials to the dark days, as well as reminders of the many centuries of Dutch-Jewish cultural history and brave acts of wartime resistance. START: **Tram 14 to Waterlooplein.**

*Inside the Jewish Museum.*

❶ ♥♥ **Jewish Museum.** This large complex was central to Jewish life in Amsterdam for centuries as it originally consisted of four synagogues, notably the magnificent Great Synagogue, in operation between 1671 and 1943. Built by Ashkenazi Jewish refugees from Germany and Poland in the 17th and 18th centuries, it was sheer luck that it survived Nazi occupation. The museum's focus is on Jewish life in the Netherlands before the Holocaust and since, with religion, art, and history taking center stage. The former *mikveh* (ritual bath), closed in 1823, was uncovered during renovations in the 1980s. The museum also displays some of the artifacts looted from the Jewish community during the war. 🕓 *1½ hr. Nieuwe Amstelstraat 1. jck.nl/en. No phone. Admission to Jewish Historical Museum, Portuguese Synagogue, and Nationaal Holocaust Museum 30€ adults (20€ Historical Museum and Synagogue only), 10€ students, 8€ kids 13–17, 6€ kids 6–12. Daily 11am–5pm. Closed Apr 27, Rosh Hashanah, and Yom Kippur.*

*Holocaust Memorial of Names.*

## Nazis in the Netherlands

**The Dutch government surrendered on May 15, 1940, after** intense Nazi bombing of Rotterdam in breach of a neutrality pact. The picture thereafter was a complex one. Holland had its share of enthusiastic Fascists, but also from the start it had a significant opposition movement mostly led (at first) by Communists and Socialists. Slowly the Nazis clamped down on more open-minded Dutch society. When additional brutal laws were enforced, taking away individual freedoms, underground resistance mounted. Amsterdam's Jews were increasingly brutalized by street thugs, then officially persecuted, forced to wear yellow stars, barred from public spaces, and stripped of their jobs. In 1942, the roundups of Jewish families began; thousands of people were deported to labor and extermination camps, often Bergen-Belsen in Germany or Auschwitz in Poland. Of the 140,000 Sephardic and Ashkenazi Jews who lived in Amsterdam before World War II, less than 30,000 survived until Liberation on May 5, 1945. The scale of the occupation's horror is impossible to capture, but Oscar-winning director Steve McQueen's 2023 documentary *Occupied City* makes a mighty attempt.

**2 ♥♥♥ Holocaust Memorial of Names.** Just down Weesperstraat, once a busy shopping street at the heart of the Jewish Quarter, this mazelike, moving memorial was unveiled in 2021. Its giant mirrored-glass shards seem to slice open the sky. ***Weesperstraat (next to the Hoftuin). www.holocaustnamenmonument.nl/en.*** ***See also p 19, 2.***

**3 ♥ Deaf Memorial.** This small bronze sculpture, just across the water from the Botanical Garden (6, below), commemorates deaf victims of the Holocaust. ***Hortusplantsoen.***

**4 ♥ *The Dockworker.*** Back up Weesperstraat, walk across Mr. Visserplein toward the Portuguese Synagogue. Just to the left side of the complex is Jonas Daniël Meijerplein, where many Jews were herded while waiting to be deported to the camps. The bronze figure surrounded by wreaths of flowers is by Mari Andriessen and was erected in 1952 in commemoration of the February 1941 strike by workers protesting the deportations, which was violently suppressed by the Nazis. ***Jonas Daniël Meijerplein.***

**5 ♥♥ Portuguese Synagogue.** Across the street from the Jewish Museum stands Europe's largest synagogue (1675), constructed by Sephardic Jews from Spain and Portugal. The building was restored in the 1950s, and today the *Esnoga* looks essentially as it did 3 centuries ago, complete with a women's gallery supported by 12 stone columns representing the Twelve Tribes of Israel. It's still lit by candles, rather than electricity. The synagogue's treasure chambers display precious *menorahs*, Torah scrolls, and linen wall-hangings from the mid-1700s found by accident in 2022, in a secret chamber below the holy ark. ◷ ***30 min. Mr. Visserplein. jck.nl/en. No phone. Admission to Portuguese Synagogue, Jewish Historical Museum, and Nationaal Holocaust Museum***

*The interior of the Portuguese Synagogue.*

*30€ adults (20€ Synagogue and Historical Museum only), 10€ students, 8€ kids 13–17, 6€ kids 6–12. May–Sept Sun–Fri 11am–5pm; Mar–Apr and Sept–Oct Sun–Thurs 11am–5pm, Fri 11am–4pm; Nov–Feb Sun–Thurs 11am–4pm, Fri 11am–2pm. Closed Apr 27 and most Jewish holidays (check website for dates).*

6 ♥ kids **Hortus Botanicus (Botanical Garden).** Amsterdam's botanical gardens were established in 1638 and create a calm oasis with 4,000 species of plants and trees; in summer, the manicured landscape explodes with colors and scents. The multi-climate greenhouse was renovated in 2025 and houses plants from Australia and South Africa. There's also an herb garden, a desert greenhouse, and a butterfly house with giant, free-flying butterflies that kids love. ⏱ *1 hr. Plantage Middenlaan 2A. www.dehortus.nl/en.* ☎ *020/625-9021. Admission 13.50€ adults, 7€ students and kids 5–17. Daily 10am–5pm. Closed Jan 1 and Dec 25. Tram: 14 to Mr. Visserplein.*

7 ♥ **Auschwitz Memorial.** In the center of Wertheim Park is a 1993 memorial by sculptor Jan Wolkers, dedicated to the victims of Auschwitz. Six large cracked-glass pieces laid flat on the ground reflect a shattered sky and cover a buried urn containing ashes of the dead from the extermination camp. The glass memorial reads, NOOIT MEER AUSCHWITZ ("Never again, Auschwitz"), with the words reflecting back at you. *Plantage Middenlaan.*

8 ♥ **coffeecompany.** A popular pit stop for students from the Business School across the road: Grab a coffee, a toastie, or a chai masala. *Plantage Muidergracht 69–71.* ☎ *020/237-4330. $.*

9 ♥♥♥ **Nationaal Holocaust Museum.** It's shocking that this museum only opened in 2024, but it finally does justice to a dark chapter in Dutch and European history. During World War II, a teaching college stood on the site. At great personal risk, staff smuggled as many as 600 Jewish kids through the building from the temporary kindergarten next door, saving them from certain death in Nazi extermination camps. Exhibits explain the ruse and lead you along the escape route. ⏱ *1½ hr. Plantage Middenlaan 27.* *See also p 19, 1.*

*Display at the Nationaal Holocaust Museum.*

*Interactive exhibits at the Resistance Museum Junior, part of the Dutch Resistance Museum and aimed at children 9 and older.*

**10 ♥♥ Hollandsche Schouwburg.** Opposite the museum, this imposing white building was originally a theater, and still has the appearance of one. In fact, it's partly an illusion: Most of the interior has been stripped away and left as a memorial to around 46,000 Jews who passed through this makeshift detention point en route to Nazi extermination camps. Local "Jew hunters" would also drop their captives here and collect the 7.50 Guilder reward. The memorial itself is simple and moving: a cast column with a Star of David and a peaceful garden. Glass "droplets" embedded in the walls activate audio commentaries about the theater compiled from witness statements and letters sent home. *30 min. Plantage Middenlaan 24. jck.nl/en. No phone. Free admission. Daily 10am–5pm. Closed Apr 27, Rosh Hashanah, and Yom Kippur.*

**11 ♥ Civil Registry Plaque.** Around the corner, a plaque on the wall of what's now De Plantage restaurant marks the former Civil Registry, at no. 36, which in the early 1940s held the records of around 70,000 Amsterdam Jews. Knowing what those records would mean in the hands of Nazi authorities, 14 members of the Resistance torched the building on March 27, 1943. The attack was partially successful but led to the execution of 12 of the attackers. *Plantage Kerklaan.*

**12 ♥♥♥ Verzetsmuseum (Dutch Resistance Museum).** Farther along Plantage Kerklaan, with its entrance almost opposite ARTIS Zoo, is Amsterdam's Dutch Resistance Museum, where dioramas and interactive exhibits unfold the absorbing story of Dutch resistance. They fought against increasingly violent and murderous occupiers, led by a puppet government under Austrian Nazi Arthur Seyss-Urquhart. Sensitive and engaging, the essential free audioguide leads you through a world of clandestine printing presses and forged ID cards; spies and spy-hunters; and the logistics of going into hiding. Indonesian Resistance against Japanese occupation is also covered. About 20,000 Dutch were sent to labor camps in Germany; of those, 2,000 were executed and several thousand more did not survive. *1½ hr. Plantage Kerklaan 61. www.verzetsmuseum.org. 020/620-2535. Admission 16€ adults, 8.50€ students and kids 7–17, 36.50€ family ticket (2+3). Mon–Fri 10am–5pm, Sat–Sun and public holidays 11am–5pm. Closed Jan 1, Apr 27, and Dec 25. Tram: 14 to ARTIS/Holocaustmuseum.*

# 4 The Best Shopping

# Shopping **Best Bets**

Best for **Buying Wine to Go**
♥♥ Wijnhandel De Ware Jacob, *Herenstraat 41 (p 80)*

Best for **Antiques**
♥♥♥ Kramer Kunst & Antiek, *Prinsengracht 807 (p 74)*

Best **Range of Delft Blue**
♥♥ Heinen Delfts Blauw, *Prinsengracht 440 (p 76)*

Best **English-Language Bookstore**
♥♥ American Book Center, *Spui 12 (p 74)*

Best **Place to Score a Stogie**
♥♥ P.G.C. Hajenius, *Rokin 92–96 (p 75)*

Best for **Diamonds**
♥♥ Gassan Diamonds, *Nieuwe Uilenburgerstraat 173–175 (p 78)*

Best **Place to Pick Up a Hunk of Gouda**
♥♥♥ De Kaaskamer, *Runstraat 7 (p 75)*; or ♥♥ Amsterdam Cheese Museum, *Prinsengracht 112 (p 75)*

Best for **Outrageous Footwear**
♥♥ United Nude, *Molsteeg 10 (p 80)*

Best **Street Market**
♥♥♥ Albert Cuypmarkt, *Albert Cuypstraat (p 78)*

Best **Thrift Store**
♥♥ Kilo Store, *Jodenbreestraat 158 (p 77)*

*Shopping for antiques at Kramer Kunst & Antiek.*

*Previous page: Heinen Delfts Blauw.*

*Amsterdam's most celebrated cheese emporium, De Kaaskamer.*

Best for **Flower Bulbs You Can Take Home**
♥♥ Amsterdam Tulip Museum, *Prinsengracht 116 (chapter 1, p 14)*

Best for **Picnic Provisions**
♥♥ Bio Noordermarkt, *Noordermarkt (p 79)*

Most **Ridiculous Gift for Friends Back Home**
♥ Rubber Duck Store, *Oude Doelenstraat 2 (p 78)*

Best **Department Store**
♥♥ de Bijenkorf, *Dam 1 (p 76)*

Freshest **Urbanwear for Men & Women**
♥♥♥ Number Nine, *Elandsgracht 34 (p 77)*; or ♥♥♥ Denim City, *De Hallen (p 77)*

Most **Luxurious Scents & Moisturizers**
♥♥♥ Marie-Stella-Maris, *Keizersgracht 357 (p 80)*

## Windowbrowsing Advice

Sometimes you don't know what you want—we totally understand. We recommend the following neighborhoods to roam and see what takes your fancy from Amsterdam's plethora of independent stores. Beyond the **Nine Streets** shopping district (p 9), the **Jordaan** is a retail gift that keeps on giving: Indie boutiques are everywhere, Tweede Anjeliersdwarsstraat being a personal favorite. The length of **Haarlemmerstraat/Haarlemmerdijk** from close to Centraal Station almost to Westerpark has numerous clothing and thrift stores, bakeries, and bars. Between Albert Cuypstraat and the **Heineken Experience** (p 63), and around De Hallen, are also fun places to browse.

# Amsterdam Shopping

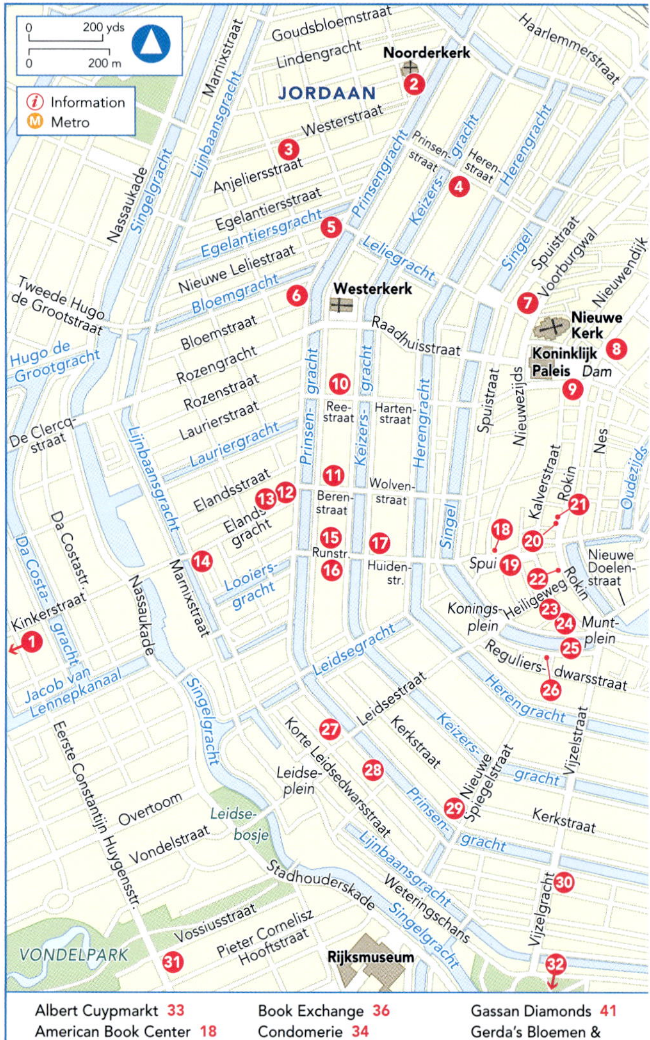


Albert Cuypmarkt 33
American Book Center 18
Amsterdam Cheese Museum 5
Antiekcentrum 14
ArtAmsterdam Spui 19
Azzurro Due 31
Bloemenmarkt (Flower Market) 25
Book Exchange 36
Condomerie 34
de Bijenkorf 8
De Kaaskamer 16
De Pindakaaswinkel 23
Denim City 1
Episode 38
Galleria d'Arte Rinascimento 6
Gassan Diamonds 41
Gerda's Bloemen & Planten 15
Heinen Delfts Blauw 27
HEMA 24
Kilo Store 40
Kramer Kunst & Antiek 29

La Savonnerie 12
Magic Mushroom Gallery 26
Marie-Stella-Maris Boutique 17
Marlies Dekkers 11
Mathieu Hart Antiques 22
Noordermarkt 2
Number Nine 13
Patisserie Holtkamp 30
Peek & Cloppenburg 9
Penny Lane 32
P.G.C. Hajenius 21
Pipeshop 28
Polspotten 3
Pontifex Kramer 10
Premsela & Hamburger 20
Rubber Duck Store 35
United Nude 7
Waterlooplein Flea Market 39
Webers Holland 37
Wijnhandel De Ware Jacob 4

# Amsterdam Shopping A to Z

American Book Center.

## Antiques & Collectibles

**♥ Antiekcentrum** JORDAAN Long-running indoor art and antiques market that is home to friendly dealers in everything from Royal Delft and Art Deco to vintage toys and '60s memorabilia. Closed Tuesdays. *Elandsgracht 109 www.antiekcentrumamsterdam.nl.* ☎ *020/624-9038. Tram: 5, 7, or 19 to Elandsgracht.*

**♥♥♥ Kramer Kunst & Antiek** CANAL RING On the edge of the Spiegelkwartier, this gloriously old-fashioned Aladdin's cave of bric-a-brac hawks everything from Christmas decorations and silver teaspoons to costume watches and, a specialty, Delft Blue tiles. Most items stocked here are portable and packable size. *Prinsengracht 807. www.antique-tileshop.nl/en.* ☎ *020/626-1116. Tram: 1, 2, 7, 12, 17, or 19 to Rijksmuseum.*

**♥♥ Mathieu Hart Antiques** OLD CENTER Since 1878, this refined store has been selling high-quality color etchings of Dutch cities, rare old prints, Delftware, pewter, and grandfather clocks. *Rokin 122. www.hartantiques.com. No phone. Tram: 2, 4, 14, or 17 to Rokin.*

**♥♥ Premsela & Hamburger** OLD CENTER Opened in 1823, this antique silver specialist boasts a great collection of Old Dutch silver by 17th-century craftsmen. Also an excellent choice for antique jewelry. *Rokin 98. premsela.com.* ☎ *020/624-9688. Tram: 2, 4, 14, or 17 to Rokin.*

## Books

**♥♥ American Book Center** OLD CENTER From English-language novels and Frommer's guides to the latest magazine issues, this general bookstore, part of a small Dutch chain, is well stocked. *Spui 12. abc.nl.* ☎ *020/625-5537. Tram: 2, 12, or 17 to Koningsplein.*

**♥♥ Book Exchange** OLD CENTER A warrenlike store of many

Book Exchange.

Cheeses for sale at the Amsterdam Cheese Museum.

levels and hidden rooms stocks secondhand English-language books on every topic imaginable. They also do trade-ins for store credit. *Kloveniersburgwal 58. www.bookexchange.nl. ☎ 020/626-6266. Metro: 51, 53, or 54 to Nieuwmarkt.*

## Candles

**♥♥ Pontifex Kramer** CANAL RING All kinds of candles, from elaborately carved melting works of art to kitsch designs. Pick up scented candles and votives for a romantic dinner in your vacation rental. *Reestraat 20. www.pontifex-kaarsen.com. ☎ 020/626-5274. Closed Sun–Mon. Tram: 13 or 17 to Westermarkt.*

## Cheese

**♥♥ Amsterdam Cheese Museum** JORDAAN Dutch cheese masters. It has a small museum in the basement, but the first-floor Gouda range is the star. Taste smoked, goat, and beer-cured varieties, but none surpass the classic vintage Gouda. Staff will pack anything ready to fly. *Prinsengracht 112. www.cheesemuseumamsterdam.com. ☎ 020/331-6605. Tram: 13 or 17 to Westermarkt.*

**♥♥♥ De Kaaskamer** CANAL RING Amsterdam's most famous cheese emporium is in the heart of the Nine Streets shopping district (p 9). Choose from hundreds of cheeses (they vacuum-pack for travelers), including rows of Gouda wheels stamped with their farm of origin. They also suggest (and sell) wine pairings if you're planning a Vondelpark picnic. *Runstraat 7. www.kaaskamer.nl. ☎ 020/623-3483. Tram: 2, 12, or 17 to Koningsplein.*

## Cigars & Pipes

**♥♥ P.G.C. Hajenius** OLD CENTER In business since 1826, this refined store is the best place to shop for Cuban cigars—an entire room is stocked with Havanas. You'll also find handmade Dutch clay pipes. *Rokin 92–96. www.hajenius.com/en. ☎ 020/623-7494. Tram: 2, 4, 14, or 17 to Rokin.*

**♥ Pipeshop** CANAL RING For anyone intending to cosplay the cerebral European detective, this pipe store sells just about every kind of pipe imaginable, from the antique to the exotic to the kitsch to the downright weird. Open afternoons only; closed Sundays.

*Cigar lovers can pick up some fine Cubans at P.G.C. Hajenius.*

*Prinsengracht 488. pipeshop.nl. ☎ 020/421-1779. Tram: 2, 12, or 17 to Prinsengracht.*

## Confectionery

**♥♥ kids De Pindakaaswinkel** OLD CENTER All-natural peanut butter with no nasty additives. Comes in a range of sizes and flavors, including of course original (and best). *Kalverstraat 210. No phone. depindakaaswinkel.nl. Tram: 4 or 14 to Muntplein. Also at: Sint Luciënsteeg 20.*

**♥ Patisserie Holtkamp** CANAL RING Art Deco patisserie with all manner of sweet treats boxed beautifully to go: biscuits, cakes, meringues, macarons, and more. *Vijzelgracht 15. www.patisserieholtkamp.nl. ☎ 020/624-8757. Metro: 52 to Vijzelgracht.*

## Delftware

**♥♥ Galleria d'Arte Rinascimento** JORDAAN This emporium sells porcelain of every type, notably genuine handpainted Delftware from Koninklijke Porceleyne Fles (Royal Delft Porcelain Factory; p 147)—the real deal. Opening hours can be extremely erratic. *Prinsengracht 170. ☎ 020/622-7509. Tram: 13 or 17 to Westermarkt.*

**♥♥ Heinen Delfts Blauw** CANAL RING This family-owned mini-chain designs, makes, and sells its own porcelain, a mix of high-end, handpainted items, including collaboration collections with leading Dutch pottery designers, and larger production-run souvenirs made in Heinen's own Chinese factory. *Prinsengracht 440. www.heinendelftsblauw.com. ☎ 020/627-8299. Tram: 2, 12, or 17 to Prinsengracht. Also at: De Munt, Muntplein 12; Damrak 65; Markt 45, Delft.*

## Department Stores

**♥♥ kids de Bijenkorf** OLD CENTER The Netherlands' best-known department store sports the largest variety of goods. From handbags and cosmetics to childrenswear, it's all here. *Dam 1. www.debijenkorf.nl/amsterdam. ☎ 020/808-9333. Tram: 4 or 14 to Dam.*

**♥ kids HEMA** OLD CENTER This budget retail chain store is a great place to find emergency basics like a toothbrush, socks, picnicware, or back-to-school stationery. *Kalverpassage, Kalverstraat 212. winkels.hema.nl. ☎ 020/422-8988. Tram: 4 or 14 to Muntplein. Also at: Ferdinand Bolstraat 93; De Ruijterkade 42A in Centraal Station.*

## Design & Home Accessories

**♥♥ Polspotten** JORDAAN Bright and colorful interior-design concept store; a good place to pick up striking home accessories, kitchenware, and household knickknacks

*Pick up some handpainted Delftware at Heinen Delfts Blauw.*

*The showroom at Polspotten, which sells striking and colorful homewares.*

by hip young designers. *Westerstraat 187. www.polspotten.com.* ☎ *020/261-2900. Tram: 5 or 13 to Marnixplein.*

## Fashion & Thrift Stores

♥♥ **Azzurro Due** MUSEUM DISTRICT The ultimate address for finding a pair of designer pants or that elusive Balenciaga accessory. For men and women, very chic, very exclusive. *Van Baerlestraat 3. azzurrodue.com.* ☎ *020/671-9708. Tram: 3 to Van Baerlestraat.*

♥♥♥ **Denim City** OUD-WEST Temple of high-quality denim with selvedge jeans and other items from select Japanese and European brands, including Dutch labels Kings of Indigo, Denham, and Muur. *Hannie Dankbaarpassage 22, De Hallen. denimcity.org. No phone. Tram: 7 or 17 to Nicolaas Beetsstraat.*

♥♥ **Episode** JEWISH QUARTER Find jackets, dresses, scarves, belts, funky brooches, boots, and leather jackets at this unisex vintage store which has grown to multiple venues—across Amsterdam and beyond. It's all properly cleaned, in good shape, and reasonably priced. *Waterlooplein 1. episode.eu. No phone. Metro: 51, 53, or 54 to Waterlooplein. Also at: Berenstraat 1; Spuistraat 96; Nieuwe Spiegelstraat 37H.*

♥♥ **Kilo Store** JEWISH QUARTER Thrift or vintage clothing is a big deal in Amsterdam. There's a wide selection here, for men and women, at reasonable prices—somewhere between "thrift" and "vintage." Tops, skirts, and denim are a good value, especially if you can pull something out of the bargain buckets. They also have branches in De Pijp and close to Centraal Station. *Jodenbreestraat 158. kilostore.nl. No phone. Metro: 51, 53, or 54 to Waterlooplein. Also at: Haarlemmerstraat 78; Albert Cuypstraat 100.*

♥♥♥ **Marlies Dekkers** CANAL RING This Nine Streets boutique is the place to head for date-night lingerie and designer swimwear, all crafted by Dutch icon Marlies. The shop also stocks a selection of her seasonal ranges countrywide in **de Bijenkorf** department stores (p 76). Closed Mondays. *Berenstraat 18. www.marliesdekkers.com.* ☎ *06/1547-0841. Tram: 2, 12, or 17 to Keizersgracht.*

♥♥♥ **Number Nine** JORDAAN Independent retailer founded in Haarlem that specializes in casual European workwear brands, kitting out women and men from head to toe. *Elandsgracht 34. www.numbernine.nl.* ☎ *020/337-4715. Tram: 5, 7, or 19 to Elandsgracht. Also at: Haarlemmerdijk 151–155.*

♥ kids **Peek & Cloppenburg** OLD CENTER Mainstream, mostly smart-casual fashionwear for men, women, and children—at a range of price levels. Multiple European and global brands are under one roof, with regular discount sales. *Dam 20. www.peek-cloppenburg.nl. No phone. Tram: 4 or 14 to Dam.*

**♥♥ Penny Lane** DE PIJP Expertly curated vintage clothing store with a bit of everything, although better stocked for women than men. Note, this is high-end designer vintage fashion, incorporating several unique pieces, not thrift. *Eerste van der Helststraat 11A. pennylanevintage.nl. No phone. Tram: 4 or 24 to Marie Heinekenplein.*

**♥♥ Webers Holland** OLD CENTER The venerable 17th-century Klein Trippenhuis (Little Trippenhuis), one of the narrowest houses in Amsterdam, is a delightfully incongruous setting for imaginative, avant-garde clothing for women, much of it designed by Amsterdammer Desiree Webers. Specialists in kinkwear and fetish. *Kloveniersburgwal 26. www.webersholland.nl. ☎ 020/638-1777. Metro: 51, 53, or 54 to Nieuwmarkt.*

## Flowers

**♥♥ Gerda's Bloemen & Planten** CANAL RING This elegant florist in the Nine Streets shopping district has a fantastic selection of exotic flowers and unusual plants artfully arranged and presented. It can accommodate last-minute bouquet orders and offers local delivery. *Runstraat 16. gerdasbloemen.com. ☎ 020/624-2912. Tram: 2, 12, or 17 to Koningsplein.*

## Offbeat Items & Original Gifts

**♥ Condomerie** OLD CENTER Handily situated on the edge of the Red Light District, this condom boutique stocks a vast range, in all shapes, sizes, and flavors, from common brands to flashy designer and novelty fittings—including in the guise of an F1 car. *Warmoesstraat 141. condomerie.com. ☎ 020/627-4174. Tram: 4 or 14 to Dam.*

**♥♥ Magic Mushroom Gallery** OLD CENTER This smart shop (p 43) sells everything from liquid psychoactives and psilocybin mushrooms to tonics and supplements for men and women that allegedly improve your sex life. Take advice from the knowledgeable staff, but come to your own informed decision. It's not for everyone; plus it goes without saying, nothing you buy here is to be transported outside of the Netherlands. Ages 18 and over only. *Spuistraat 249. www.magicmushroom.com. No phone. Tram: 2, 12, or 17 to Paleisstraat.*

**♥ kids Rubber Duck Store** OLD CENTER A bewildering range of novelty ducks for floating in your bath. Includes such themed special editions as Mad Quax and ZZ Flock. *Oude Doelenstraat 2. ☎ 06/4719-6776. Tram: 2, 4, 14, or 17 to Rokin.*

## Jewelry & Gems

**♥♥ Gassan Diamonds** JEWISH QUARTER Look for the brick smokestack: This is home base for the House Of Gassan. In addition to shopping for diamonds in the showroom, you can take a free 1-hour tour of the stunning 1879 factory that shows you how the jewels are cut. Tax-free shopping is available (p 170). *Nieuwe Uilenburgerstraat 173–175. www.gassan.com. ☎ 020/622-5333. Tram: 14 to Mr. Visserplein. Also at: Rokin 1–5.*

## Markets

**♥♥♥ Albert Cuypmarkt** DE PIJP Amsterdam's busiest, buzziest, and

*Fresh flower bouquets at Gerda's Bloemen & Planten.*

*You can watch a jeweler cutting diamonds in the factory tour at Gassan Diamonds.*

best all-purpose street market stretches for 1km (½ mile). From ready-to-eat herring, cannabis edibles, fresh *stroopwafels*, and halal chicken street food to casual bags, funky jewelry, and hand-knitted hats, you'll find it all here Monday through Saturday from 9am to 5pm. Amsterdammers love it, and so will you. *Albert Cuypstraat btw. Ferdinand Bolstraat & Van Woustraat. albertcuyp-markt.amsterdam. No phone. Tram: 4 to Albert Cuypstraat.*

♥ **ArtAmsterdam Spui** OLD CENTER Every Sunday (10am–6pm) from March to December, local artists mount outdoor exhibits of their paintings, ceramics, and handmade jewelry—and it's possible to find something special. There's often a secondhand book market in the same square on Fridays. *Spui. artamsterdam-spui.com. ☎ 06/4020-9891. Tram: 2, 4, 14, or 17 to Rokin.*

♥ **Bloemenmarkt (Flower Market)** CANAL RING Partly floating on a row of platforms and permanently moored barges, this is Amsterdam's most popular flower market. It's incredibly touristy and always busy, but you will find fresh-cut flowers, rows of tulip bunches, and ready-to-travel packets of tulip bulbs—make sure they are certified if you plan to bring them home. Open daily. *Along the south bank of Singel btw. Muntplein and Koningsplein. No phone. Tram: 4 or 14 to Muntplein.*

♥♥ **Noordermarkt** JORDAAN The Noorderkerk (North Church) was built the same year this market was inaugurated, in 1623, and was the final masterpiece of Hendrik de Keyser. The square that envelops the church is home to a sprawling flea market on Saturdays and a less extensive market on Monday mornings. Stalls show off a mixed bag of paintings, a few antiques, handmade jewelry, rugs, and old books at rock-bottom prices. Everything starts to close up around 2pm so get here at 9am to snap up a genuine find. The **Bio Noordermarkt** farmers market (Sat 9am–2pm only) is adjacent, the place to find fresh vegetables, fruit, honey, cheeses, and organic breads for a picnic. *Noordermarkt. www.noordermarkt-amsterdam.nl. No phone. Tram: 5 to Willemsstraat.*

♥♥ **Waterlooplein Flea Market** JEWISH QUARTER The oldest and most famous Amsterdam flea market is a jumble of everything from bargain-basement souvenirs to old CDs, rubber raincoats, and 10€ Levi's. Stalls generally open Monday through Saturday from 9am to 5:30pm. *Waterlooplein. No phone. Metro: 51, 53, or 54 to Waterlooplein.*

*A fresh batch of* stroopwafels *at Albert Cuypmarkt.*

*Amsterdam's most popular flower market, Bloemenmarkt, has everything from dried flowers to bags of tulip bulbs.*

## Shoes

**♥♥ United Nude** OLD CENTER "Outrageous" and "avant-garde" doesn't begin to encapsulate the women's shoes on sale at this brand flagship store. Some styles still incorporate the award-winning Mobius heel, inspired by design icon Mies van der Rohe. Budget for around 300€ a pair. *Molsteeg 10. unitednude.eu. No phone. Tram: 2, 12, or 17 to Dam.*

## Skincare, Scents & Soap

**♥ kids La Savonnerie** JORDAAN You'll smell the store before you arrive: Artisanal soaps of all shapes and sizes are made and sold here. Kids may appreciate the animal-shaped soaps. *Prinsengracht 294. www.savonnerie.nl. ☎ 020/428-1139. Tram: 5, 7, or 19 to Elandsgracht.*

**♥♥♥ Marie-Stella-Maris Boutique** CANAL RING Exquisite scents for you and your home—and without microplastics or other damaging ingredients. This boutique sells luxury with a mission, supporting sustainable clean water projects all over the world. *Keizersgracht 357. marie-stella-maris.com. ☎ 085/273-2845. Tram: 2, 12, or 17 to Koningsplein. Also at: Van Baerlestraat 34.*

## Wine & Liquor

**♥♥ Wijnhandel De Ware Jacob** CANAL RING Since 1970, this small but charming wine store has carried the finest vintages from wineries around the world, as well as several boutique and limited-release Scotch whiskies. *Herenstraat 41. warejacob.com. ☎ 020/623-9877. Tram: 2, 12, or 17 to Nieuwezijds Kolk.*

*Wijnhandel De Ware Jacob.*

# 5 The Best of the **Outdoors**

# Strolling in Vondelpark

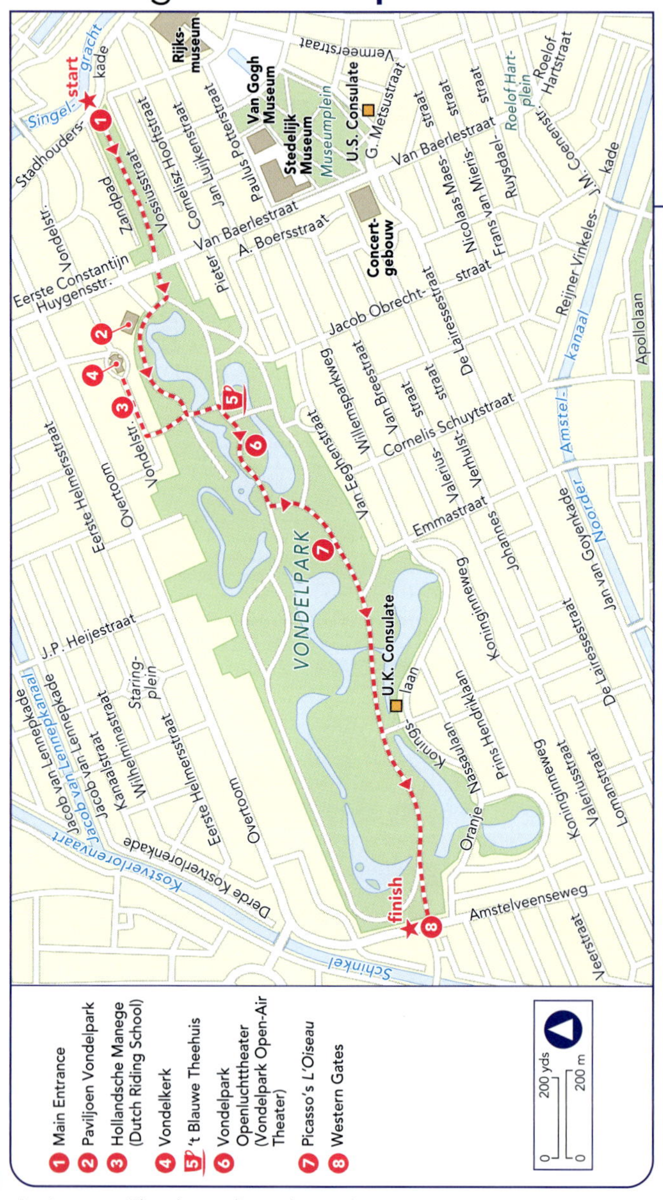


*Previous page: Bikes along an Amsterdam canal.*

**Central Amsterdam is a densely packed city,** but several large parks provide tranquil refuges from the crowds of tourists if not from the marauding cyclists. Of these, Oosterpark is the oldest, Westerpark is a hive of music and concerts, and Sarphatipark is Amsterdam's best-kept neighborhood secret. But the Vondelpark is the biggest and most loved. A step away from Museumplein, it encompasses 47 hectares (116 acres) of lawn set in an English-style park where manicured rose gardens and ponds are set amid trails for joggers, bikers, and in-line skaters. START: **Tram 1, 2, 5, 12, or 17to Leidseplein.**

*Picnicking in Vondelpark.*

❶ ♥♥ **Main Entrance.** Enter the park through the main gates at 1e Constantijn Huygensstraat, less than a 10-minute walk from Leidseplein. The sculpture *Maid of Amsterdam,* a symbol of the city, sits over these gates. The park opened to the public in 1865. Jan David Zocher and Louis David Zocher (a father-and-son operation) landscaped what was then a much smaller space, using rose gardens, ponds, and pathways to create an English-style garden. Over the years, as the park grew to its present size, some 130 different species of trees were planted. The park is home to squirrels, rabbits, wading birds, and a colony of bright-green parakeets. ***Note:*** Wherever you walk in the park, keep to your right to avoid zooming bikes.

❷ ♥ **Paviljoen Vondelpark.** From the gates, head southwest, keeping to the path on your right. After about 500m (550 yards), you'll see this grand pavilion to your right. Constructed

*Paviljoen Vondelpark.*

## Revitalizing Vondelpark

**The 10 million–plus visitors to Vondelpark every year are seriously impacting the earth.** The park was built on peat, and now the ground is 0.6m (2 ft.) lower than the surrounding buildings. Indeed, the **Paviljoen Vondelpark** (p 83) is at the city's lowest point, well below the water level. In the past, when it rained, some areas were prone to collect water, resulting in large, unwanted ponds. A renovation project has created a new drainage system. Landscapers have also planted new varieties of water-absorbing trees and bushes.

in a flamboyant Italian neo-Renaissance style, it opened in 1881 as a cafe and restaurant and then in 1947 became an international cultural center. From 1972 until 2011, the pavilion housed the country's main film museum, **Eye Filmmuseum** (p 21), which now has a shiny home on the north shore of the IJ. The pavilion is currently occupied by the IDFA Institute, dedicated to documentary filmmaking, and hosts regular movie screenings, exhibitions, and events. *Vondelpark 3. www.idfa.nl/paviljoen.*

**3 ♥ Hollandsche Manege (Dutch Riding School).** When you exit the cafe, stay on the path to the right and you'll see the glorious neoclassical facade of the Dutch Riding School, which was built in 1882 by A.L. van Gendt. Restored in the 1980s, it still operates as a stable and arena. The building was modeled after the Spanish Riding School in Vienna. A tour includes the vaulted *manège* with its orchestra pits, gilded mirrors, and molded horses' heads; the stables; and a short documentary. You can also take lessons here; e-mail ahead to book. *Vondelstraat 140 (stables' entrance on Overtoom). levendpaardenmuseum.nl. No phone. Admission 12.50€ adults, 8€ kids 3–12. Tues–Sun 11am–5pm. Tram: 1 to Eerste Constantijn Huygensstraat.*

**4 ♥ Vondelkerk.** Close to the Riding School is a tall neo-Gothic Catholic church designed by Pierre Cuypers, architect of **Centraal Station** (p 30) and the **Rijksmuseum** (p 7). It was completed in 1880, but a fire in 1904 destroyed its original tower; a new one was added by the architect's son. In 1985, the church was partially converted into offices, to fund restoration, but the towering main nave still hosts chamber music concerts and other events (see the website for listings). *Vondelstraat 120-D. www.vondelkerk.nl. ☎ 020/520-0090. Free admission to the public 1st Wed of month (noon–4pm) and 3rd Sun of month (1–4pm). Tram: 1 to Eerste Constantijn Huygensstraat.*

*The spire of Vondelkerk.*

*Vondelpark Open-Air Theater.*

5 ♥ **'t Blauwe Theehuis.** "The Blue Teahouse" is a functionalist-style spaceship of a cafe-bar run by Amsterdam's Brouwerij 't IJ. It's a fine all-day place for a coffee and croissant; a light lunch; or bites and local brews. Closed Mondays. *Vondelpark 5. www.brouwerijhetij.nl/proeflokaal-het-blauwe-theehuis.* ☎ *020/235-7170. $.*

6 ♥ kids **Vondelpark Openluchttheater (Vondelpark Open-Air Theater).** Another couple of minutes' stroll brings you to this dome-shaped open-air stage, where music festivals, concerts, theater, comedy, and children's shows are staged free of charge. Performances take place Friday evening to Sunday afternoon from late May through late August; check the website for program details. *Vondelpark 5a. www.openluchttheater.nl.* ☎ *020/673-1499. Free admission.*

7 ♥ **Picasso's L'Oiseau.** It looks like a fish and everyone calls it "The Fish," but it's actually a cut-out, 16-foot bird sculpture as seen by the Cubist eye of Pablo Picasso. It was donated by the great Spanish artist to mark Vondelpark's centenary in 1965.

8 **Western Gates.** By the time you reach the western gates on Amstelveenseweg, you'll have walked a little over 2km (1¼ miles). Exit here and jump on tram 1 from Overtoom or tram 2 from Koninginneweg to go back into the city, or you can head back east, staying to your right to take the path back to the entrance gates close to Leidseplein. The entire loop measures about 4km (2½ miles).

## Friday Night Skate

If you're game for a little rollerblading, try joining the many skaters (one time a record 3,000) who strap on their 'blades for Amsterdam's regular—and free—**Friday Night Skate** (www.fridaynightskate.com). This event, which started in 1997, begins at 8:30pm, weather permitting (check the website), from outside Paviljoen Vondelpark. It takes one of a series of possible routes through the city (around 20km, or 12½ miles), returning to the starting point in approximately 2 hours. You can rent blades nearby (15€/day; protective gear included) from **Thisissoul,** Overtoom 327 (www.thisissoul.com; ☎ **06/2835-0976;** Tram: 1 to J.P. Heijestraat), which closes at 6pm on Fridays (return them in the morning).

# Touring Amsterdam by Canal Bike

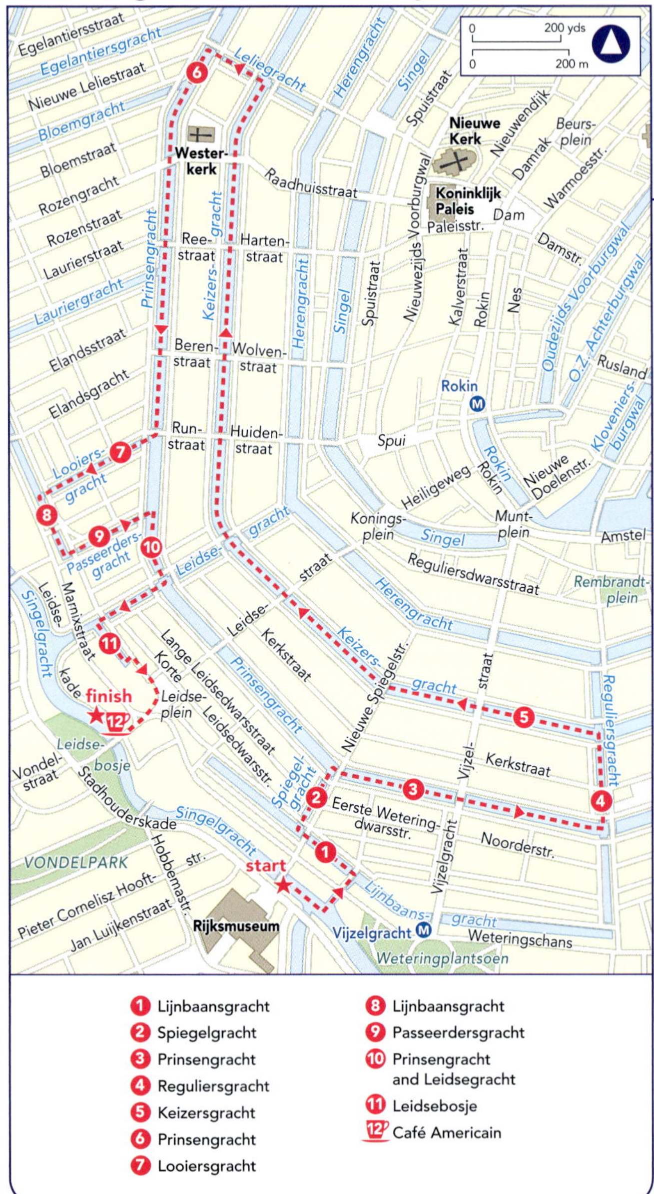


1. Lijnbaansgracht
2. Spiegelgracht
3. Prinsengracht
4. Reguliersgracht
5. Keizersgracht
6. Prinsengracht
7. Looiersgracht
8. Lijnbaansgracht
9. Passeerdersgracht
10. Prinsengracht and Leidsegracht
11. Leidsebosje
12. Café Americain

**Canal biking down the city's myriad interlocking waterways** is an outdoor activity peculiar to Amsterdam. These pedal boats (or pedalos) let you glide quietly down the canals for a close-up look at houseboats and bridges. You'll also get a different vantage point from which to admire the 17th- and 18th-century houses that line the canals. Early on a summer's evening or late on a winter's afternoon is the best time for a trip, when the slanting sun hits the buildings and bridges, affording rich opportunities for photos. START: **Tram 1, 2, 7, 12, 17, or 19 to Rijksmuseum.**

*Renting a pedal boat is a great way to see the canals.*

1 **Lijnbaansgracht.** From the Rijksmuseum mooring on Singelgracht, take a left into Lijnbaansgracht, with its very low bridge and rows of neck-gabled houses. This long canal goes all the way to Haarlemmerpoort and is where 17th-century rope-makers (Lijnbaansgracht translates as "ropewalk") used to stretch and twist the ropes they made for the Dutch shipbuilding industry.

2 ♥ **Spiegelgracht.** Turn right onto this short canal lined with antiques shops. There are 100 or so specialized antiques dealers behind the gabled facades in the **Spiegelkwartier** neighborhood (p 52), selling everything from barometers and clocks to brass and copper ornaments. If you choose to stop and have a look, have one person in your party stay with the canal bike—don't leave it unattended.

3 ♥♥♥ **Prinsengracht.** Turn right onto one of Amsterdam's Golden Age canals. Many of the houses here were built between 1635 and 1700. The houses along this stretch of canal all belonged to

*Prinsengracht canal.*

*From Reguliersgracht canal, you can see seven identical arched bridges in perfect alignment.*

rich families and have ornate facades and steps up to their doors—an indication of wealth.

4 ♥ **Reguliersgracht.** Turn left onto Reguliersgracht. As you swing the boat around, look directly forward: Seven identical arched bridges, perfectly aligned, span this canal. These date back to the 17th century. It's a famous spot for photographs—brides and grooms are a common sight—and the waterway can get pretty crowded.

5 ♥♥♥ **Keizersgracht.** Turn left onto Keizersgracht, the ring's widest canal at 28m (92 ft.). Some of the houses lining the canal were originally built as coach houses for the mansions of the prosperous "Golden Bend" stretch of nearby Herengracht. You'll be pedaling for quite some time (30–45 min.) on Keizersgracht: To cut your loop shorter (to around 1 hr.), make a left into Leidsegracht, and skip forward to stop 10. Otherwise, head northwards along the edge of the old city center, bisecting the heart of the **Nine Streets** shopping district (p 9), and towards the Jordaan. To begin looping back, turn left on tiny Leliegracht, just after the tall spire of the **Westerkerk** (p 51), and then left again on Prinsengracht.

6 ♥♥♥ **Prinsengracht.** You are back on Prinsengracht, now in the heart of the charming Jordaan neighborhood. The **Anne Frank Huis** (p 13) is immediately on the left. You'll see many houseboats lining the banks of Prinsengracht; most have been here since just after World War II, when the housing shortage forced some people to find alternative dwellings. There are currently some 2,500 houseboats in Amsterdam, and they cost as much to buy as houses on land.

7 **Looiersgracht.** Just after you pass the **Houseboat Museum** (p 51), turn right at the "Tanners' Canal"; not surprisingly, this is where leather was tanned.

8 **Lijnbaansgracht.** Turn left and you're back on to Lijnbaansgracht.

9 ♥♥♥ **Passeerdersgracht.** Turn left here and notice the low railing on the bridge, installed to stop cars from falling into the water. Before the railing was built, cars frequently fell into the canal, and in the 18th century, horses and carriages also tumbled into the water. Railings were not installed on

*Keizersgracht canal at night.*

*Anne Frank Huis and museum, far right, along the Prinsengracht canal.*

any of Amsterdam's 100km (62 miles) of canals until the 1960s.

⑩ **Prinsengracht and Leidsegracht.** Turn right and you're on Prinsengracht again. Turn right onto Leidsegracht. Notice the four houses at nos. 72–78, which display four different kinds of gables: No. 72 has a neck gable, 74 a cornice gable, 76 a spout gable, and 78 a step gable (p 32).

⑪ **Leidsebosje.** Turn left and you've reached the end! Return your canal bike here and head for a restorative drink at the Art Nouveau **Café Americain** (see below) opposite the mooring.

12 ♥ **Café Americain.** Abutting Leidseplein, this cafe is a national monument to Dutch Art Nouveau. Don't forget to look up to admire the frosted-glass Tiffany chandeliers. It's quite touristy but offers plenty of salads and sandwiches to choose from as well as afternoon tea daily. *Leidseplein 28. cafeamericain.nl/en.* ☎ *020/556-3010. $$.*

## Pedal Boat Rentals & Rules

Pedal boats can seat up to four people (a child can be carried as a fifth passenger in some circumstances), and they are stable and comfortable. The charge per boat is between 19.50€ and 33€ for 1 hour, depending on whether you book online or walk up (morning rentals are often cheaper). If you prebook using your **I amsterdam City Card** (p 8), there's also 25% off. Our suggested itinerary takes about 2 hours. A free map is given with every trip. Rental hours are 10:30am to between 5 and 9:30pm, depending on the weather and time of year. Rent from **Stromma** at its Rijksmuseum mooring, Stadhouderskade 520 (www.stromma.com; ☎ **020/217-0501**). In addition to this mooring, Stromma operates docks in front of the Anne Frank Huis on Prinsengracht (Apr–Sept only), and at the Leidsebosje facing the American Hotel (p 130). If you get tired, drop off your canal bike at one of these moorings.

Always stay to the right when navigating the canals—this is especially important when going under bridges in narrow canals. All other traffic has right of way. The port area and the Amstel River are off-limits to canal bikes. If you need a break, stop at one of the mooring docks. ***Never*** leave your canal bike unattended—it will be towed away.

# Biking Along the **Amstel River**

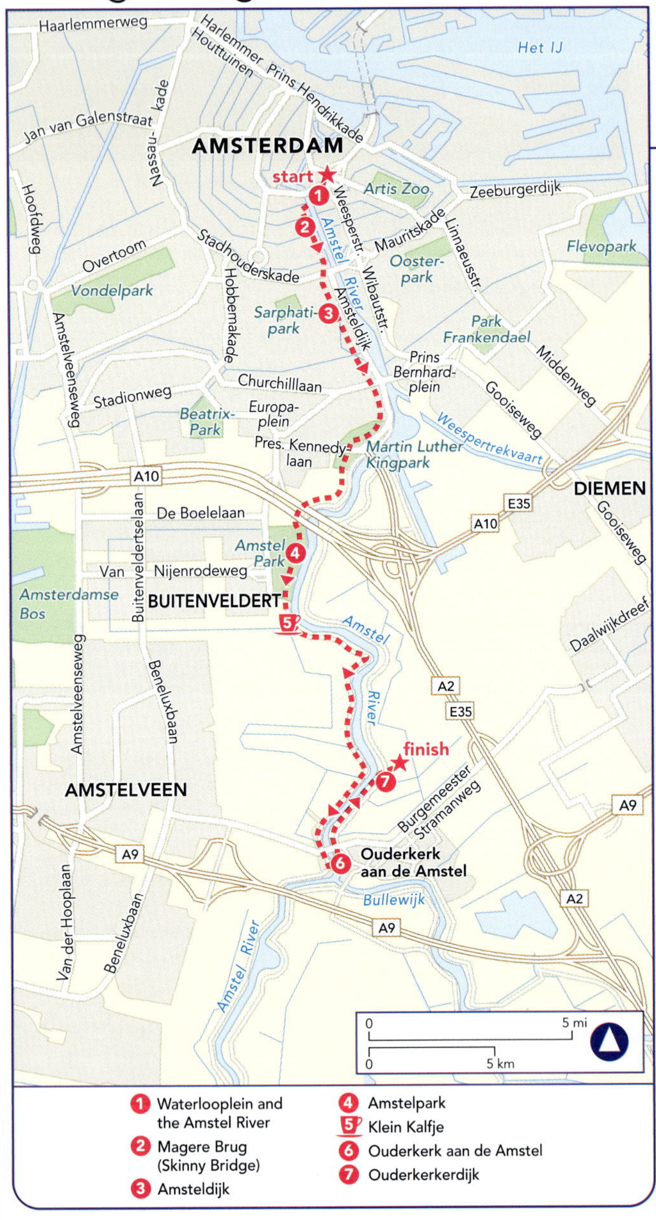


1 Waterlooplein and the Amstel River
2 Magere Brug (Skinny Bridge)
3 Amsteldijk
4 Amstelpark
5 Klein Kalfje
6 Ouderkerk aan de Amstel
7 Ouderkerkerdijk

**Amsterdammers go everywhere on their bikes** and make no concessions for inexperienced visitors on rented *fiets* (bicycles) who attempt to navigate the inner city's complicated streets, alleyways, and one-way systems while dodging the trams. This bike route takes you away from the city center and into the tranquil countryside. You will likely want to leave most of the day to complete this loop at a gentle pace. START: **Tram 14 to Waterlooplein.**

*Views of the National Opera & Ballet on the Amstel River.*

❶ **Waterlooplein and the Amstel River.** Once you've rented your bikes (see the box "Renting Your Bikes," p 92), head away from the center and Waterlooplein; the **National Opera & Ballet** (p 122) will be on your left, on the opposite bank of the Amstel. Follow the riverside Amsteldijk; on your return, you'll be on the opposite bank, with the river again on your left. Look for **H'ART** (p 25), houseboats moored along both banks, and lots of maritime bustle on the river.

*Biking across the Skinny Bridge.*

❷ ♥♥ **Magere Brug (Skinny Bridge).** The Skinny Bridge over the Amstel is an 18th-century replacement of the original 17th-century bridge. It's a double drawbridge that opens every 10 minutes or so to let river traffic through and is floodlit with hundreds of lights at night. The **Carré** (p 124), one of the city's largest cultural venues, is visible from the bridge.

❸ **Amsteldijk.** As you pedal south, you'll negotiate busy Stadhouderskade. Continue on Amsteldijk south to the Berlagebrug (Berlage Bridge), where the traffic thickens again. Stay on Amsteldijk—most of the traffic swings away to the right on President Kennedylaan. The road becomes noticeably quieter, and you can relax and admire the many houseboats lined up along the river.

❹ ♥ **Amstelpark.** Cycle under the highway bridge (A10 ring road) and continue along the riverbank until you reach this tranquil park. Continue south until you see the

*A bronze statue of Rembrandt and Rieker windmill in Amstelpark.*

Rieker windmill, built in 1636, and a bronze statue of Rembrandt, who used to sketch the landscapes here. Look for storks' nests, pheasants, and squirrels. It's a perfect spot for a rest and a photo or two, so stretch your legs and have a snack.

5 **Klein Kalfje.** This traditional Dutch cafe-restaurant has a sheltered terrace along the water. Try soup, a poke bowl, or a filling salad and fuel up for your ride back with a strong Dutch coffee. *Amsteldijk 355. kleinkalfje.nl. ☎ 020/823-1844. $$–$$$.*

6 ♥ **Ouderkerk aan de Amstel.** Ride south past villas and cottages to this charming little village. If you have time, lock up your bikes and meander the village streets before heading back; roam past brightly painted gabled cottages to the Beth Haim Jewish cemetery, the oldest in the Netherlands.

7 ♥ **Ouderkerkerdijk.** Head back north on the opposite bank of the Amstel. This is quieter and narrower than the Amsteldijk, with much less traffic. Follow the Amstel all the way to Spaklerweg, where you will cross right by a bridgekeeper's station, now rentable as part of the **SWEETS** suites network (p 138), then turn left again onto Omval. When you reach the Berlagebrug and the road name changes to Weesperzijde, you'll know you're getting close to your starting point. The streets are busier here, but stay on the right bank and enjoy the different city vistas until you pass H'ART and reach Waterlooplein. ●

## Renting Your Bikes

The rental outlet closest to your starting point is A-Bike Rembrandtplein, Amstel 140 (www.a-bike.nl; ☎ **020/895-0268**). You'll need to leave a credit card deposit, which is returned when you bring the bike back. Rates (including insurance) vary by day and pickup time but run between 13.50€ and 18.50€ for 1 day for a bike with a regular hand-operated brake. A valid **I amsterdam City Card** (p 8) entitles you to 24 hours' free rental from A-Bike, but you **must reserve a timeslot** via iamsterdam.com. A-Bike is open daily 9:30am to 6pm. It also rents eBikes (35€–42€/day) and kids' bikes (14€–16€/day). If you just want to putter around the canal ring in the saddle, go for a 1- or 3-hour rental instead. A-Bike has other central outlets: at Centraal Station, Oosterdoksstraat 106; Kerkstraat 27A at Leidseplein; and Tesselschadestraat 1E, near Vondelpark.

# 6 The Best Dining

# Dining Best Bets

Best **Grill**
♥♥♥ Pelusa $$$ *Leen Jongewaardkade 41 (p 102)*

Best **When Money Is No Object**
♥♥♥ Vinkeles $$$$$ *Keizersgracht 384 (p 104)*

Best for **Street Food**
♥♥ Foodhallen $$ *Bellamyplein 51 (p 100)*

Best for a **Business Dinner**
♥♥ Amstel $$$$ *Professor Tulpplein 1 (p 98)*

Best **Ethiopian-Eritrean Cuisine**
♥♥♥ Fenan Klein Afrika $$ *Jan Pieter Heijestraat 147 (p 99)*

Best **Indonesian Rijsttafel**
♥♥ Blauw $$$ *Amstelveenseweg 158–160 (p 98)*; or ♥♥♥ Tujuh Maret $$$ *Utrechtsestraat 73 (p 103)*

Best **Burger**
♥♥ IJver $$$ *Scheepsbouwkade 72 (p 100)*

Best for **Fish the Dutch Way**
♥♥ Stubbe's Haring $ *Nieuwe Haarlemmersluis (p 103)*; or ♥♥ Volendammer Vishandel Koning $ *Eerste van der Helststraat 60 (p 104)*

Best **All-You-Can-Eat**
♥ Miss Korea BBQ $$ *Albert Cuypstraat 70 (p 101)*

Best **Vegetarian and Vegan Food**
♥♥ Café de Ceuvel $$$ *Korte Papaverweg 4 (p 98)*

Best **Farm-to-Table Dining**
♥♥♥ De Kas $$$$ *Kamerlingh Onneslaan 3 (p 99)*

Best for **Kids**
♥ Pancake Bakery $$ *Prinsengracht 191 (p 101)*

Best for **Smoked Everything**
♥♥♥ Frank's Smoke House $$ *Wittenburgergracht 303 (p 100)*

Best for a **Taste of Traditional Dutch** ♥♥ Heemelrijck $$$ *Van Woustraat 23 (p 100)*

*This page: Chef Hendra of Blauw.*

*Previous page: Café de Ceuvel.*

# Oud-West & De Pijp Dining

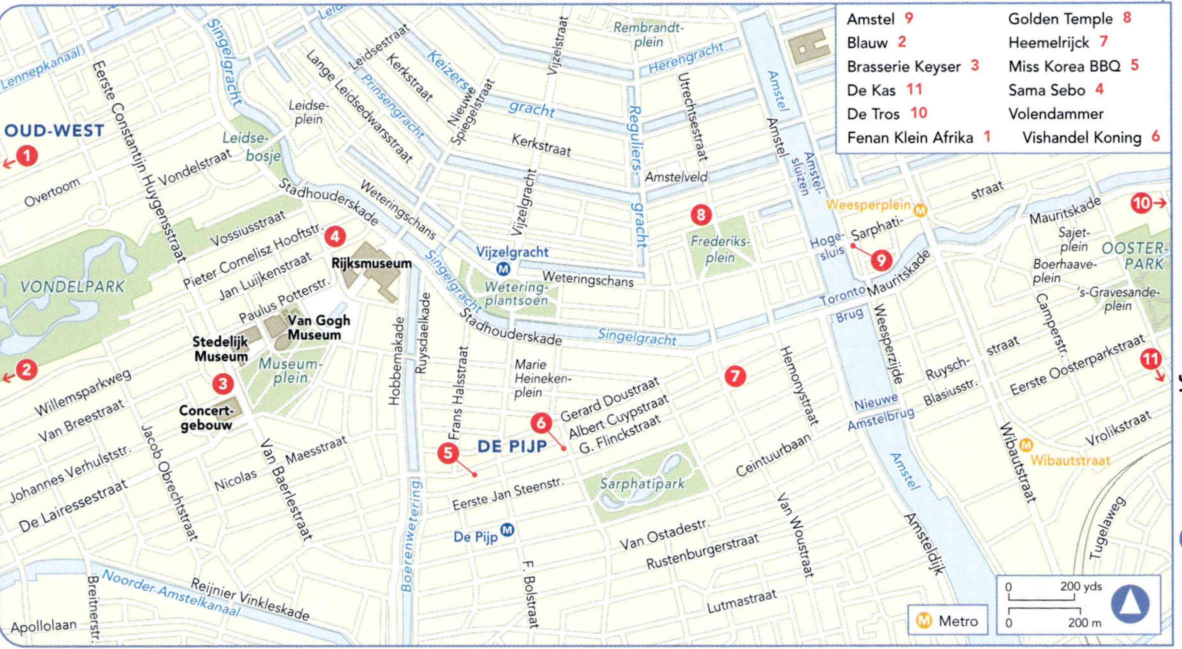

# Central Amsterdam **Dining**

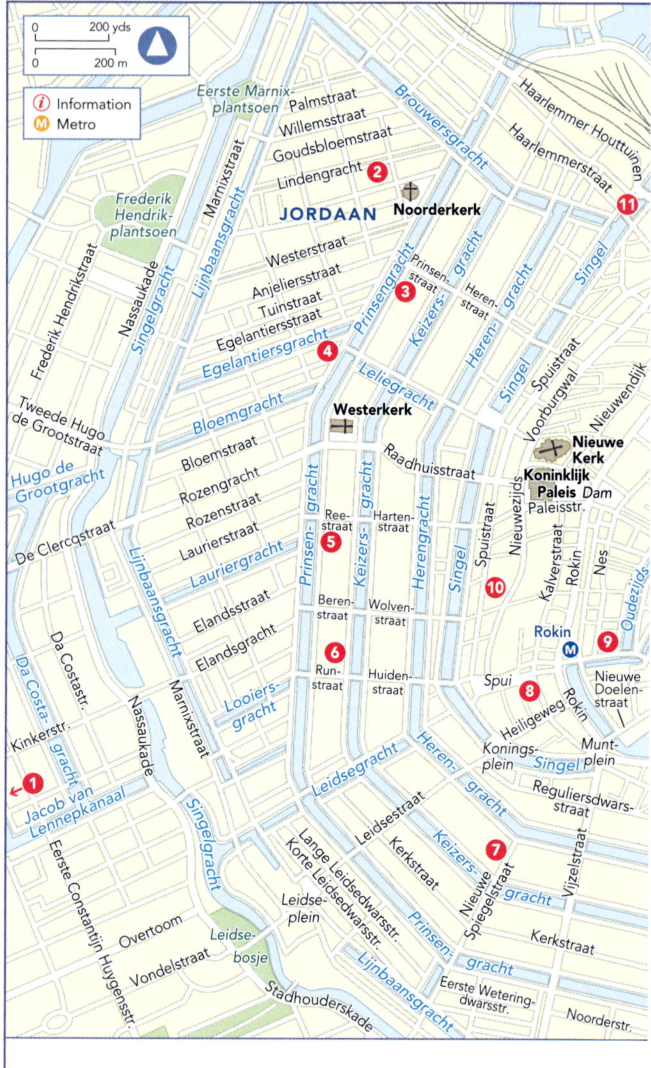


| | | |
|---|---|---|
| Café de Ceuvel 16 | Foodhallen 1 | Kapitein Zeppos 9 |
| De Jaren 12 | Frank's Smoke House 15 | Lucius 10 |
| De Prins 4 | IJver 17 | Pancake Bakery 3 |

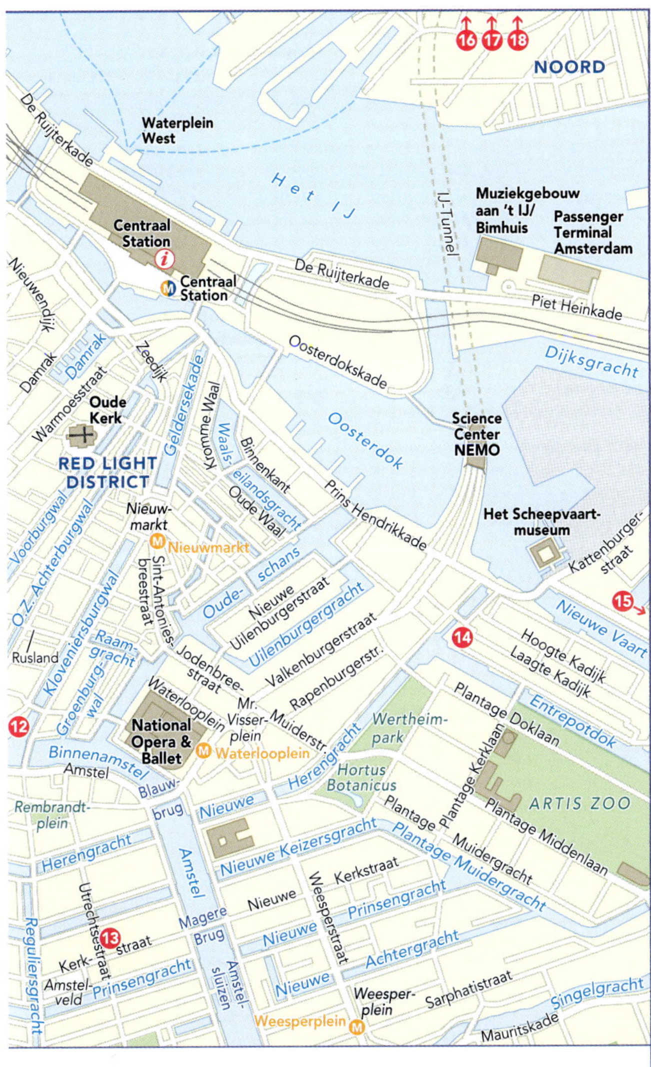


Pasta e Basta 2.0 **7**
Pelusa **18**
The Seafood Bar **8**

Sotto **14**
Stubbe's Haring **11**
Toscanini **2**

Tujuh Maret **13**
Van Puffelen **5**
Vinkeles **6**

# Amsterdam Restaurants A to Z

♥♥ **Amstel** OOST *FRENCH/MEDITERRANEAN* The dining room is tranquil and elegant, with gorgeous picture windows overlooking the river. The menu is understated French with a contemporary international twist, in such dishes as poached sole filet with zucchini and lobster or chocolate crémeux with matcha ice cream. Reservations are required at dinner. *Amstel Hotel, Professor Tulpplein 1. www.amstelhotel.com/restaurant-bar. ☎ 020/622-6060. Mains 31€–54€. Dinner daily; lunch Fri–Sun. Tram: 1, 7, or 19 to Weesperplein. Map p 95.*

♥♥ **Blauw** VONDELPARK *INDONESIAN* For many years now, Blauw has been rated one of the city's top *rijsttafel* spots: It shows no signs of getting knocked off its perch and is packed to the rafters every night, so reserve ahead. The 17-dish special comes in meat, fish, and vegan variants; prepare your tastebuds for the classic flavors of rendang, sayur, satay, and sambal on each one. *Amstelveenseweg 158–160. restaurantblauw.nl/en. ☎ 020/675-5000. Mains 24€–29€; rijsttafel 40€–48€. Dinner daily. Tram: 2 to Amstelveenseweg. Map p 95.*

♥ **Brasserie Keyzer** MUSEUM DISTRICT *EUROPEAN* This century-old brasserie with a dusky decor and starched linens serves French-inspired European classics such as fresh seabass filet or tournedos Rossini. The lunch menu is simpler: veal croquettes, Caesar salads, and the like. *Van Baerlestraat 96. brasseriekeyzer.nl/en. ☎ 020/675-1866. Dinner mains 26€–38€, lunch mains 16€–19€. Breakfast, lunch, and dinner daily. Tram: 3, 5, or 12 to Concertgebouw. Map p 95.*

♥♥ **Café de Ceuvel** NOORD *MODERN VEGAN* With tables inside and out, and a dockside location, this casual bar-restaurant has the feel of a seafood shack, except that everything on the menu is plant-based. The cuisine has a global heritage: perhaps beet polenta with pumpkin cream or curried paneer cheese with nettles. You can also stop by for a beer or carafe of rosé and a plate of their zingy house pickles. *Korte Papaverweg 4. deceuvel.nl/en/cafe. ☎ 020/229-6210. Mains 20€. Dinner Tues–Sun. Bus: 391 or 394 to Mosplein. Map p 96.*

*Dockside dining at Café de Ceuvel.*

*East African dishes served atop* injera *(flatbread) at Fenan Klein Afrika.*

♥ **De Jaren** OLD CENTER *GASTROPUB* On the Binnen Amstel waterfront, this perennial visitor favorite is light and airy, with a panoramic terrace for dining on sunny days. It has an enormous two-story bar and a menu of sandwiches, salads, and such bistro classics as salmon filet with hollandaise sauce. No reservations. *Nieuwe Doelenstraat 20. cafedejaren.nl/en.* ☎ *020/625-5771. Mains 15€–26€. Breakfast, lunch, and dinner daily. Metro: 52 to Rokin. Map p 96.*

♥♥♥ **De Kas** OOST *CONTEMPORARY DUTCH* The focus here hasn't shifted for more than 2 decades: it's all about seasonal, minimal intervention, and as much produce from their own greenhouses and market gardens as humanly possible. Allergies and vegan/vegetarian variations aside, diners follow a fixed menu of dishes that change daily with the harvest and are constructed with a light touch to let individual ingredients sing. Reservations highly recommended. *Kamerlingh Onneslaan 3, Park Frankendael. restaurantdekas.com.* ☎ *020/462-4562. Fixed-price lunch (3/4/5 courses) 50€/62€/71€; fixed-price dinner (5/6 courses) 84€/93€. Lunch and dinner Mon–Sat. Tram: 19 to Hogeweg. Map p 95.*

♥ **De Prins** JORDAAN *GASTROPUB* A popular canalside Dutch *eetcafé* (cafe with food) in a sunny spot just across from the Anne Frank Huis. Choose from classics like steak and frites or chicken satay and take your pick from a great selection of Dutch and Belgian beers. Lunch is more informal: a choice of croquettes, salads, or burgers. *Prinsengracht 124. deprins.nl/en.* ☎ *020/624-9382. Mains 18€–22€. Breakfast, lunch and dinner daily. Tram: 13 or 17 to Westermarkt. Map p 96.*

♥♥ **De Tros** OOST *DUTCH/ASIAN* There's a short menu of mains here, but the real stars are the eclectic Asian-inspired small plates—the likes of tuna tataki or steak tartare with char siu dressing—and a renowned straight-up smashburger. *Linnaeusstraat 63. www.detrosamsterdam.nl. No phone. Mains 21€–26€; small plates 6€–17€. Dinner daily; lunch Thurs–Sun. Tram: 1, 3, or 14 to Linnaeusstraat. Map p 95.*

♥♥♥ **Fenan Klein Afrika** VONDELPARK *ETHIOPIAN/ERITREAN* This casual neighborhood eatery serves knockout East African food at tasty prices: Call ahead or DM their Insta (@fenankleinafrika) to secure a table. Carnivores and vegetarians are treated equally, with dishes spiced in a range from delicate to feisty, all served traditionally on *injera* (spongelike flatbread) to scoop up—but of course they have cutlery if you prefer. The meat or veggie *beyaynetu* is a three-dish combo with sides—and the perfect introduction to the kitchen's skills. *Jan Pieter Heijestraat 147. ☎ 020/ 412-4442. Mains 15€–21€. Dinner daily. Tram: 1 to J.P. Heijestraat. Map p 95.*

♥♥ **Foodhallen** OUD WEST *STREET FOOD* Former tram depots turned all-day covered street-food market. Inside you'll find everything from shellfish and bao buns to Peruvian tacos and the traditional Dutch beer snack *bitterballen*—plus wine, beer, and cocktails galore. It's far enough from the heart of the center to tip the clientele balance towards locals. *Bellamyplein 51. www.foodhallen.nl. No phone. Dishes 5€–15€. Lunch and dinner daily. Tram: 7 or 17 to Osdorp Dijkgraafplein. Map p 96.*

♥♥♥ **Frank's Smoke House** OOST *DELI* If you can eat it, Frank smokes it—all on site. Offering up to 30 different types of smoked fish, cheese, meat, and vegetables, he'll build a gourmet sandwich you'll never forget. A couple of tables outside and some wines in the fridge create a memorable no-fuss lunch. *Wittenburgergracht 303. www.smokehouse.nl. ☎ 020/585-7107. Sandwiches 6.50€–13.50€. Lunch Tues–Sun. Tram: 7 to Eerste Coehoornstraat. Map p 96.*

*Bitterballen sample platter at Foodhallen.*

♥♥ **Golden Temple** CANAL RING *VEGETARIAN ASIAN* Lovers of vegetarian and Asian food who cannot make up their minds will appreciate the menu's unlikely roster of Indian (North and Goa), Mexican, and Middle Eastern plates. Multi-dish Indian *thalis* are often the way to go, or combine appetizers to create a global journey of discovery: Nepalese *momos* (dumplings), Japanese nori tempura, and spring rolls served with a tamarind chutney. *Utrechtsestraat 126. www.restaurantgoldentemple.com. ☎ 020/626-8560. Mains 19€–25€. Dinner daily; lunch Sat–Sun. Tram: 4 to Prinsengracht. Map p 95.*

♥♥ **Heemelrijck** DE PIJP *DUTCH* Although this place only opened in 2023, the family's restaurant heritage dates to 1949. Its rebirth echoes tradition in both decor and recipes. The dining room is outfitted in dark wood with plush drapes and Delft Blue platters on the wall; the menu showcases such old Dutch favorites as *stamppot* (mashed potato and vegetable with gravy, bacon, and meatballs), ox tartare, and slip sole served with seasonal vegetables. Reserve ahead—it's small and popular. *Van Woustraat 23. www.heemelrijck.nl/en. ☎ 020/722-0390. Mains 15€–30€. Dinner daily. Tram: 4 to Albert Cuypstraat. Map p 95.*

♥♥ kids **IJver** NDSM *GASTROPUB* Familiar bistro dishes here are split into categories of Big and Small, to match anyone's appetite. Of the former, standouts are the juicy house burger and *coq a la bière*, a twist on the classic French chicken stew. The neo-industrial space gets more inviting as darkness falls and low-watt lighting fires

*Savory pancakes with a range of toppings at the Pancake Bakery.*

up inside, with fairy lights twinkling on the terrace. A fine range of wines and beers includes collaborations with local brewer Oedipus and up to eight alcohol-free brews. *Scheepsbouwkade 72. ijveramsterdam.nl/en. ☎ 020/247-1001. Mains 17€–27€. Lunch and dinner daily. Ferry: F4 to NDSM. Map p 96.*

♥♥ **Kapitein Zeppos** OLD CENTER *FRENCH/FLEMISH* A kitsch restaurant tucked away down a pretty little alley in one of the oldest parts of the center, Zeppos offers an eclectic menu of authentic Dutch-Flemish and French classics, with plenty of fish. Expect fish soup, salads, and great pots of mussels by day and the likes of venison steak with chestnut puree or Coquille St.-Jacques by night. *Gebed Zonder End 5. zeppos.nl/en. ☎ 020/624-2057. Mains 14€–34€. Lunch and dinner daily. Metro: 52 to Rokin. Map p 96.*

♥♥ **Lucius** OLD CENTER *SEAFOOD* For more than 50 years, this place has been a reliable choice for fresh, well-sourced seafood prepared in a classic style. The showpiece *fruits de mer* platter includes langoustine, oysters, clams, shrimp, and North Sea crab—and if you're feeling flush, add a Canadian half lobster at market price. *Spuistraat 247. www.lucius.nl/en. ☎ 020/624-1831. Entrees 22€–32€; seafood and shellfish platters 38€–40€. Lunch and dinner daily. Tram: 2 or 12 to Paleisstraat. Map p 96.*

♥ **Miss Korea BBQ** DE PIJP *KOREAN* A longstanding staple in an area where restaurants come and go, Miss Korea is large and yet always packed with families loading their tabletop BBQ with meats and seafood, devoured with as many stir-fries, stews, and sides as they can eat. Despite the crowds, the waitstaff is happy to explain the menu: You choose up to three items per person for as many courses as you can eat in 2 hours. To reduce waste, there's a supplementary charge of 1€ to 3€ per dish that you leave. A solid choice with hungry teens. *Albert Cuypstraat 70. www.misskorea.nl. ☎ 020/679-0606. Fixed-price menu Mon–Wed 37€, Thurs–Sun and public holidays 38€; kids ages 3–10 19€. Dinner daily. Metro: M52 to De Pijp. Map p 95.*

♥ kids **Pancake Bakery** CANAL RING *PANCAKES* A 17th-century canal warehouse is home to a perennially popular temple to pancakes with all kinds of toppings and stuffings. Go simple or go wild, with Indonesian chicken, melted goat's cheese with thyme, or honey, nuts, and whipped cream. It also serves omelets. Reserve ahead or expect to wait in line. *Prinsengracht 191. pancake.nl/en. ☎ 020/625-1333.*

*Pancakes 10€–20€. Breakfast, lunch, and dinner daily. Tram: 13 or 17 to Westermarkt. Map p 96.*

♥ **Pasta e Basta 2.0** CANAL RING *ITALIAN* A boisterous Italian restaurant with the best opera-singing waiters this side of La Scala. A rotating seasonal set menu includes a range of appetizers, pasta and traditional meat and/or fish courses, and a dessert. But it's the effusive, energetic staff and the full-throttle entertainment you're likely here for. *Nieuwe Spiegelstraat 8. pastaebasta.nl/en.* ☎ *020/422-2222. Fixed-price set menu (4/5 courses) 65€/75€. Dinner Wed–Sun. Tram: 2 or 12 to Koningsplein. Map p 96.*

♥♥♥ **Pelusa** NOORD *GRILL* Noord is now one of Amsterdam's hottest dining neighborhoods. Here the open South American–style *parrilla* takes center stage—sociable counter seats with a front-row view are available—and a starring role is given to sharing dishes (meat, fish, and vegetarian) grilled to order. Alternatively, creative small plates draw on fine Dutch produce like Zeeland oysters. The extensive drinks list includes rare lambic beers and natural wines; pairing suggestions are gladly offered. There are homemade beer snacks for those who just want to sit and sip. *Leen Jongewaardkade 41. pelusa.amsterdam.* ☎ *020/303-1468. Mains 17€–22€; small plates 8.50€–12€; chef's menu (3/4/5 courses) 37€/45€/53€. Dinner Wed–Sun; lunch Sat–Sun. Bus: 38 to Distelweg. Map p 96.*

♥ **Sama Sebo** MUSEUM DISTRICT *INDONESIAN* This upmarket Indonesian restaurant serves its tasty *rijsttafel* (a feast consisting of a range of Dutch-Indonesian meat dishes, fish, vegetables, and nuts served with rice) in two different sizes, with 9 or 18 dishes. It's also just a few steps from the **Rijksmuseum** (p 7). Reservations recommended. *Pieter Cornelisz Hooftstraat 27. www.samasebo.nl/en.* ☎ *020/662-8146. Mains 10€–22€; rijsttafel 25€–40€ (2 sizes). Lunch and dinner Mon–Sat; closed 2 weeks Dec–Jan. Tram: 2, 5, or 12 to Museumplein. Map p 95.*

♥♥ **The Seafood Bar** OLD CENTER *SEAFOOD* Its evolution from a fishmonger's store in the 1980s to this mini-chain of highly rated brasserie-style seafood restaurants is an impressive backstory. The food is even more impressive: Strong on classic shellfish in particular, it also features fresh catch grilled, cooked on the plancha, or even as Brit-style fish and chips. If

*Dining room at Pelusa.*

Diners at the Seafood Bar.

it's not available fresh, you won't see it on the menu. Reservations are recommended, but they only book out 60% of tables: A walk-up is always worth trying. *Spui 15. www.theseafoodbar.com. ☎ 020/233-7452. Mains 20€–36€; fruits de mer platters 36€–57€. Lunch and dinner daily. Tram: 4 or 14 to Rokin. Map p 96. Also at: Damrak 213; Van Baerlestraat 5H; Ferdinand Bolstraat 32H.*

♥ kids **Sotto** OOST *PIZZA* Classic Neapolitan-style pizzas—plus a few offbeat combos and monthly specials—cooked in a gas-fired oven. There's also a short menu of Italian antipasti including burrata. It's all fast, filling, and reliably tasty. *Kadijksplein 4. ☎ 020/773-3120. www.sottopizza.nl. Pizzas 10€–18€. Dinner daily; lunch Fri–Sun. Bus: 22, 305, 314, or 316 to Kadijksplein. Map p 96. Also at: Amstelveenseweg 89.*

♥♥ kids **Stubbe's Haring** OLD CENTER *FISH* Raw herring is a Dutch specialty, especially favored in summer months, and there are several *haring* stands in town. This one, located on a bridge near Centraal Station, is a great spot for raw herring served naked, or in a bread roll, with pickles and chopped sweet onions. Mackerel is also usually available. *Nieuwe Haarlemmersluis, Singel. No phone. Sandwiches 6€. No credit cards. Hours vary. Tram: Take any line to Centraal Station. Map p 96.*

♥ **Toscanini** JORDAAN *ITALIAN* This charming eatery with unembellished country-style decor is flooded with natural light during the day. Authentic Italian regional dishes always include fresh homemade pasta with seasonal and regional sauces, as well as braised and grilled meat dishes. If you only crave a light bite, their next-door deli serves snacks, charcuterie, and cheese platters. *Lindengracht 75. restauranttoscanini.nl/en. ☎ 020/623-2813. Mains 22€–31€. Dinner Mon–Sat; lunch Fri–Sat. Tram: 5 to Nieuwe Willemsstraat. Map p 96.*

♥♥♥ **Tujuh Maret** CANAL RING *INDONESIAN* Specialists in the dishes of North Sulawesi—at the spicier end of Indonesian food—this place nevertheless has plenty to offer even the most timid of palates. It's small, friendly, family-run, and serves one of Amsterdam's tastiest 18-plate *rijsttafels*. Vegetarian dishes are a standout, but whatever you eat, you will not leave hungry: Portions are generous, and the pandan rice far too moreish. *Utrechtsestraat 73. tujuhmaret.nl. ☎ 020/427-9865. Mains 23€–26€; rijsttafel 35€–39€. Late lunch and dinner daily. Tram: 4 to Prinsengracht. Map p 96.*

*North Sulawesi Indonesian dishes at Tujuh Maret.*

♥ **Van Puffelen** CANAL RING *EUROPEAN* This former brown cafe has grown to become a popular restaurant that rambles through two adjacent, wood-adorned canal houses. Lunch is mainly familiar staples like omelet or salad. Dinner fare consists of more elaborate, but still traditional, European dishes, such as confit duck leg with orange port sauce and grilled fresh fish. *Prinsengracht 375–377. restaurantvanpuffelen.com/english. ☎ 020/624-6270. Mains 21€–27€. Lunch and dinner daily. Tram: 13 or 17 to Westermarkt. Map p 96.*

♥♥♥ **Vinkeles** CANAL RING *CONTEMPORARY FRENCH* Ensconced inside **The Dylan** (p 133), one of Amsterdam's best luxury hotels, this elegant restaurant is also a destination in its own right. Multi-award-winning and many-starred chefs whip up artistic seasonal a la carte dishes and a daily signature menu featuring the likes of pigeon with ponzu, sour cherry, and cacao or turbot with clams, smoked eel, and Dutch potatoes. Reservations required. *Dylan Hotel, Keizersgracht 384. www.vinkeles.com. ☎ 020/530-2010. Entrees 75€–80€; fixed-price menus (vegetarian or meat) 165€–220€. Dinner Tues–Sat. Tram: 2 or 12 to Koningsplein. Map p 96.*

♥♥ kids **Volendammer Vishandel Koning** DE PIJP *FISH* One of the city's real bargain lunches, as long as you don't mind perching out front or eating on the go. This fish shop turns out a Dutch street-food specialty: *kibbeling,* freshly deep-fried pieces of white fish served with a tangy mustard-tartare dip. It also serves herring or mackerel rolls, plus raw and smoked fish, all presented simply with pickled garnishes, at equally keen prices. *Eerste van der Helststraat 60. ☎ 020/676-0394. Dishes 3€–7.50€. Lunch Mon–Sat. Tram: 24 to Marie Heinekenplein. Map p 95.*

# 7 The Best Nightlife

# Nightlife Best Bets

Best **Place to Sample Boutique European Wines**
♥♥ Wijnbar Paulus, *Ceintuurbaan 348H (p 113)*; or ♥♥♥ Wijnbar Vindict, *Docklandsweg 3 (p 113)*

Best for a **Drink with the Locals**
♥♥ Café Chris, *Bloemstraat 42 (p 110)*; or ♥ Proeflokaal de Ooievaar, *Sint Olofspoort 1 (p 112)*

Friendliest **Gay Bar**
♥♥ Amstel Fifty Four, *Amstel 54 (p 114)*

Best **Brewery Tap**
♥♥ Brouwerij 't IJ, *Funenkade 7 (p 110)*

Best **Dutch Beer Selection**
♥♥♥ Proeflokaal Arendsnest, *Herengracht 90 (p 111)*

Most **Iconic Dance Club**
♥♥♥ Paradiso, *Weteringschans 6 (p 114)*

Best for **Romance**
♥♥ Vesper, *Vinkenstraat 57 (p 113)*

Best for **Gezelligheid (Dutch Hospitality)**
♥♥ De Drie Fleschjes, *Gravenstraat 18 (p 110)*

Best **Lesbian Bar**
♥♥ Saarein, *Elandsstraat 119 (p 114)*

Most **Creative Cocktails**
♥♥♥ Zum Barbarossa, *Voetboogstraat 1 (p 113)*; or ♥♥ Dutch Courage, *Zeedijk 12 (p 112)*

Best **Pub to Watch the Game**
♥ Molly Malone's, *Oudezijds Kolk 9 (p 111)*

Best for **Jenever Tasting**
♥♥♥ Wynand Fockink, *Pijlsteeg 31 (p 113)*

*This page: Patrons at Bubbles & Wines.*

*Previous page: Cocktails at Zum Barbarossa.*

# De Pijp, Leidseplein & Vondelpark Nightlife

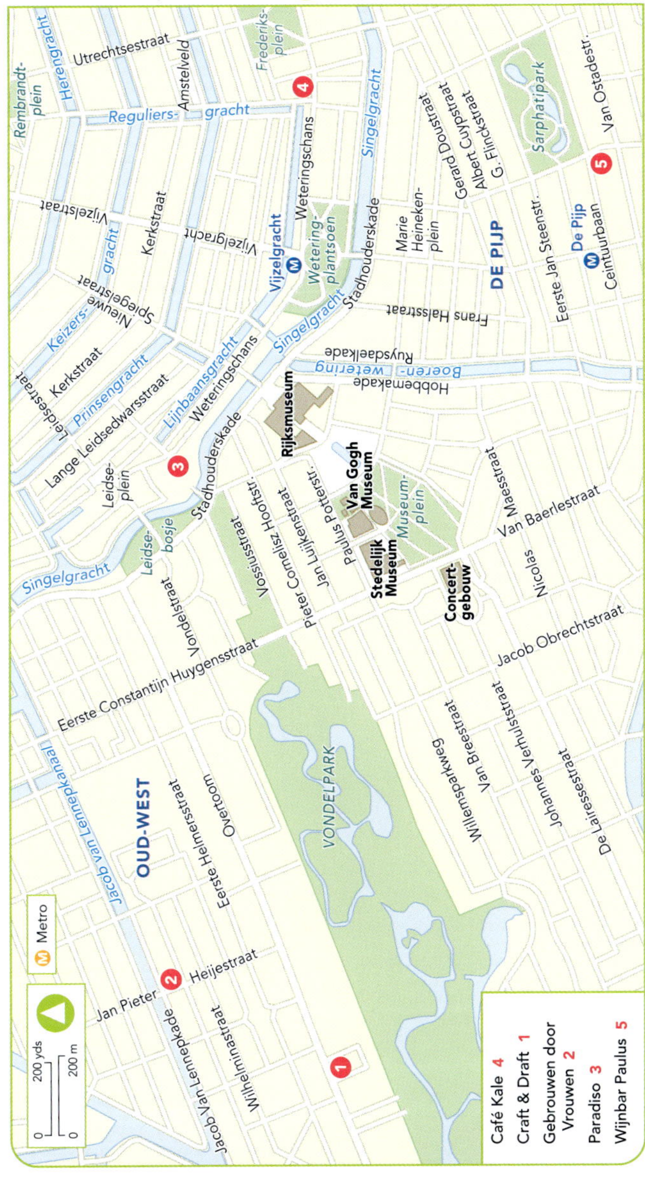

# Center, Jordaan & Noord Nightlife

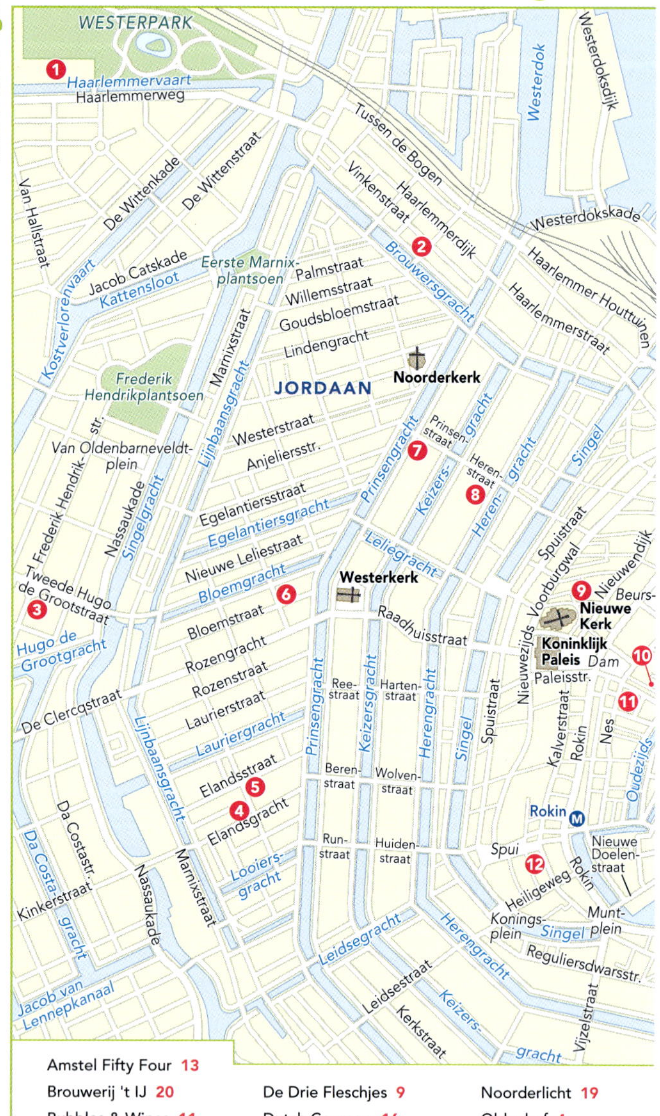


Amstel Fifty Four 13
Brouwerij 't IJ 20
Bubbles & Wines 11
Café Chris 6
Cafe Twee Prinsen 7
De Drie Fleschjes 9
Dutch Courage 16
Escape 14
Molly Malone's 15
Noorderlicht 19
Oldenhof 4
Proeflokaal Arendsnest 8

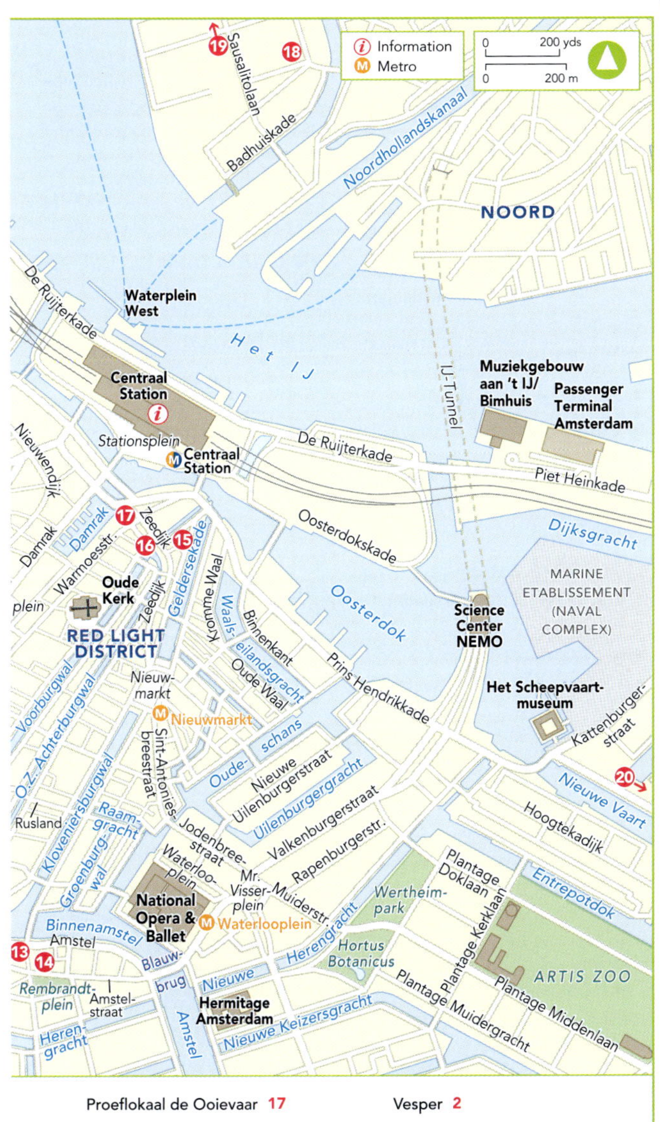


Proeflokaal de Ooievaar **17**
Saarein **5**
Troost Westergas **1**
Two Chefs Taproom **3**
Vesper **2**
Wijnbar Vindict **18**
Wynand Fockink **10**
Zum Barbarossa **12**

# Amsterdam Nightlife A to Z

## Brown Cafes, Pubs & Taprooms

♥♥ **Brouwerij 't IJ** OOST Ideal for a sunny afternoon, this pub-taproom has a pretty terrace overlooking the IJ waterway. Many beers are made in the onsite brewery, next to the landmark De Gooyer Windmill; Belgian-style *tripels*, *wit* (wheat), and blondes are specialties. The same brewery operates **'t Blauwe Theehuis** in Vondelpark (p 85). *Funenkade 7. www.brouwerijhetij.nl. ☎ 020/261-9801. Tram: 7 to Hoogte Kadijk. Map p 108.*

♥ **Café Kale** MUSEUM DISTRICT Expect a friendly welcome, a range of draft beers and cocktails, and a mixed bunch of locals grazing on snacks as they drink. Also open for brunch. *Weteringschans 267. www.cafekale.nl. ☎ 020/622-6363. Tram: 1, 4, 7, 12, 19, or 24 to Frederiksplein. Map p 107.*

♥♥ **Café Chris** JORDAAN This old brown cafe has been serving the Jordaan's thirsty burghers for over 400 years, so they are clearly doing something right. Its wood and cut-glass interior is often packed with a friendly mix of boisterous—but never rowdy—locals and visitors. *Bloemstraat 42. No phone. Tram: 13 or 17 to Westermarkt. Map p 108.*

♥♥ **Craft & Draft** OUD-WEST/VONDELPARK With 40 European small-batch brews on tap; friendly, knowledgeable staff to guide you to the right ones; and a straight-outta-Brooklyn interior, this is a strong choice for every visiting beer geek. A small terrace out front catches the late afternoon sun. *Overtoom 417. www.craftanddraft.nl. ☎ 020/223-0725. Tram: 1 to Rhijnvis Feithstraat. Map p 107.*

♥♥ **De Drie Fleschjes** OLD CENTER The "Three Little Bottles" has been around in some form since 1619. It specializes in Bols *jenever*, a triple-distilled grain spirit flavored with juniper berries: It's a

### Brown Cafes

A friendly neighborhood *bruine kroeg* (brown cafe) can be a great place to mix with locals. Some Amsterdammers even start their day at their favorite brown cafe, have lunch there, and then go back to socialize after work. The brown cafe gets its name because of the centuries-old tobacco stains that have dyed the walls brown—although smoking is no longer permitted indoors. It embodies *gezelligheid* (coziness) and evokes a bygone era. Opening hours for brown cafes are somewhere between 8 and 10am and 1 and 3am the following day. They're found all over town and often have a snack menu featuring sandwiches *(broodjes)* made with everything from *Amsterdamse osseworst* (smoked beef sausage) to cheese, vegetables, and salami; *toost* (toasted white bread) with ham and cheese, smoked eel, or beef tartare; *bitterballen* (croquettes, traditionally meat-filled but also now widely available as vegetarian snacks); and simple salads.

*Proeflokaal Arendsnest.*

forerunner of gin but tastes nothing like it, exhibiting in multiple different varieties, flavors of grain spirit like vodka, a hint of Cognac's elegance, or, when barrel-aged, the spicy sweetness of rye whiskey. Staff is happy to talk you through the range. *Jenever* is traditionally taken as a *kopstootje* (literally, "headbutt") with a small glass of pilsner beer on the side. There are wines, cocktails, and *borrel* (drinking snacks), too. *Gravenstraat 18. www.dedriefleschjes.nl/en.* ☎ *020/624-8443. Tram: 2, 12, or 17 to Dam. Map p 108.*

♥ **Gebrouwen door Vrouwen** OUD-WEST/VONDELPARK The cheerful "Brewed by Women" bar showcases the brewery's particularly adept fruit-accented beer styles. *Jan Pieter Heijestraat 119D-h. www.gebrouwendoorvrouwen.nl.* ☎ *020/854-5277. Tram: 1 to J. P. Heijestraat. Map p 107.*

♥ **Molly Malone's** OLD CENTER This lively Irish pub is a go-to for live sports on three projector screens. There's Guinness and Kilkenny, as you'd expect, and if you settle in, pub grub and too many whiskeys to count. *Oudezijds Kolk 9. mollyinamsterdam.com.* ☎ *020/624-1150. Bus: 305, 314, 316, or 391 to Prins Hendrikkade. Map p 108.*

♥♥ **Noorderlicht** NOORD Bar, cafe, restaurant, and summer weekend venue for DJs and live music. Whatever time of day you call in, there's a seat beside the IJ waiting for you. *NDSM plein 102. noorderlichtcafe.nl/en.* ☎ *020/492-2770. Bus: 391 or 394 to Klaprozenweg. Map p 108.*

♥♥♥ **Proeflokaal Arendsnest** CANAL RING The best place in town for a crash course in Dutch beer: More than 50 on tap, all brewed in the Netherlands, are poured by knowledgeable, waistcoated staff. A youngish tourist and expat after-work crowd enjoy everything from blondes and dubbels to modern raspberry porters or a brett pale. There are cheese and sausage platters to munch while you drink. *Herengracht 90. www.arendsnest.nl.* ☎ *020/421-2057. Tram: 2, 12, 13, or 17 to Nieuwezijds Kolk. Map p 108.*

*Taproom at Troost Westergas.*

♥ **Proeflokaal de Ooievaar** OLD CENTER  Small wood-paneled corner bar where, despite the location, you'll still hear more Dutch than English being spoken. It's right below a stepped gable that leans, appropriately, like it's had one too many. *Sint Olofspoort 1. proeflokaaldeooievaar.nl.* ☎ *06/1971-1380. Metro/Tram: any service to Centraal Station. Map p 108.*

♥ **Troost Westergas** WESTERPARK  Beerhall-style taproom for Amsterdam's Brouwerij Troost, with its range of global- and European-style beers, craft lemonade, and tasty, carb-filled food to soak it up. Its sister brewery-bar is in De Pijp. Weekend table reservations (online) are recommended, although if you want a seat on the terrace, you'll have to turn up early. *Pazzanistraat 25–27. brouwerijtroost.nl.* ☎ *020/737-1028. Tram: 5 to Haarlemmerplein. Map p 108. Also at: Cornelis Troostplein 21.*

♥♥ **Two Chefs Taproom** JORDAAN  The freshest brews from local craft beer pioneers Two Chefs amid a riot of neon and in-your-face-painted decor. Expect the whole range, including low/no alcohol beers, plus a never-ending carousel of special beers. *Hugo de Grootplein 7. twochefsbrewing.com.* ☎ *020/772-2795. Tram: 3 to Hugo de Grootplein. Map p 108.*

## Cocktail Bars & Wine Bars

♥♥ **Bubbles & Wines** OLD CENTER  Just a few minutes' walk from Dam Square, this fancy champagne and wine bar—all subdued lighting, dark wood surfaces, and red tones—serves a roster of champagne and 50 wines by the glass, alongside snacks of caviar, oysters, and charcuterie plates. Closed Mondays. *Nes 37. bubblesandwines.com.* ☎ *020/422-3318. Tram: 4 or 14 to Dam. Map p 108.*

♥ **Cafe Twee Prinsen** CANAL RING  Once a historic brown cafe (see p 110), the "Two Princes" is now a bright, glass-fronted wine bar and a lovely spot for whiling away summer evenings overlooking Prinsengracht, including on outside tables. *Prinsenstraat 27. tweeprinsen.nl. No phone. Tram: 13 or 17 to Westermarkt. Map p 108.*

♥♥ **Dutch Courage** OLD CENTER  A gem among the sometimes overbearing streets of the Old Center. Friendly staff and a cocktail menu that proves traditional Dutch liquor *jenever* has the versatility for a vast range of modern flavor combinations. It also offers curated *jenever* flights. *Zeedijk 12. www.dutchcouragecocktails.com.* ☎ *06/4739-8467. Metro/Tram: any service to Centraal Station. Map p 108.*

♥♥ **Oldenhof** JORDAAN  Small American-style bar serving classic and fun house cocktails in a cozy, refined atmosphere reminiscent of a gentleman's club. Service and staff knowledge are top-drawer. No reservations. *Elandsgracht 84. www.bar-oldenhof.com.* ☎ *020/751-3273. Tram: 5, 7, or 19 to Elandsgracht. Map p 108.*

♥♥ **Vesper** JORDAAN A super-smooth cocktail bar with a seasonal menu crammed with wacky and wonderful concoctions, widely regarded as employing some of the coolest mixologists in Amsterdam. Open Wednesday through Saturday only; no reservations. *Vinkenstraat 57. www.vesperbar.nl.* ☎ *020/846-4458. Tram: 5 to Haarlemmerplein. Map p 108.*

♥♥ **Wijnbar Paulus** DE PIJP Overseen by owner Paul who cannot do enough to point you in the right direction, this place offers a range of carefully chosen European wines by the glass, including natural and kosher labels. Snacks to accompany your sipping include the likes of Iberico ham and burrata cheese. Reserve ahead on weekends; closed Mondays. *Ceintuurbaan 348H. No phone. www.wijnbarpaulus.nl. Tram: 3 or 4 to van der Helststraat. Map p 107.*

♥♥♥ **Wijnbar Vindict** NOORD Knowledgeable and approachable staff make this another outstanding place to drink unusual European wines, with 70 available by the glass including grassy Dutch whites from the Brabant region. Clientele are mostly the local residents of a fast-changing neighborhood. The kitchen also turns out Mediterranean-inspired small plates. *Docklandsweg 3. wijnbarvindict.nl.* ☎ *020/331-1394. Closed Sun–Tues. Bus: 38 to Grasweg. Map p 108.*

♥♥♥ **Wynand Fockink** OLD CENTER It's *jenever* heaven at this tasting room operated by a city distiller founded in 1679, the same year this tiny gabled bar was built. Staff is knowledgeable and always eager to help you find the right liquor to drink (or take home—the shop is next door). *Pijlsteeg 31. wynand-fockink.nl.* ☎ *020/639-2695. Tram: 4 or 14 to Dam. Map p 108.*

♥♥♥ **Zum Barbarossa** OLD CENTER Chic basement cocktail bar with low-watt lighting and mid-century furnishings. Mixology com-

*Zum Barbarossa.*

*The owners of Saarein.*

bines the classic and hyper-creative, as in their "Our Fashioned" made with aged rum, PX sherry, chocolate bitters, and an oyster. Reserve ahead on weekends or you won't get past the rope: It's tiny. *Voetboogstraat 1. www.zumbarbarossa.com/amsterdam.* ☎ *020/700-8337. Tram: 4 or 14 to Rokin. Map p 108.*

## Dance Clubs

♥ **Escape** REMBRANDTPLEIN This perennial superclub isn't quite operating at EDM's cutting-edge, as it once was, but it remains an iconic venue with a great sound system that still draws a mix of local and international DJs. *Rembrandtplein 11. escape.nl.* ☎ *06/3922-8876. Admission 5€–15€. Tram: 4 or 14 to Rembrandtplein. Map p 108.*

♥♥♥ **Paradiso** LEIDSEPLEIN An Amsterdam institution, this former church building is a majestic club and live music venue(s) with lofty ceilings and high balconies. Over almost 6 decades it has hosted everyone from big-name house music DJs to Nirvana. The lineup of bands and club nights remains stubbornly eclectic and gloriously un-pigeonhole-able. *Weteringschans 6. www.paradiso.nl.* ☎ *020/626-4521. Admission 10€–30€. Tram: 1, 2, 7, 12, 17, or 19 to Leidseplein. Map p 107.*

## LGBTQ+

♥♥ **Amstel Fifty Four** REMBRANDTPLEIN One of Amsterdam's venerable gay bars has a definite sense of style, even if it isn't exactly hip anymore. It remains engagingly convivial, with singalongs and drag shows. *Amstel 54. amstel-fifty-four.metro.rest.* ☎ *020/623-4254. Tram: 4 or 14 to Rembrandtplein. Map p 108.*

♥♥ **Saarein** JORDAAN This bar-cafe is a longtime favorite on Amsterdam's lesbian scene, although it now draws a mixed gay crowd. A great brown cafe location in the Jordaan, a pool table, a fine range of beer, and a friendly atmosphere make this an appealing choice. *Elandsstraat 119. cafesaarein.nl.* ☎ *020/623-4901. Tram: 5, 7, or 19 to Elandsgracht. Map p 108.*

# 8 The Best Arts & Entertainment

# Arts & Entertainment Best Bets

Best **Concert Acoustics**
♥♥♥ The Royal Concertgebouw Amsterdam, *Concertgebouwplein 10 (p 120)*

Best for **Contemporary Live Music**
♥♥ Paradiso, *Weteringschans 6 (p 121)*

Best for **Opera**
♥♥♥ Dutch National Opera & Ballet, *Amstel 3 (p 122)*

Best for **Midweek Techno**
♥♥ Melkweg, *Lijnbaansgracht 234A (p 121)*

Best for **Lavish Shows & Musicals**
♥♥ Carré, *Amstel 115–125 (p 124)*

Best **Movie Theater**
♥♥♥ Eye Filmmuseum, *IJpromenade 1 (p 122)*; or
♥♥ Pathé Royal Theater Tuschinski, *Reguliersbreestraat 26–34 (p 123)*

Best for **Summer Beachtime Fun**
♥♥ Strand IJburg, *Pampuslaan 1001 (p 123)*

Best for **Modern Dutch Theater**
♥ Internationaal Theater Amsterdam, *Leidseplein 26 (p 124)*

Best **Blues Venue**
♥♥ Maloe Melo, *Lijnbaansgracht 163 (p 124)*

*The Royal Concertgebouw Amsterdam, home of the Royal Concertgebouw Orchestra.*

*Previous page: Performance of Tosca at the Dutch National Opera & Ballet.*

*Permanent exhibition on the technology of film at the Eye Filmmuseum.*

Best for **Experimental Classical Music**
♥♥♥ Muziekgebouw aan 't IJ, *Piet Heinkade 1 (p 121)*

Best **Free Open-air Concerts**
♥♥ Vondelpark Openluchttheater, *Vondelpark (p 122)*

Best for **Laughing the Night Away**
♥♥ Boom Chicago, *Rozengracht 117 (p 120)*

Best for **Last-Minute Tickets**
♥♥ Iamsterdam.com

*Paradiso nightclub.*

# Amsterdam A&E

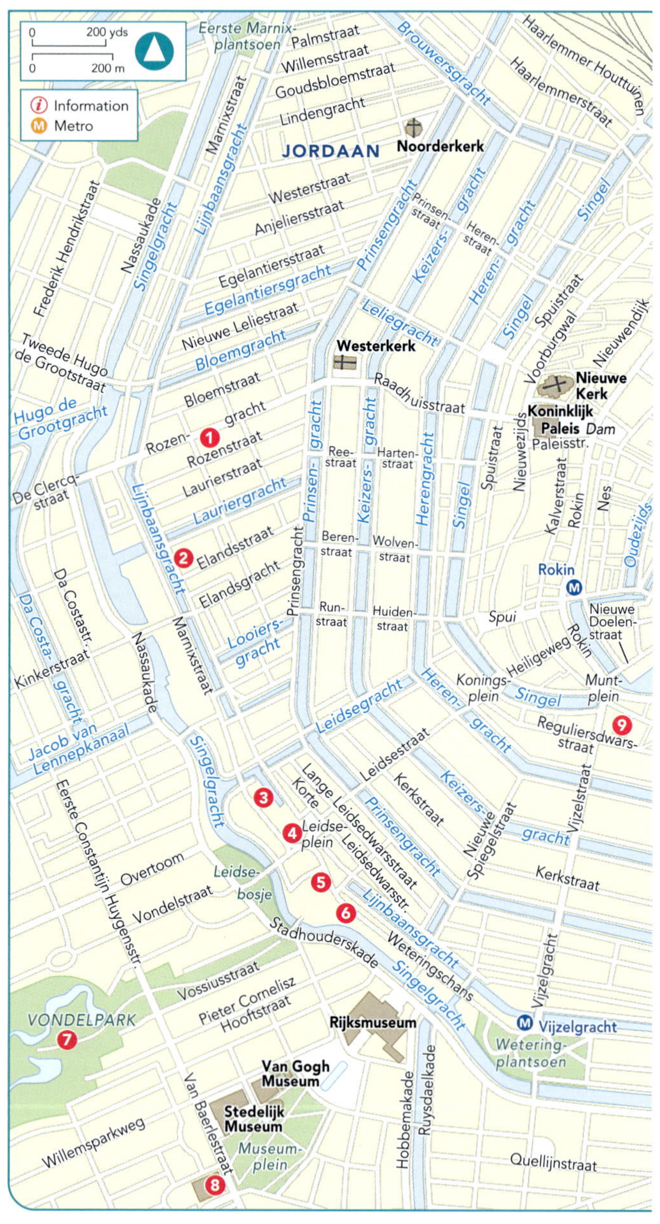

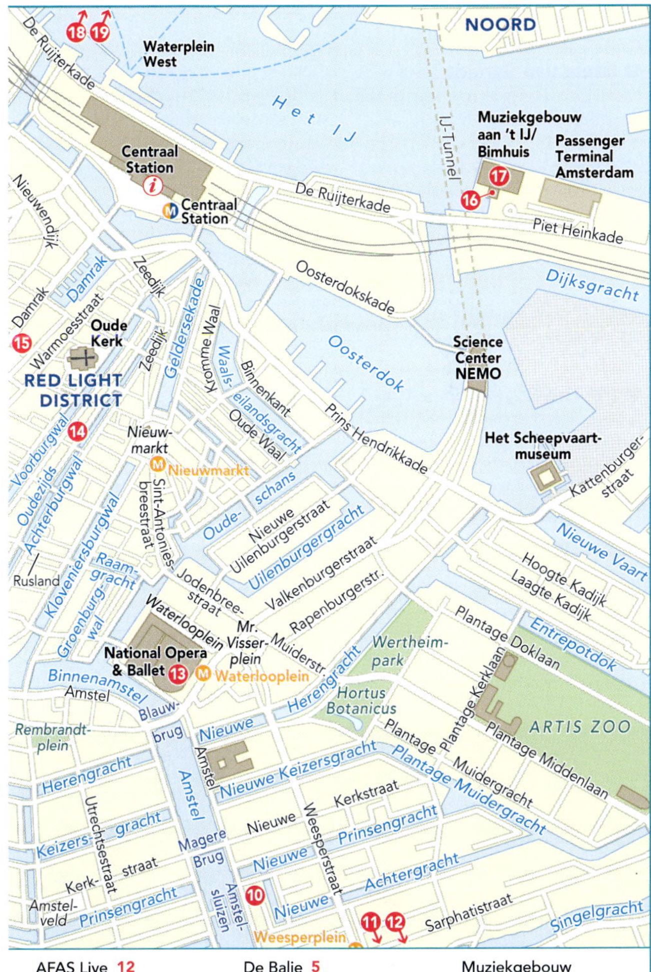


AFAS Live 12
Beurs van Berlage 15
Bimhuis 16
Boom Chicago 1
Carré 10
Casa Rosso 14
The Royal Concertgebouw Amsterdam 8
De Balie 5
Dutch National Opera & Ballet 13
Eye Filmmuseum 18
Internationaal Theater Amsterdam 4
Johan Cruijff ArenA 11
Maloe Melo 2
Melkweg 3
Muziekgebouw aan 't IJ 17
Paradiso 6
Pathé Royal Theater Tuschinski 9
Tolhuistuin 19
Vondelpark Openluchttheater 7

# Arts & Entertainment A to Z

## Classical Music

♥ **Beurs van Berlage** OLD CENTER The former home of the Amsterdam Stock Exchange, an architectural marvel from 1903 designed by Hendrik Berlage, is now a conference and eclectic exhibition center, plus sometime concert venue with two halls hosting classical concerts and rock festivals. Many events are free to enter. *Beursplein 1. www.beursvanberlage.nl. ☎ 020/531-3355. Tram: 2, 4, 12, 13, 14, or 17 to Dam.*

♥♥♥ **The Royal Concertgebouw Amsterdam** MUSEUM DISTRICT The home of the Royal Concertgebouw Orchestra, the Netherlands Philharmonic, and the Netherlands Chamber Orchestra first opened its doors in 1888 and is still touted as one of the most acoustically accurate concert halls in Europe. The world's finest conductors, orchestras, ensembles, and soloists regularly perform here. There are two halls: the main auditorium and a recital hall, which hosts smaller concerts. Free concerts every Wednesday at 12:30pm. *Concertgebouwplein 10. www.concertgebouw.nl. ☎ 020/671-8345. Tickets 10€–85€. Tram: 3, 5, or 12 to Concertgebouw.*

## Comedy

♥♥ **Boom Chicago** JORDAAN Amsterdam's premier comedy theater has been going strong since 1993. The partly scripted, partly improvised humor takes aim at life in Amsterdam, the Dutch, tourists, and any other convenient target. Most performances are in English. You can attend one show for free with an I amsterdam city card (p 8). *Rozengracht 117. www.boomchicago.nl. ☎ 020/217-0004. Tickets 20€–30€. Tram: 5, 13, or 17 to Rozengracht/Marnixstraat.*

## Concerts

♥ **AFAS Live** ZUIDOOST Near the ArenA, this smaller venue hosts midsize concerts, headline

*Bruce Springsteen performs at the Johan Cruijff ArenA.*

*Terrace bar at Muziekgebouw aan 't IJ.*

comedians, darts, and other events. Recent performers have included Kaytranada, Camila Cabello, and Ricky Gervais. *Johan Cruijff Boulevard 590. www.afaslive.nl. ☎ 0900/687-4242. Tickets 35€–95€. Metro: 54 to Bijlmer ArenA.*

**♥♥ Johan Cruijff ArenA** ZUIDOOST Named after Holland's most famous soccer player, this is the home of Ajax during the season (Aug–May). Off-season, expect big-name rock, rap, and pop concerts filling the city's biggest events arena. It is located in southeast Amsterdam with efficient transport connections. *Johan Cruijff Blvd. 1. www.johancruijffarena.nl. Tickets 18€–165€. Metro: 54 to Bijlmer ArenA.*

**♥♥ Melkweg** LEIDSEPLEIN A contemporary multipurpose venue which hosts all kinds of music, cinema, concerts, club nights, and exhibitions. Its program tends to showcase new groups, both international and local, with lashings of experimentalism, documentary music cinema, techno, punk, and a whole lot more. *Lijnbaansgracht 234A. www.melkweg.nl. ☎ 020/531-8181. Tickets free–28€. Tram: 1, 2, 5, 7, 12, 17, or 19 to Leidseplein.*

**♥♥♥ Muziekgebouw aan 't IJ** WATERFRONT This award-winning modern glass construction, located on the IJ waterfront east of Centraal Station, is the hub of contemporary and experimental classical music in Amsterdam. Top local and international musicians perform across two halls. Its terrace bar is an epic spot for a city sundowner. Jazz venue **Bimhuis** (p 123) is adjacent. *Piet Heinkade 1. www.muziekgebouw.nl. ☎ 020/788-2000. Tickets 10€–51€. Tram: 26 to Muziekgebouw Bimhuis.*

**♥♥ Paradiso** LEIDSEPLEIN An Amsterdam nightlife icon, this former church is a multipurpose venue, great for dance events (on weekends; p 114), and a concert venue for zeitgeist-y artists. The Rolling Stones, Nirvana, and Adele have all played here. *Weteringschans 6. www.paradiso.nl. ☎ 020/626-4521.*

*Concert tickets 15€–62€. Tram: 1, 2, 5, 7, 12, or 19 to Leidseplein.*

♥♥ **Tolhuistuin** NOORD Eclectic multi-arts and culture space with a strong roster of edgy contemporary sounds: from Afrobeat and soul to folk, jazz, and EDM. Or just grab a beer and a bite to eat in its cafe-restaurant. *IJpromenade 2. tolhuistuin.nl. ☎ 020/760-4820. Tickets 17€–30€. Ferry: F3 to Buiksloterweg.*

♥♥ **Vondelpark Openluchttheater** MUSEUM DISTRICT This open-air venue comes to life on weekends from May through September, when pop, rock, dance, comedy, or classical artists give free concerts in the midst of peaceful, green Vondelpark (p 83). Bring a picnic and enjoy an evening under the stars. *Vondelpark. www.openluchttheater.nl. ☎ 020/428-3360. Free admission. Tram: 2to Cornelis Schuytstraat.*

## Dance & Opera

♥♥♥ **Dutch National Opera & Ballet** WATERLOOPLEIN One of the city's stellar performance venues, this place has a superbly equipped 1,600-seat auditorium and is the home base of both the highly regarded Dutch National Opera and the National Ballet. Operatic surtitles are in Dutch and English. *Amstel 3. www.operaballet.nl. ☎ 020/625-5455. Tickets 28€–168€. Metro: 51, 53, or 54 to Waterlooplein.*

## Erotic Shows

♥ **Casa Rosso** OLD CENTER In its own words, Casa Rosso puts on "a variety of short erotic shows, performed by talented artists." You may (or may not) describe it in this way, but this live sex-show joint is perennially popular with tourists of every age and gender. No prebooking. *Oudezijds Achterburgwal 106–108. www.casarosso.nl. ☎ 020/627-8954. Cover 65€ including 1 drink. Metro: 51, 53, or 54 to Nieuwmarkt.*

## Film

♥♥ **De Balie** LEIDSEPLEIN This all-purpose cultural center has an eclectic calendar of workshops, lectures, and film festivals as well as a cafe-restaurant (open daily). You can see controversial and award-winning features or documentaries and interesting movies from around the world that don't make it to your local multiplex. *Kleine-Gartmanplantsoen 10. debalie.nl. ☎ 020/553-5100. Movie tickets 13€; lectures 16€–25€. Tram: 1, 2, 5, 7, 12, 17, or 19 to Leidseplein.*

♥♥♥ **Eye Filmmuseum** NOORD Much more than a film museum, this arthouse cinema complex moved in 2012 from its old location in Vondelpark to a striking contemporary building in Amsterdam-Noord. The new building houses four movie theaters, exhibitions, a store, and a bar-restaurant. Newly restored and 35mm classics are a specialty. *IJpromenade 1.*

*Performance of Don Quixote ballet at the Dutch National Opera & Ballet.*

*Restaurant at the Eye Filmmuseum.*

*www.eyefilm.nl.* ☎ *020/589-1400. Movie tickets 12.50€ adults, 7.50€ kids 11 and under. Ferry: F3 to Buiksloterweg.*

♥♥ **Pathé Royal Theater Tuschinski** REMBRANDTPLEIN Six screens of 1920s opulence, fully restored to original Art Deco and Art Nouveau splendor. Movie program combines Hollywood, arthouse, and classics. Self-guided audio tours run daily. *Reguliersbreestraat 26–34. www.pathe.nl. Movie tickets 16€ adults, 8€ kids 11 and under. Audio tour (45 min.) 11.50€. Tram: 4 or 14 to Rembrandtplein.*

### Jazz & Blues

♥♥ **Bimhuis** WATERFRONT Next door to the Muziekgebouw aan 't IJ (p 121), this 400-capacity space is the city's premier jazz, blues, and improvisational music venue. *Piet Heinkade 3. www.bimhuis.nl.* ☎ *020/788-2188. Tickets free–30€. Tram: 26 to Muziekgebouw Bimhuis.*

## Amsterdam's Urban Beaches

Yes, that's right: beaches. Amsterdam has no natural beaches of its own, so it decided to create some. Admission is generally free to many facilities and daily entertainment programs—usually running May through September only. **Strand IJburg** ♥♥ (Pampuslaan 1001; tram 26) is in the eastern suburbs, a man-made sandy strip with a bohemian vibe, campfires, and late-night summertime partying. Sophisticated **Strandzuid** ♥♥ at Europaplein 22 (strandzuid.nl; ☎ **020/639-2589**) attracts a more mature clientele with restaurants, a cocktail lounge, and beach bars on the wooden boardwalk. It's south of De Pijp, close to the Zuid financial district; catch metro 54 or tram 4.

## Buying Last-Minute Tickets

Although the reception staff at some hotels can help you book tickets, the most convenient outlet in the city is the **I amsterdam website** (www.iamsterdam.com). Their "What's On" section is updated monthly and is searchable by categories including Clubbing, Concerts, Festivals, and more. In addition, they also produce monthly previews of coming highlights and weekend preview guides. Holders of an **I amsterdam City Card** (p 8) get 25% off same-day tickets for Bimhuis, Muziekgebouw, and the Dutch National Opera and Ballet.

♥♥ **Maloe Melo** JORDAAN This small, grungy bar-club presents live blues and rock every night, interspersed with evenings of jazz and country, plus DJs sometimes on the weekend. ***Lijnbaansgracht** 163. www.maloemelo.com.* ☎ *020/420-4592. Cover 7.50€–10€. Tram: 5, 7, 17, or 19 to Elandsgracht.*

### Theater

♥♥ **Carré** OOST This big, plush theater on the Amstel used to be a circus arena; now a circus performs here only over Christmas. The theater hosts lavish Dutch- and English-language musical productions, modern dance, and ballet, as well as touring shows such as *War Horse* and well-known international acts like comedian Nate Bargatze and Brit singer-songwriter David Gray. *Amstel 115–125. carre.nl.* ☎ *020/524-9453. Tickets 21€–120€. Tram: 1, 7, or 19 to Weesperplein.*

♥ **Internationaal Theater Amsterdam** LEIDSEPLEIN This 950-seat municipal venue is Amsterdam's premier stage for Dutch dance and theater. Classic and modern plays in English are also occasionally staged—think *Hamlet* or *Angels in America*. ***Leidseplein** 26. ita.nl.* ☎ *020/624-2311. Tickets 10€–50€. Tram: 1, 2, 5, 7, 12, 17, or 19 to Leidseplein.*

*Musical performance at Carré.*

# 9 The Best Lodging

# Lodging **Best Bets**

*Previous page: Library in the De L'Europe hotel. This page: Loft guest room in the Ambassade.*

Best **Canal House Hotel**
♥♥♥ Ambassade $$$$
*Herengracht 341 (p 130)*

Best **Float-el**
♥♥ Asile Flottant $$–$$$
*Korte Papaverweg 2 (p 131)*

Best for **Beatles Fans**
♥ Hilton Amsterdam $$$–$$$$
*Apollolaan 138 (p 134)*

Best for **Business Travelers**
♥♥ citizenM Amsterdam South $$–$$$ *Prinses Irenestraat 30 (p 132)*

Best for **Gamers**
♥♥ The Arcade Hotel $–$$
*Sarphatipark 106 (p 130)*

Best **When Money Is No Object**
♥♥ De L'Europe $$$$$ *Nieuwe Doelenstraat 2–14 (p 133)*

Best for **Travelers Who Like to Spread Out**
♥♥♥ Hendrick's $$–$$$$ *Prins Hendrikkade 139 (p 134)*

Most **"Only in Amsterdam" Lodgings**
♥♥ SWEETS $$–$$$$ *Various locations (p 138)*

Best **Location for Families**
♥ Lancaster Amsterdam $$–$$$
*Plantage Middenlaan 48 (p 135)*

Best for **Young Party Animals on a Budget**
♥ St. Christopher's Inn at the Winston $$ *Warmoesstraat 129 (p 137)*

Best for **Museumgoers on a Budget**
♥♥ Keizershof $ *Keizersgracht 618 (p 135)*

Best for a **Luxury Romantic Getaway**
♥♥♥ The Pulitzer $$$$$
*Prinsengracht 315–331 (p 136)*; or
♥♥♥ The Dylan $$$$$
*Keizersgracht 384 (p 133)*

Best **Interior Design**
♥♥♥ Volkshotel $$$ *Wibautstraat 150 (p 138)*

Best for **Affordable Elegance**
♥♥♥ Seven Bridges $–$$$ *Reguliersgracht 31 (p 138)*

Best for **Sustainable Travel**
♥♥ Conscious Westerpark $$–$$$
*Haarlemmerweg 10 (p 132)*; or
♥♥♥ Mr. Jordaan $$–$$$
*Bloemgracht 102 (p 135)*

Best for **Showing Return Visitors a Different Amsterdam**
♥♥♥ BUNK Amsterdam $–$$$
*Hagedoornplein 2 (p 131)*

# Oud-West & De Pijp Lodging

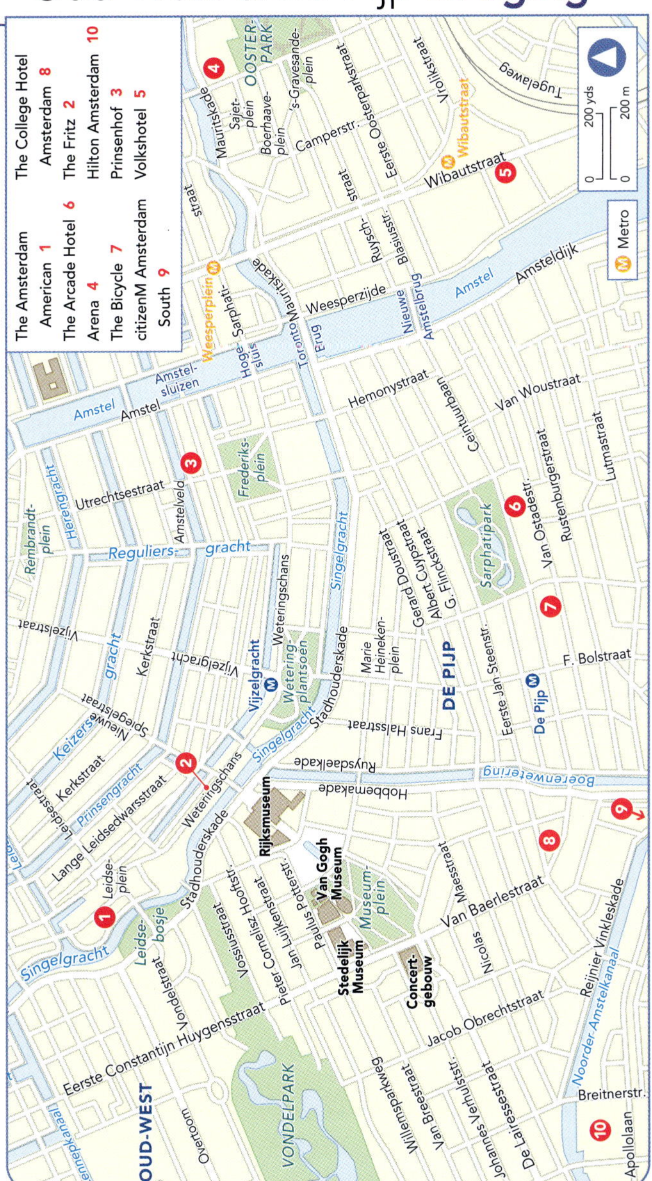

# Central Amsterdam Lodging

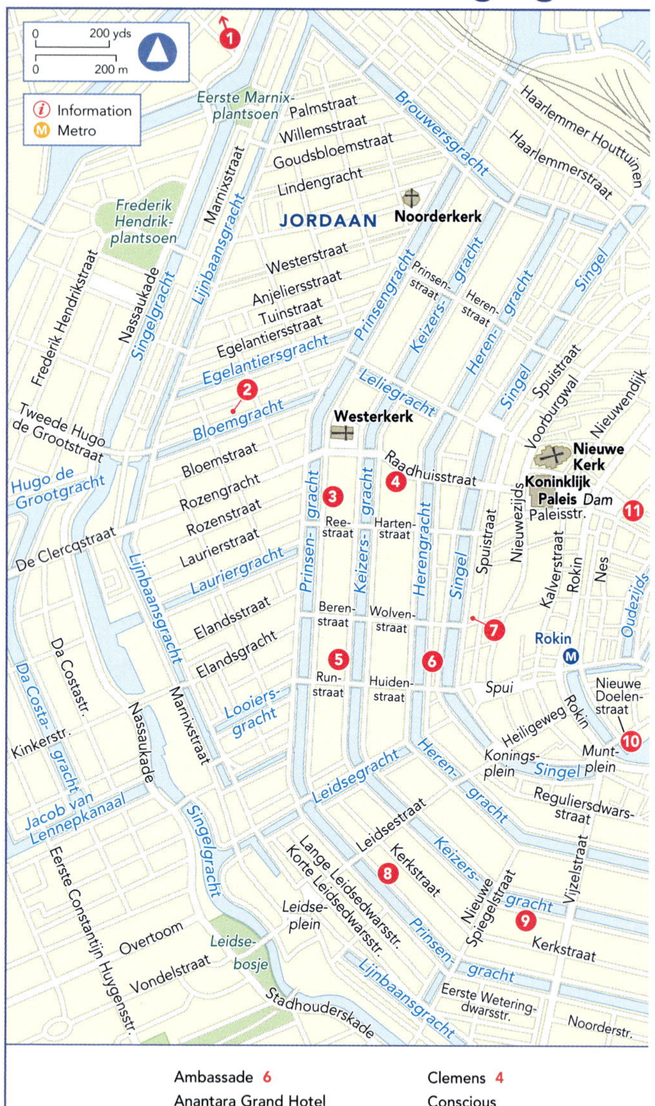


Ambassade 6
Anantara Grand Hotel Krasnapolsky 11
Asile Flottant 18
BUNK Amsterdam 19
Clemens 4
Conscious Westerpark 1
De L'Europe 10
The Dylan 5

Estheréa 7
Grand Hotel Amrâth 17
Hendrick's 16
Hotel 717 8
Keizershof 9
Lancaster Amsterdam 15
Mr. Jordaan 2
The Pulitzer 3
Radisson Blu 13
St. Christopher's Inn at the Winston 12
Seven Bridges 14
SWEETS 20

# Amsterdam Hotels A to Z

♥♥♥ **Ambassade** CANAL RING Ten elegant 17th- and 18th-century canal houses have been renovated over 70 years to create this perfectly located gem with a rich literary heritage (and large library). Individually decorated rooms and suites are furnished in lavish Louis XV and XVI styles, and CoBrA artworks hang in public spaces. Not all rooms are accessible by elevator. *Herengracht 341. ambassade-hotel.nl. ☎ 020/555-0222. 56 units. Doubles 219€–530€. Tram: 2, 12, or 17 to Koningsplein. Map p 129.*

♥♥ **The Amsterdam American** LEIDSEPLEIN Built in 1900, this hotel with Venetian Gothic and Art Nouveau architectural features may be showing its age just a little, but it remains a quality stalwart in the center's liveliest neighborhood. Thoughtfully modernized rooms are subdued, refined, and furnished for comfort. Take your pick from views of the Singelgracht canal or kaleidoscopic Leidseplein. Its Art Deco **Café Americain** (p 89) is perennially popular with international visitors. *Leidsekade 97. www.claytonhotels.com/amsterdam. ☎ 020/556-3000. 175 units. Doubles 189€–509€. Tram: 2 or 12 to Leidseplein. Map p 127.*

♥♥♥ **Anantara Grand Hotel Krasnapolsky** OLD CENTER "The Kras" has got its buzz back. With a luxe refit (including an award-winning spa) and still at the heart of it all, facing the **Royal Palace** (p 29), it remains an Amsterdam landmark. Room sizes and views vary, but calm, muted tones reign throughout. There may be hipper hotels in town—there are *certainly* cheaper ones—but once again, this has a claim to being Amsterdam's #1 address. *Dam 9. www.anantara.com/en/grand-hotel-krasnapolsky-amsterdam. ☎ 020/554-9111. 402 units. Doubles 340€–740€. Tram: 4 or 14 to Dam. Map p 128.*

♥♥ **The Arcade Hotel** DE PIJP The theme hotel you never knew you needed: Every room comes with a classic games console, and the lobby has a video arcade, modern consoles, a comic library, and even old-school board games. Rooms themselves are unpolished, with mismatched modern furniture and suitably nerdy embellishments like wall art assembled from old floppy disks (decent showers, though). It's a fun reinvention of the budget hotel format, and in a great location. Book direct for goodies

*Relaxation room at the Anantara Spa.*

*Superior double room at the Arcade.*

like free 1pm checkout. ***Sarphatipark 106. www.arcadehotel.nl.*** *☎ 020/ 667-0310. 42 units. Doubles 94€–250€. Tram: 3 to van der Helststraat. Map p 127.*

**♥♥ Arena** OOST Formerly an orphanage dating to 1890, the Arena is now a stylish hotel catering to travelers who love a sense of warm minimalism within an old frame. Rooms and suites are each individually decorated by Dutch designers with clever use of natural materials and light. There's a smart bar and eatery and a cute terrace bar (with firepit) that directly abuts Oosterpark. ***'s-Gravesandestraat 55. hotelarena.nl.*** *☎ 020/850-2400. 141 units. Doubles 140€–410€. Tram: 1, 3, 7 or 19 to Korte 's-Gravesandestraat. Map p 127.*

**♥♥ Asile Flottant** NOORD Named after a boat crafted by architect Le Corbusier, this floating hotel delivers on its design promise: Six boats of various sizes, most rescued from the scrapyard, have been repaired and individually refitted with diverse 20th-century nautical interiors. For the game traveler, it's a unique place to stay, plus one of our favorite bar-restaurants, **Café De Ceuvel** (p. 98), is directly quayside. Minimum stay 2 nights. ***Korte Papaverweg 2. www.asileflottant.com.*** *☎ 06/1521-1299. 6 units. Boat for 2 (Anneliese) from 185€. Bus: 391 or 394 to Mosplein. Map p 128.*

**♥ The Bicycle** DE PIJP Located a few blocks from the **Albert Cuypmarkt** (p 78), this eco-friendly budget hotel caters to visitors who wish to explore Amsterdam by bike. (You can rent and stable your trusty steed indoors.) Guest rooms have plain but comfortable modern furnishings; some have shared bathrooms; and there are large rooms for families. No elevator. ***Van Ostadestraat 123. bicyclehotel.com.*** *☎ 020/679-3452. 16 units. Doubles 89€–280€ w/breakfast. Metro: 52 to De Pijp. Map p 127.*

**♥♥♥ BUNK Amsterdam** NOORD Once a church, now a thoughtfully converted "posh-tel" with a mix of sleeping pods and comfortable, "urban-contemporary" ensuite rooms sleeping up to five. Staff is young and friendly; clientele spans couples, cost-conscious families, and businesspeople. Rooms are compact but cleverly designed to maximize storage space. Location is great for exploring Noord—perhaps

*Terrace of BUNK Amsterdam room.*

better suited to return visitors than to Amsterdam first-timers. *Hagedoornplein 2. wearebunk.com/amsterdam. ☎ 088/6969-869. 159 units. Doubles 63€–270€. Metro: Noorderpark. Map p 129.*

♥♥ **citizenM Amsterdam South** NIEUW ZUID Proximity to the Zuid business district often makes weekend rates here very tempting. It's a sterile neighborhood, but transport links are superb. Rooms at this Amsterdam-founded boutique design-hotel chain are tech-forward—an iPad controls everything—with comfortable mattresses, underbed storage, and free cycle rental. ***Note:*** Pod-style toilets may not suit everyone's taste. *Prinses Irenestraat 30. www.citizenm.com. ☎ 020/811-7090. 215 units. Doubles 120€–290€. Tram: 5 to Prinses Irenestraat. Map p 127.*

*Lobby at citizenM Amsterdam South.*

♥ **Clemens** JORDAAN Comfy, friendly, and close to many of the city's main attractions. All of the fairly spacious rooms are bright, clean, and homey, and some have tiny balconies facing the Westerkerk. The hotel occupies four floors in a steep-staired building, and there's no elevator. *Raadhuisstraat 39. www.clemenshotel.nl. ☎ 020/624-6089. 14 units. Doubles 144€–385€ w/ breakfast. Tram: 13 or 17 to Westermarkt. Map p 129.*

♥♥ **The College Hotel Amsterdam** MUSEUM DISTRICT Renovated in 2024, this glammy boutique hotel is housed in a 19th-century school building (hence the name) just a short walk from the major museums. It's now part of Marriott's Autograph Collection, with rooms styled in sympathy with the school architecture and two restaurants. *Roelof Hartstraat 1. www.thecollegehotel.com. ☎ 020/571-1511. 40 units. Doubles 260€–549€. Tram: 5 to Roelof Hartplein. Map p 127.*

♥♥ **Conscious Westerpark** WESTERPARK The opposite of stuffy, this remodeled former gasworks building feels more like a hip co-working space than a chain hotel. Rooms inside the 19th-century shell

Courtyard at the College Hotel Amsterdam.

are fresh and modern with California king-size beds. Triple rooms and the adjacent park suit families; for others, there's 24/7 entertainment on the doorstep, although you're a little outside Amsterdam's traditional center. A sister hotel is near Vondelpark. Two-night minimum on summer weekends. *Haarlemmerweg 10. conscioushotels.com/stay/westerpark. ☎ 020/820-3333. 89 units. Doubles 92€–279€. Tram: 5 to Haarlemmerplein. Map p 129.*

♥♥♥ **De L'Europe** OLD CENTER This classic luxury hotel commands a prime riverside location. Rooms and suites are spacious and bright, and all have sumptuous linens and marble bathrooms. There's a stellar restaurant, a spa, and a summer terrace overlooking the Amstel. Service from dedicated staff is top-class. *Nieuwe Doelenstraat 2–14. www.deleurope.com. ☎ 020/531-1777. 107 units. Doubles 468€–800€. Tram: 4 or 14 to Rokin/Muntplein. Map p 129.*

♥♥♥ **The Dylan** CANAL RING Amsterdam's swankiest boutique hotel is set in 17th-century buildings beside one of the city's most scenic canals. Modern elegance reigns—many rooms have four-poster beds and spacious bathrooms. Each room is individually decorated with natural materials, rich fabrics, and bold accent colors. *Keizersgracht 384. www.dylanamsterdam.com. ☎ 020/530-2010. 41 units. Doubles 495€–795€. Tram: 2, 12, or 17 to Koningsplein. Map p 129.*

♥♥ **Estheréa** CANAL RING This quirky boutique hotel, built within neighboring 17th-century houses on the city's oldest canal, has been owned by the same family since it opened. Wood paneling, chandeliers, and dresser-desks lend warmth to the bold-hued guest rooms, many of which were renovated in 2025. *Singel 303–309. www.estherea.nl. ☎ 020/624-5146. 93 units. Doubles 179€–730€. Tram: 2 or 12 to Paleisstraat. Map p 128.*

♥ **The Fritz** LEIDSEPLEIN A traditional townhouse renovated in

Junior suite at De L'Europe.

*Spacious guest room at the Dylan.*

2024, and (bizarrely) with a sister hotel in Miami Beach, the Fritz has an enviable location for combining culture and nightlife: **Paradiso** (p 114) and the **Rijksmuseum** (p 7) are each within 2 minutes' walk. Rooms are small by North American standards but are well equipped and cleverly designed—fine for those who travel light. Stairs are steep, but there's an elevator. *Weiteringschans 67. thefritzamsterdam.com. ☎ 020/248-0562. 20 units. Doubles 80€–240€. Tram: 1, 7, or 19 to Rijksmuseum. Map p 127.*

♥♥ **Grand Hotel Amrâth** WATERFRONT It may not be the most luxurious government-rated five-star in town, but this former shipping HQ is a genuine architectural landmark: an icon of Amsterdam School design by Van der Meij. Its grand interior now offers rooms you will sink into—canal views beat those out front—and a decadent spa. *Prins Hendrikkade 108. www.amrathamsterdam.com. ☎ 020/552-0000. 205 units. Doubles 225€–425€. Bus: 305 to Prins Hendrikkade. Map p 128.*

♥♥♥ **Hendrick's** WATERFRONT The many cultural venues of the IJ docks are out front, the canals of the Old Center in back, and Centraal Station is a 5-minute walk away. But the real joy is what's inside this converted Golden Age canal house: serene interiors, spacious rooms flooded with natural light, large heritage-tiled bathrooms with his-and-hers sinks, and a free welcome drink. *Prins Hendrikkade 139. www.thehendrickshotel.com. ☎ 020/260-3000. 25 units. Doubles 169€–455€. Bus: 305 to Prins Hendrikkade. Map p 128.*

♥ **Hilton Amsterdam** NIEUW ZUID The light-drenched room no. 902 is where John Lennon and Yoko Ono had their "Bed-in for Peace" in 1969. Designers consulted Yoko when renovating the room, and it now features extensive use of natural materials. The hotel has modern facilities and a location in a leafy, almost suburban district. *Apollolaan 138. www.hilton.com. ☎ 020/710-6000. 271 units. Doubles 202€–439€. Bus: 357 or 397 to Emmastraat. Map p 127.*

♥♥ **Hotel 717** CANAL RING One of the Netherlands' original luxe boutique hotels, this palace of style has been wonderfully renovated in bright whites, creams, and bold heritage colors, with butler service on tap for all guests. An elegant drawing room, a sunspot terrace, canal views, original artworks, and a flower-filled room serving a la carte breakfast, all contribute to a truly unforgettable experience, far removed from impersonal chain hotels. Small "Little Prince" double

## A Canal House Warning

**Elevators are difficult things to shoehorn into the cramped confines** of a 17th-century canal house and cost more than some hotels can afford. Consequently, many budget properties don't have them. If lugging your old wooden sea chest up six flights of steep, narrow stairs is liable to void your life insurance, better make sure an elevator is in place and working. Should there be no such amenity, you might want to ask for a room on a lower floor.

rooms bring the luxury of their canal-view suites within reach of more modest budgets, too. *Prinsengracht 717. 717hotel.nl. ☎ 020/427-0717. 23 units. Doubles 200€–570€. Tram: 2 or 12 to Prinsengracht. Map p 128.*

♥♥ **Keizershof** CANAL RING This four-story canal house dates to 1672 and offers guests a gloriously old-fashioned, B&B-style welcome. Rooms are on the upper floors (no elevator), beamed and cozy with simple, modern furnishings and large windows. Not all have private bathrooms. In summer, you can enjoy a legendary breakfast in the flower-filled courtyard garden. *Keizersgracht 618. hotelkeizershof.nl. ☎ 020/622-2855. 5 units. Doubles 140€–180€ w/breakfast. Tram: 2, 12, or 17 to Keizersgracht. Map p 128.*

♥ **Lancaster Amsterdam** JEWISH QUARTER A stone's throw from the zoo and **Micropia** (p 37), this hotel is in a great location for families. The quiet neighborhood seems far from the crowds and noise of the old center, but it's just a 10-minute tram ride away. Attractive triples and quads are perfect if you're traveling with kids—crane your necks and you might just see the flamingoes across the road. *Plantage Middenlaan 48. www.thelancasterhotelamsterdam.com. ☎ 020/535-6888. 121 units. Doubles 135€–345€. Tram: 14 to Artis. Map p 128.*

♥♥♥ **Mr. Jordaan** JORDAAN They really squeeze the most they can out of the typical canal house mazy layout. While the interior is completely modernized with warm

*Grand Heritage room at Hotel 717 overlooks the Prinsengracht canal.*

*Gabled wooden headboard in a guest room at Mr. Jordaan.*

natural materials and some contemporary panache (like wooden headboards carved into Amsterdam gables), rooms are smaller than you are likely accustomed to. But location and staff are perfect. *Bloemgracht 102. mrjordaan.nl. ☎ 020/626-5801. 34 units. Doubles 97€–445€. Tram: 13 or 17 to Westermarkt. Map p 128.*

♥ **Prinsenhof** CANAL RING This canal-house hotel offers basic but bright and comfortable rooms with beamed ceilings and private bathrooms. Front rooms look out onto the Prinsengracht, where colorful houseboats are moored. There's no elevator. *Prinsengracht 810. www.hotelprinsenhof.com. ☎ 020/623-1772. 10 units. Doubles 150€–360€ w/breakfast. Tram: 4 to Prinsengracht. Map p 127.*

♥♥♥ **The Pulitzer** CANAL RING The multi-award-winning Pulitzer offers its lucky guests pure luxury and the best of Dutch design without being ostentatious. A superior location on a canal at the edge of the Jordaan, rooms so plush they envelop you, a spa, two restaurants, and a cocktail bar make this an incredible place to splurge on a romantic getaway. It's also close to the tourist hotspots and Nine Streets shopping. *Prinsengracht 323.*

## Money-Saving & More Hotel Tips

Alas, Amsterdam's hotels can be expensive. If a particular place strikes your fancy but is out of your price range, ask whether off-season (Nov, Jan–Feb; sometimes Aug in business hotels), weekday, or other packages will bring the cost down. Sunday night stays are sometimes *much* cheaper and you may earn a discount for staying 3 nights or more. Pretty much every hotel these days uses dynamic pricing, so another money-saving route, if your dates are flexible, is to hunt down a bargain with patient, date-by-date searching.

With most hotels, it's cheaper to book direct online rather than through an agency website, sometimes up to 10% cheaper—you'll also get more sympathy if something goes wrong with your plans and perhaps inclusive goodies like free late checkout. Note that Wi-Fi is free and reliable pretty much everywhere; breakfast is rarely included in quoted rates (we note some exceptions in this chapter), but may be available cheaper if you prebook it with the room. Some hotels quote room rates without including 12.5% local tax: Ask if unclear. A minimum 2-night stay on summer weekends is increasingly common. For something totally different, and *very* Amsterdam, don't neglect the self-explanatory **BookaHouseboat.com**.

## Summer Stays: Reserve Ahead

Despite there being more than 500 hotels in the city, May through September are tough months for finding good (and good-value) rooms here. Try to reserve as far ahead as possible for this period. If you have problems getting a reservation, sit it out on the web or use the live chat feature to contact tourism promotion agency **I amsterdam** (p 8), who may be able to help.

*www.pulitzeramsterdam.com.* ☎ *020/523-5235. 225 units. Doubles 396€–990€. Tram: 13 or 17 to Westermarkt. Map p 128.*

♥ **Radisson Blu** OLD CENTER This sprawling hotel is close to everything. There are multiple room categories and price points, which are divided design-wise into Scandi-inspired Naturally Cool and richer Golden Age schemes. The hotel is bursting with amenities: a gym, sauna, bar, restaurants, and even its own 24/7 convenience store. *Rusland 17. www.radissonhotels.com.* ☎ *020/623-1231. 252 units. Doubles 186€–350€. Metro: 52 to Rokin. Map p 128.*

♥ **St. Christopher's Inn at the Winston** OLD CENTER Young partygoers flock to this bouncing hostel-cum-art-hotel with a popular bar-diner, **Belushi's,** on-site: Book direct for a free welcome drink and 25% off food. Ensuite private rooms and dorms are available. It's on a slightly seedy street, steps from the Red Light District, so families may want to look elsewhere, but it's a great choice for young party people. *Warmoesstraat 129. www.st-christophers.co.uk/amsterdam.* ☎ *020/623-1380. 60 units. Doubles 110€–380€. Tram: 4 or 14 to Dam. Map p 128.*

*Family suite at the Pulitzer.*

*Guest suite in a former bridgekeeper's house at SWEETS.*

**♥♥♥ Seven Bridges** CANAL RING This canal-house gem is a rare combo of gorgeous and great value. Each individually decorated room has genuine antique furnishings (Art Deco, Biedermeier, Louis XVI), handmade Italian drapes, and wooden floors topped with Oriental rugs. Attic rooms have sloped ceilings and exposed beams. It's a real romantic escape, and very reasonable in price considering its only-in-Amsterdam style. No elevator. *Reguliersgracht 31. www.sevenbridgeshotel.nl. ☎ 020/623-1329. 8 units. Doubles 150€–250€. Tram: 4 to Keizersgracht. Map p 128.*

**♥♥ SWEETS** OLD CENTER You'll likely never get the chance to stay in a place like this again. It's not a single hotel but a collection of former bridgekeeper's houses built over 4 centuries along Amsterdam's water thoroughfares. Each has been converted into a contemporary suite for two people (one sleeps four) and is accessed by a smartphone key delivered on check-in day. Location, size, and ambience vary enormously, from a peaceful lake in Amsterdam-Noord to a bustling road in De Pijp. Those numbered between 201 and 207 are all fairly central, ranged along the Amstel. Ages 21 and over only. *Locations around the city. sweetshotel.amsterdam. ☎ 020/740-1010. 28 units. Doubles 125€–515€.*

**♥♥♥ Volkshotel** OOST Once a renowned newspaper HQ, now a hotel renovated with flair using natural materials like concrete and wood to create a midcentury-meets-industrial vibe. Rooms in all sizes are bright, with compact bathrooms and quality firm mattresses. Public spaces are a real draw, for guests and Amsterdammers: There's a restaurant, cafe, rooftop sauna and hot tubs (guests only), a coworking space, and a nightclub in the basement. *Wibautstraat 150. www.volkshotel.nl. ☎ 020/661-2100. 196 units. Doubles 76€–340€. Metro: 51, 53, or 54 to Wibautstraat. Map p 127.* ●

# 10 The Best Day Trips & Excursions

# Haarlem

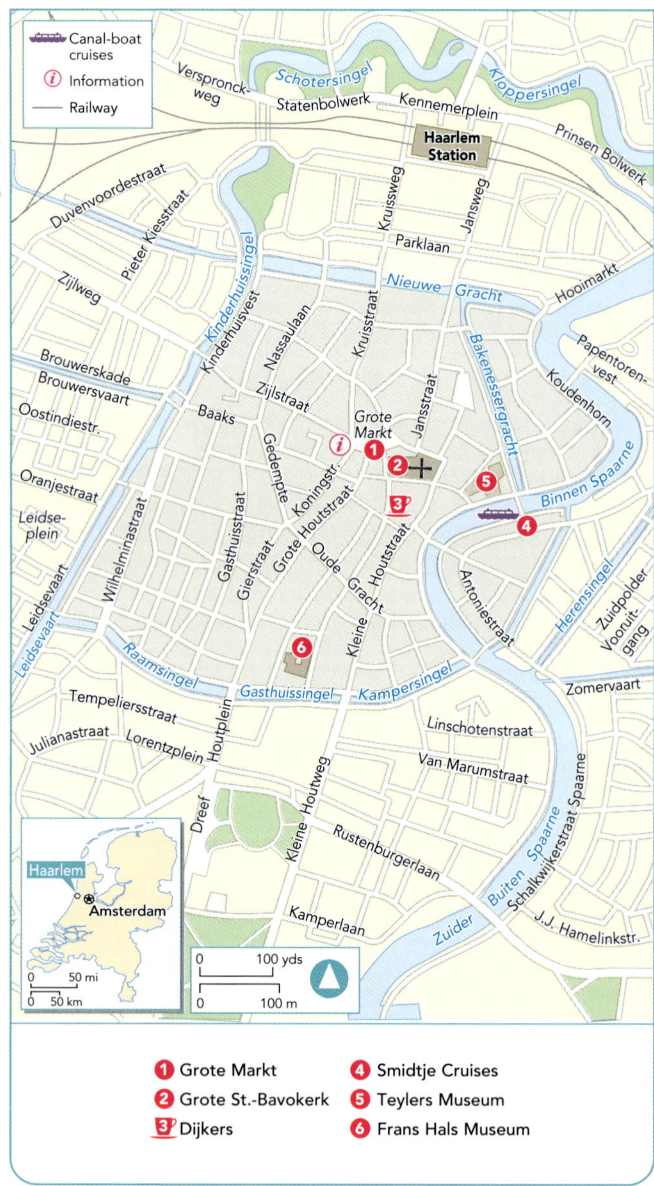


1. Grote Markt
2. Grote St.-Bavokerk
3. Dijkers
4. Smidtje Cruises
5. Teylers Museum
6. Frans Hals Museum

*Previous page: Crew rowing on a canal in Haarlem.*

**Handsome Haarlem is today virtually a suburb of Amsterdam,** but in the 17th-century Dutch Golden Age it was a thriving town and cultural center, home of Rembrandt's contemporaries Frans Hals, Jacob van Ruisdael, and Pieter Saenredam, who were famous for domestic and civic portraits, landscapes, and church interiors. Despite its diminutive size, a day in Haarlem reveals one of the finest churches in the Netherlands, a charismatic muddle of architecture, and one of the best art museums in Europe. START: **A walk of a ½ mile south from the rail station along Kruisweg, Kruisstraat, and Smedestraat to Grote Markt.**

*Cafe in front of Town Hall on Grote Markt.*

❶ ♥♥♥ **Grote Markt.** The monumental buildings around this tree-lined market square, which date from the 15th to 19th centuries, are a delightful visual mini-course in the development of Dutch architecture. The oldest building is the 14th-century gabled, balconied, and spired **Stadhuis (Town Hall),** a former hunting lodge that was rebuilt in the 17th century. 🕔 *30 min. Main market Sat 8:30am–5pm; smaller market Mon 9am–4pm.*

❷ ♥ **Grote St.-Bavokerk (Great St. Bavo's Church).** Completed in 1520, this magnificent Gothic church dominates the Grote Markt with a rare unity of structure and proportion. Its elegant wooden tower is adorned with gilt and topped with a gilded crown. The light and airy church interior has rood-screen and sandstone pillars, but the standout feature is a soaring Christian Müller

*Great St. Bavo's was completed in 1520.*

*Teylers is the oldest museum in the Netherlands, continually open since 1784.*

organ (1738), which has 5,068 pipes and is nearly 30m (98 ft.) tall. Mozart played the organ in 1766 when he was just 10 years old, and Handel and Liszt both made pilgrimages to play here. You can hear the organ in action in a program of recitals that run from May to October (tickets 4€), usually on Tuesday evening and/or Thursday afternoon, plus occasional weekends. Check the church website for details and **PHIL Haarlem** (philhaarlem.nl) for additional concerts. *45 min. Grote Markt 22. www.bavo.nl/en. 023/553-2040. Admission 4€ adults, 2€ ages 12–16. Guided tour (Sat 2pm) 7€. Mon–Sat 10am–5pm.*

3 ♥ **Dijkers.** This cozy little restaurant offers light lunches from a menu of burgers, hearty salads, daily sandwiches, and flammkuchen (Alsatian pizzalike flatbreads) for a lunchtime pit stop. If you prefer to eat on the move, friendly Friethuis La Petite ♥ next door sells classic Dutch fries with toppings. *Warmoesstraat 5–7. www.restaurantdijkers.nl. 023/551-1564. Closed Mon. $–$$.*

4 ♥ kids **Smidtje Cruises.** A river cruise is the ideal way to explore Haarlem if you're time-deprived. The dock is on the River Spaarne just beside the Gravenstenenbrug, a handsome lift bridge. You'll see historical buildings and pass close to an 18th-century Dutch windmill, Molen de Adriaan—a great photo op. *50 min. Spaarne 11a on the riverside. www.smidtjecanalcruises.nl. 023/535-7723. Tickets 21.50€ adults, 11.50€ kids 4–12, 55€ family 2+2 (free with I amsterdam City Card). Boats depart frequently throughout the day.*

5 ♥♥ kids **Teylers Museum.** Quirky but oddly compelling, this museum is the oldest in the Netherlands, continually open since 1784. It's named after the 18th-century merchant Pieter Teyler van der Hulst, who willed his entire fortune to the advancement of science and the arts. You'll find a diverse collection here: drawings by Michelangelo, Raphael, and Rembrandt; fossils, minerals, and skeletons; instruments of physics; and an assortment of inventions, including the largest electrostatic generator in the world. *1¼ hr. Spaarne 16. teylersmuseum.nl/en. 023/516-0960. 17.50€ adults, 8.75€ young adults 18–24, 2.50€ kids 6–17 (free with I amsterdam City Card). Tues–Sun 10am–5pm. Closed Jan 1, Dec 25.*

6 ♥♥♥ **Frans Hals Museum.** Quite simply the highlight of many art lovers' trips to Holland, this

## Haarlem Essentials

Haarlem is so easily accessible from Amsterdam that many people commute daily: This charming town is a mere 15 minutes from Amsterdam Centraal Station, and trains run between the two at regular intervals. The round-trip fare is 10.40€. Once in Haarlem, it's easy to get around on foot; the station is a flat 10-minute walk from Grote Markt.

**VVV Haarlem** (the tourist information office) is at Grote Markt 2 (www.visithaarlem.com/en; ☎ **023/531-7325**). Regular opening hours are Monday to Saturday from 10am to 5pm. It often opens on Sundays at peak times, including during spring tulip season; in winter, it's usually closed Mondays. Free admission to the Frans Hals (6) and Teylers (5) museums, plus a canal cruise (4), are included with the **I amsterdam City Card** (p 8); no advance reservations required.

museum is housed in a former *Oudemannenhuis* (elderly care home for men) dating from 1608. Consequently, the wonderful paintings by Frans Hals (1580–1666) and other masters of the Haarlem School hang in a setting reminiscent of the Golden Age houses they were intended to adorn.

*The Frans Hals Museum exhibits many celebrated works of this Golden Age master, who lived and died in Haarlem.*

(Although here, Old Masters are also hung creatively alongside "responses" by modern painters.) A short film provides informative context for this great artist, who earned a living by painting portraits of members of the local guilds (p 173). Five of his civic-guard pictures—painted between 1616 and 1639—are on display in the museum, including *A Banquet of the Officers of the Civic Guard of St George* (1616); the 1639 portrait of the same guard includes the only known Hals self-portrait (top-left). Among other highlights are the preserved original almshouse men's dining room; a dollhouse from around 1740 (not a toy!); silver and clocks; and several paintings of old Haarlem and its nearby dunes, including a couple of very early landscapes by Mondriaan. *2 hr. Groot Heiligland 62. franshalsmuseum.nl/en. ☎ 023/511-5775. Admission 17.50€ adults, 9€ young adults 19–24, free for kids 18 and under (also free with I amsterdam City Card). Tues–Sun 11am–5pm. Closed Jan 1, Apr 27, and Dec 25.*

# Delft

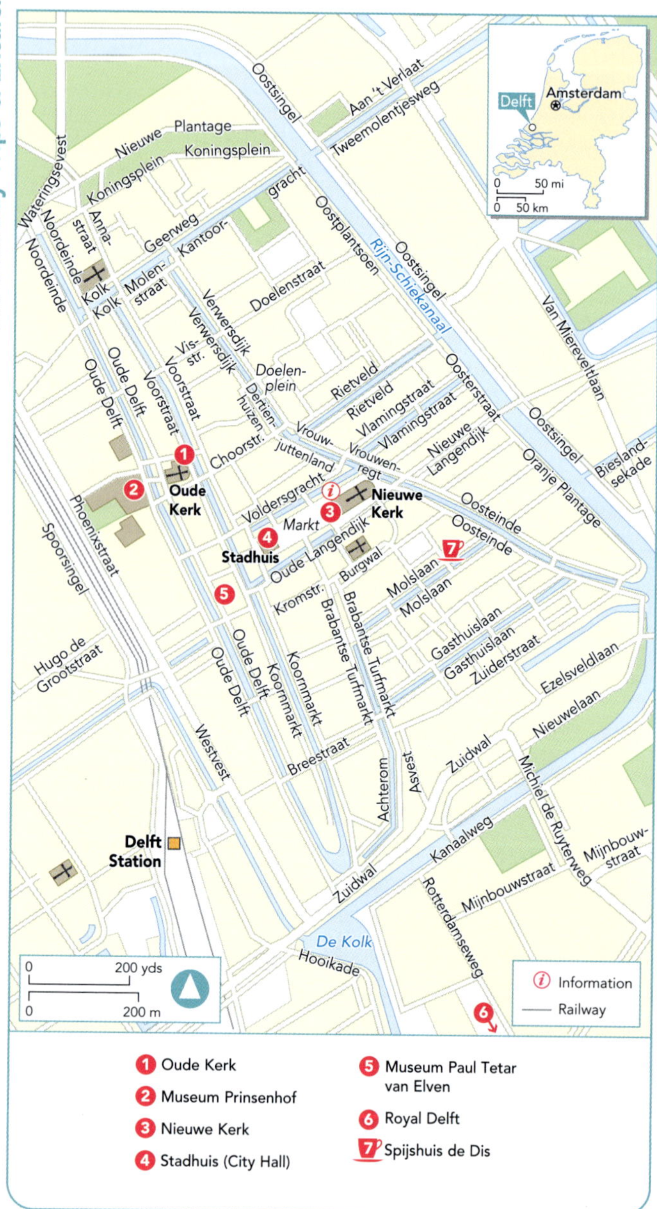


1 Oude Kerk

2 Museum Prinsenhof

3 Nieuwe Kerk

4 Stadhuis (City Hall)

5 Museum Paul Tetar van Elven

6 Royal Delft

7 Spijshuis de Dis

**Delft is best known as the home of the famous blue-and-white porcelain.** On this day out, you'll visit the factory where it's produced. Delft is a small, charming city with a leading technical university and a big history; it was the cradle of the Dutch Republic, the burial place of the royal family, and the birthplace and inspiration of artist Jan Vermeer, the 17th-century master of light and subtle emotion. Take a stroll through the streets to admire the colorful flower boxes and linden trees that bow over tranquil canals. START: **Walk north from the station along canalside Oude Delft and through the heart of the Old Town, a distance of around 800m (½ mile).**

*Stained-glass windows in Delft's Oude Kerk.*

❶ ♥♥ **Oude Kerk (Old Church).** Jan Vermeer's house is long gone, as are his paintings, but he's buried at the Oude Kerk, an immense church with 11th-century origins, an "official" inauguration year of 1246, and countless additions through the centuries. The Gothic north transept was appended in the 16th century, and the ornate, skinny clock tower was rebuilt after the local arsenal blew up and destroyed much of the town in 1654, an event known as the "Delft Thunder." The repairs left it with a distinct kink in its profile. Like that of many Dutch churches, the floors are paved with tomb slabs from the 17th century and dappled with sunlight streaming through glorious stained-glass windows, the work of 20th-century craftsman Joep Nicolas. *30 min. Heilige Geestkerkhof 25. oudeennieuwekerkdelft.nl. ☎ 015/212-3015. Admission (combined with Nieuwe Kerk; see below) 8.50€ adults, 7€ students 12–25, 4€ kids 6–11. Mon–Sat 10am–5pm (Nov–Jan closes 4pm).*

❷ ♥♥ **Museum Prinsenhof.** The "Father of the Fatherland," William of Orange (aka William the

*A study of William I of Orange hangs in the Museum Prinsenhof.*

## Delft Essentials

Delft is just under an hour by train from Amsterdam. The round-trip fare is 33€, and trains depart Centraal and Zuid stations approximately every 30 minutes. From Delft station, almost everything is just a 10-minute walk. The tourist office, **VVV Delft** is inside the rail station, Stationsplein 7 (www.indelft.nl/en; ☎ **015/ 215-4052**). Opening hours are April to September, Sunday and Monday from 10am to 4pm, Tuesday to Saturday from 10am to 5pm; October to March, Tuesday to Saturday from 10am to 4pm, Sunday and Monday from 11am to 3pm. Delft's main market is held on Thursdays.

Silent) had his headquarters in this Gothic former convent during the years he was fighting the Spanish to found the Dutch Republic. He was also assassinated here in 1584, on behalf of the King of Spain; you can still see the musket-ball holes in the stairwell. Reopening in 2027 after a major renovation, the Prinsenhof relates the story of William's life and displays paintings, tapestries, silverware, and pottery from the 17th century. Among the collection's most prized artworks is Michiel Jansz van Mierevelt's cleverly lit *Civic Guard Banquet* (1611). *1 hr. Sint Agathaplein 1. www.museumprinsenhofdelft.nl/en. ☎ 015/260-2358. See website for admission prices and opening hours.*

**3 ♥ Nieuwe Kerk (New Church).** Prince William and other members of the House of Orange-Nassau are buried in this church, built between 1384 and 1510. Like many of Delft's medieval buildings, it was restored following the Great Fire in 1536, which was probably caused by a lightning strike on the original church tower. Renowned architect Pierre Cuypers, designer of the **Rijksmuseum** in Amsterdam (p 7), added the near-109m (356 ft.) tower in 1872. After exploring the interior, fit travelers can climb 374 narrow steps to glorious views over Delft. *30 min. Markt 80. oudeennieuwekerkdelft.nl. ☎ 015/212-3025. Admission: Church (combined with Oude Kerk; see above) 8.50€ adults, 7€ students 12–25, 4€ kids 6–11; Tower only: 6€ adults, 5€ students 12–25, 3.50€ kids 6–11; both churches plus tower 13€/10.50€/5€. Mon–Sat 10am–5pm (Nov–Jan closes 4pm).*

**4 ♥ Stadhuis (City Hall).** Facing the Nieuwe Kerk across Delft's expansive market square is this ornate Renaissance building designed by Hendrick De Keyser in 1618. The tower at its center is the only surviving part of the original circa-1200 building. *10 min.*

**5 ♥♥ Museum Paul Tetar van Elven.** The 19th-century artist Van Elven (1823–96) lived and worked in this stately canal house, and the furnishings are largely as he left them—although the layout has been modified to accommodate visitors. His 17th-century-style studio looks like it's ready for the artist to enter and pick up his brushes. Van Elven's Dutch Renaissance furniture and porcelain form one of the finest collections of 19th-century decorative arts, but more interesting are the paintings. Van Elven was a noted copyist, a legitimate business in the era

Stadhuis (City Hall) on Delft's expansive market square.

before photography, and many of his reproductions are on display. Most of these fakes are excellent, especially the Rembrandts and the Paulus Potter. ⏲ *45 min. Koornmarkt 67. museumpaultetarvanelven.nl. ☎ 015/212-4206. Admission 12€ adults, free ages 18 and under. Tues–Sun 1–5pm.*

6 ♥♥ **Royal Delft.** If you like Delftware porcelain, you'll be in heaven at Royal Delft. The audio-guided experience includes a firsthand view of the business of producing and painting Delft Blue pottery; a visit to the Delft factory museum, which was renovated in 2025 and features antique multi-spouted tulip vases; and a shop with factory seconds at relative bargain prices. ⏲ *1½ hr. Rotterdamseweg 196. museum.royaldelft.com/en. ☎ 015/251-2030. Tour 17€ adults, 10€ ages 13–18, 7.50€ kids 7–12; painting workshops 36€–46€. Daily 9am–5pm. Closed Jan 1 and Dec 25–26.*

7 ♥♥ **Spijshuis de Dis.** Great Dutch cooking is dished up at this atmospheric restaurant on a popular square. Traditional plates are presented in modern variations: bokkenpot (a stew made from beef, chicken, and rabbit in beer sauce), lamb shank with fennel, and a fresh fish and seafood platter for sharing. *Beestenmarkt 36. www.spijshuisdedis.com. ☎ 015/213-1782. Tues–Sat 5–10pm. $$–$$$.*

Artist at work at Delft's porcelain factory museum.

# Rotterdam

0.2 mi
0.2 km
Canal-boat cruises
Information
Amsterdam
Rotterdam
50 mi
50 km
Maas
Nieuwe
Maas
Rijnhaven
Erasmusbrug
Posthumalaan
Maaskade
Meeuwen-str.
Wilhelminakade
Otto Reuchlinweg
Boompjeskade
Boompjes
Terwenakker
Leuvehaven
Schiedamsedijk
Leuve-haven
Willems-plein
Zalmstr.
Willemskade
Houtlaan
Westerstr.
Schiedamse Vest
Schiedamsesingel
Boomgaardsstr.
Eendrachtsstr.
Eendrachtsweg
Westersingel
Vasteland
Zalmhaven
Van Vollenhovenstr.
Veerkade
West-plein
Veerhaven
Veerhaven
Westmaaslaan
Natuurhistorisch Museum Rotterdam
Kunsthal
Museumpark
Parklaan
Parklaan
Kievitslaan
Westzeedijk
HET PARK
Parkkade
Maastunnel
Rotterdam Centraal Station
Wytemaweg
ERASMUS MC (HOSPITAL)
Zimmer-manweg
straat
Dijkzigt
Mathenesserlaan
Saftlevenstr.
Ochter-veltstr.
's-Gravendijkwal
's-Gravendijkwal
Droogleever Fortuynplein
Parkhaven
Puntegaalstr.
G.J. de Jonghweg
Binnenweg
straat
Zwaerdecroon-str.
Snellinckstr.
Rochussen-
Claes de Vrieselaan
Mathenesserlaan
Volmarijn-
Nieuwe
Hondiusstr.
De Vliegerstr.
Coolhaven
Buytewechstraat
Pieter de Hoochweg
Willem
1 Rotterdam Harbor Tour
2 Depot Boijmans Van Beuningen
3 Euromast
4 Hotel New York
5 FENIX

**Rotterdam can be tough to love at first sight:** Virtually flattened by German bombing in 1940, then Allied raids in 1941–43, it remains first and foremost a working port. But it's also an energetic, forward-looking city with innovative architecture and cultural offerings that seem to look at things differently, including a major new migration museum that opened in 2025. Plus, for many North Americans of European descent, Rotterdam harbor is where your New World family (hi)story began. With limited time in a large city, focus on two fascinating areas: Museumpark and the port.

START: **Metro D or E from Rotterdam Centraal Station to Leuvehaven.**

*Rotterdam Harbor's sleek Erasmus Bridge.*

**1 ♥♥♥ kids Rotterdam Harbor Tour.** Spido's boat tour on the River Maas shows you a small fraction of Europe's busiest port (the world's largest outside Asia) and Rotterdam's daring modern skyline. You travel under the landmark Erasmus Bridge (or Swan Bridge, as it's often called); pass historic Delfshaven, departure point for the Pilgrim Fathers in 1620; and see transatlantic steamship *SS Rotterdam*. But the most fascinating aspect of this tour is the up-close-and-personal view of the workings of an immense port; the boat zigzags around giant cranes, tankers, barges, and all sizes of boats and container ships. *1¼ hr. Willemsplein 85. www.spido.nl/en. ☎ 010/275-9999. Tickets 17.50€ adults, 10€ kids 4–11. Apr–Oct departures every 45 min. from 10:15am;*

## Rotterdam Essentials

Around six direct trains per hour depart from Amsterdam Zuid Station for Rotterdam Centraal Station; a less frequent service leaves from Amsterdam Centraal. The journey takes between 40 minutes and 1¼ hours, depending on the service. A round-trip fare is 38€. On public transportation in Rotterdam, you can tap to pay with your credit card or use OVpay (p 164). Taxis are plentiful.

The main tourist information center is at the railway station, **VVV Rotterdam Centraal,** Stationsplein 21 (www.rotterdam.info; ☎ 010/790-0185), open daily from 9:30am to 6pm. The center sells tours and tickets and offers free downloadable city maps.

*The reflective Depot Boijmans Van Beuningen.*

*Oct–Mar usually four trips per day Thurs–Sun, one per day Mon–Wed. Metro: D or E to Leuvehaven.*

**2 ♥♥ Depot Boijmans Van Beuningen.** It's impossible to miss what looks like a giant reflective soup bowl in the heart of Museumpark. It's even more extraordinary inside, although not necessarily for the artworks on display. Its six-floor interior atrium is crisscrossed by transparent walkways. Art from every era hovers above, below, and beside you as you ascend all the way to a panoramic living rooftop planted with birch and spruce trees, from where you can look down on the park's elegant geometry. This is primarily a working depot: You'll see some of its 155,000 objects being moved into and out of storage; conservators at work; and the assembly or breakdown of exhibitions where they present recent research findings into such phenomena as "weeping glass." A unique experience. *1½ hr. Museumpark 24. www.boijmans.nl/depot. ☎ 010/441-9400. Admission 20€ adults, free for ages 18 and under. Tues–Sun 11am–5pm. Closed Apr 27 and Dec 25. Tram: 7 to Museumpark.*

**3 ♥♥ kids Euromast.** This slender tower, 185m (607 ft.) tall, is the best vantage point for a panoramic view of Rotterdam and its environs, out to 30km (19 miles) on a clear day. You can stop at the viewing platform (112m/367 ft.) for perfectly enjoyable vistas of the port. From here, the **Euroscoop** glass-floored elevator departs to the top of the spire. For an additional fee (May–Sept weekends only; 67.50€), you can abseil back to the ground—definitely not for the faint of heart. *30 min. Parkhaven 20. euromast.nl/en. ☎ 010/436-4811. Full admission including Euroscoop (bought online in advance) 18.50€ adults, 15€ kids 4–11 (platform only 12.50€/9€). Daily 10am–10pm. Tram: 8 or 18 to Euromast.*

**4 ♥♥ Hotel New York.** The former HQ of the Holland-America Line, which carried hundreds of thousands of Europeans to a new life in North America, is now a hotel with intact Art Nouveau styling. It overlooks the river at Wilhelmina Pier on the south side of the Maas, 5 minutes by water taxi from Euromast (www.watertaxirotterdam.nl;

*Euromast's viewing platform offers panoramic views of Rotterdam.*

## Linger Longer?

Rotterdam has so much to see and do: Stay overnight if you have time, perhaps at the reasonably priced **Hotel New York** (4). The Museumpark has much more to offer, notably **Huis Sonneveld ♥♥**, Jongkindstraat 12 (nieuweinstituut.nl; ☎ 010/440-1200; closed Mon), an outstanding example of 1930s Functionalist architecture, preserved inside and out. Across the Maas, the **Nederlands Fotomuseum ♥♥**, Rijnhaven (www.nederlandsfotomuseum.nl/en; ☎ 010/203-0405), is the Dutch national photography collection, which relocated to a historic converted warehouse in 2025. In the **Port of Rotterdam Pavilion ♥**, Schiedamsedijk 68 (portpavilion.com; ☎ 010/252-2540; closed Mon), you can learn more about the workings of this immense operation, control port webcams, and track ships in and out on a video wall. **Spido** (1) also run a limited number of Saturday-only extended 2½-hour port tours for anyone with a greater interest; see the website for a schedule.

☎ 010/403-0303; 5€ per passenger). Enjoy afternoon tea (3–5pm; 22.50€), or splash out in the oyster bar, at the very spot where tickets to New York were once sold. *Koninginnenhoofd 1. hotelnewyork.com. ☎ 010/439-0500. $$.*

**5 ♥♥ FENIX.** Inaugurated in 2025, this new museum has a distinctive "Tornado" roof terrace that pokes above Rotterdam's warehouse district. Inside, innovative displays tell the many and varied stories of migration through art. The collection reflects the emigrant and immigrant characters of its host city. Around 3 million people departed Rotterdam bound for the U.S., Canada, Australia, and elsewhere—Albert Einstein among them. The Katendrecht neighborhood was home to Greek sailors from the 1890s, many Chinese from 1910, and Cape Verdeans from the 1960s, most of whom came to work on Rotterdam's docks or departing ships. *1¼ hr. Paul Nijghkade 5. www.fenix.nl/en. ☎ 010/313-4760. Admission 15€ adults, 7.50€ ages 18–25, free for kids 17 and under. Tues–Sun 10am–5pm (Fri until 9pm). Metro: D or E to Wilhelminaplein.*

*The distinctive roof terrace at FENIX museum.*

# The Hague & Scheveningen

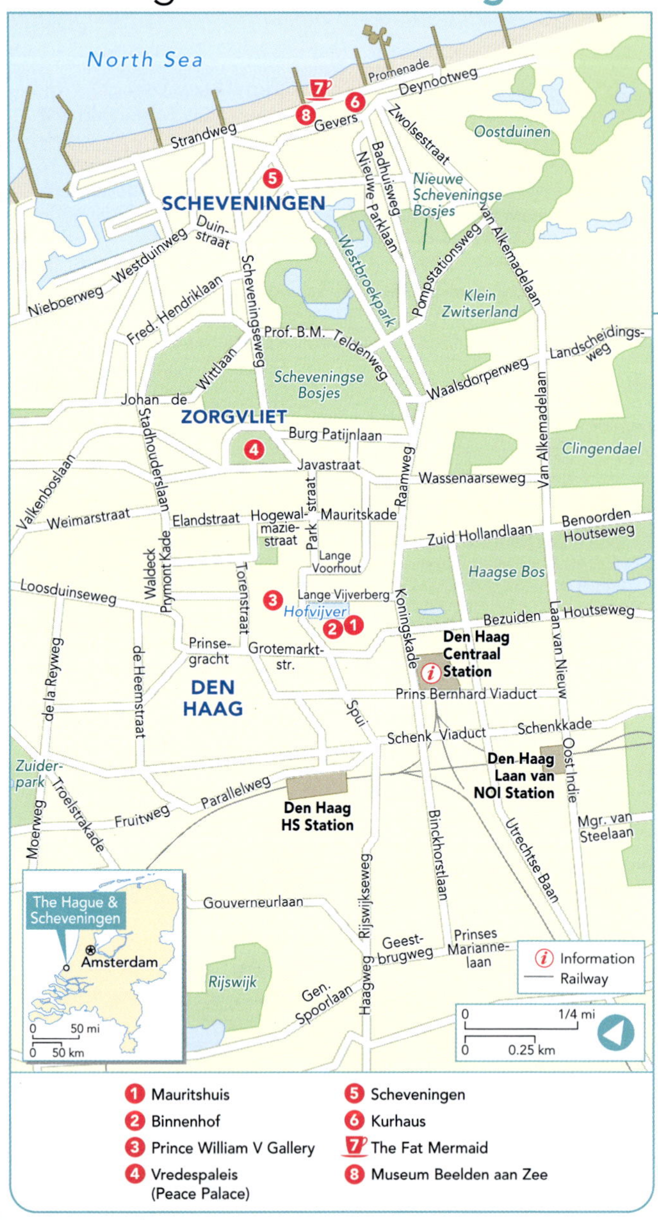


1 Mauritshuis
2 Binnenhof
3 Prince William V Gallery
4 Vredespaleis (Peace Palace)
5 Scheveningen
6 Kurhaus
7 The Fat Mermaid
8 Museum Beelden aan Zee

**The stately capital of the Netherlands** contrasts with its laid-back coastal neighbor Scheveningen, where you'll get a bracing taste of North Sea beach life. At The Hague (Den Haag in Dutch), you'll get the chance to take in the historic seat of the Dutch Parliament, visit the Peace Palace (home to the International Court of Justice), and encounter Vermeer's iconic *Girl with a Pearl Earring* at the Mauritshuis. With careful planning and a brisk schedule, you can even combine the key sights of The Hague (excluding Scheveningen) with the best of Delft's old center (p 145, 1–5), only 15 minutes away by easy rail connection. If you decide to do this, begin in The Hague by 10am, Tuesday through Saturday only.

START: **A 10-minute stroll from Den Haag Centraal Station to Plein, a pleasant square ringed by cafe-bars.**

*Vermeer's famed* Girl With a Pearl Earring *in the Mauritshuis museum.*

1 ♥♥♥ **Mauritshuis.** Overlooking Hofvijver Lake, this fine 17th-century townhouse has an astounding, heavyweight collection of Dutch Old Masters in a collection that fills just 16 small rooms. Pretty much everyone is here to see (and photograph) the *Girl with a Pearl Earring* (1665) by Jan Vermeer. But there's plenty more, including Vermeer's tranquil *View of Delft* (1661), facing her. Spread around much quieter rooms, 11 Rembrandts including a self-portrait painted the year before he died; Carel Fabritius' delicate *The Goldfinch* (1654); Paulus Potter's *The Bull* (1647), restored in 2025; and landscapes by van Ruisdael and others. *1¾ hr. Plein 29. ☎ 070/302-3456. www.mauritshuis.nl/en. Admission 20€, free ages 18 and under. Mon 1–6pm, Tues–Sun 10am–6pm. Tram: 1, 10, or 15 to Centrum.*

2 ♥♥ **Binnenhof (Inner Court).** With a massive renovation underway through at least 2029, the Binnenhof, one of Europe's prettiest parliaments, is off-limits to visitors—and indeed, even to government officials, who have been relocated around The Hague. However, a bit of thoughtful ingenuity enables you to get a glimpse of its venerable civic buildings: A 149-step viewing tower, free to climb, has been erected beside the Buitenhof entrance and looks directly down into the Binnenhof's courtyards. The many-gabled, medieval Ridderzaal (Hall of the Knights) is the most striking building, built in 1280, with a vast, vaulted ceiling. Traditionally, this hall plays a leading part in

*The medieval Hall of the Knights in the Binnenhof (Inner Court).*

Dutch politics: King Willem-Alexander delivers his annual Speech from the Throne from here on Prinsjesdag (third Tues in Sept). A Renovation Information Centre, also free to visit, has an exhibition on the buildings' 800-year history in its medieval vaulted cellar. *30 min. Information Centre Binnenhof Renovation, Plaats 22. www.binnenhofrenovatie.nl. Wed–Sat 10am–4pm, Sun noon–4pm.Viewing Tower: daily 9am–5pm. Tram: 15 or 17 to Buitenhof.*

**3 ♥ Prince William V Gallery.** Show your Mauritshuis ticket at the desk and you gain free access to this "overspill" collection in an elegant room above the old city gate. It was converted specifically in 1774 to show the private collection of stadtholder William V— the first public museum in the Netherlands. His collection later formed the basis of the Mauritshuis collection. The Golden Age paintings, including works by Steen and Rubens, are "stacked" on the walls, one above another, the style in which they were originally displayed. *30 min. Buitenhof 33. No phone. Admission free with Mauritshuis ticket; otherwise 5.50€, free ages 18 and under. Tues–Sun noon–5pm.*

## The Hague Essentials

The Hague is 50 minutes from Amsterdam's Centraal Station, and served by at least two direct trains an hour. A round-trip ticket is 29€. There are usually four direct trains per hour from Amsterdam Zuid (and it's a few euros cheaper). The Hague has two main rail stations, Den Haag Centraal and Den Haag HS; most sights are closer to Centraal, but some fast trains stop only at HS. Once you arrive at Den Haag Centraal, you'll find trams next to the station and overhead on an elevated line. To get around, you can tap to pay with your credit card or use OVpay. However, our first recommended stops are comfortably walkable from the station (p 153).

Tourist information is **VVV Den Haag,** inside Centraal Station at Koningin Julianaplein 50–51 (denhaag.com/en; ☎ **06/5537-6853**). It's open Monday to Saturday 10am to 6pm, Sunday 10am to 4pm.

❹ ♥♥ **Vredespaleis (Peace Palace).** Scottish–American philanthropist Andrew Carnegie donated more than a million dollars to the construction of this magnificent neo-Gothic palace to house the Permanent Court of Arbitration, an international judicial body established by the first Hague Peace Conference and Hague Conventions of 1899. It's also home to the International Court of Justice. The building was designed by French architect Louis Cordonnier and completed in 1913 with interior decorations in a mix of neo-Gothic and Delft Art Nouveau by Herman Rosse. Today it may be visited only occasionally by guided tour; tickets are released on a rolling basis 1 month in advance and sell out quickly. You'll be able to marvel at gifts given by participating countries: crystal chandeliers (each weighing 1,750kg/3,858 lb.) from Delft, made with rubies and emeralds; incredible mosaic floors from France; a huge Turkish carpet woven in 1926 in Izmir; and an immense 3,500kg (7,716 lb.) vase from Czar Nicholas of Russia. If the courts are not in session, your guide may take you inside the International Court of Justice, which handles United Nations judicial cases. The visitor center explains the history of the Peace Palace and purpose of its courts with an exhibition and short film. *1 hr. Carnegieplein 2. www.vredespaleis.nl. No phone. Inside the Palace Tour 16.50€ adults, free for kids 7 and under. Reservations required; take your passport on the day. Visitor Center: Wed–Sun noon–5pm. Closed Apr 27. Tram: 1 to Vredespaleis.*

*The International Court of Justice in Vredespaleis (Peace Palace).*

❺ ♥ **Scheveningen.** This relaxed beachside town known for herring fishing is only a 15-minute tram ride from the center of The Hague. It has a wide sandy beach and seasonal restaurants lining its boardwalk, whose aesthetics and sea defenses were improved in public works completed in 2025. Towering over both the small town and its beach is the 19th-century Kurhaus (❻, below). If you're in the mood for outdoor activity, you can walk for miles alongside rolling sand dunes that line the North Sea coast. *Tram: 1 or 9 to Kurhaus (20 min.).*

❻ **Kurhaus.** This grande dame of seaside spa hotels enjoyed its heyday in the early 20th century,

*The expansive beach at Scheveningen.*

*The beachfront Kurhaus hotel.*

before Northern Europeans started frequenting the Mediterranean en masse. Its vast Kurzaal public space is certainly worth a look; on breezy off-season days, when Scheveningen's boardwalk bars are shuttered for the winter, its covered terrace is an evocative spot to take tea and gaze out to sea. ⏲ *10 min. Gevers Deynootplein 30. www.amrathkurhaus.com.* ☎ *070/416-2636. Tram: 1 or 9 to Kurhaus.*

7 ♥ **The Fat Mermaid.** At the more relaxed southern end of a boisterous beachfront, you'll find a friendly vibe, tables by the sand, and sunny international dishes such as North Sea fish tacos. *Strandweg 19. www.thefat.nl.* ☎ *070/354-1729. Open mid-March to early Oct. $$.*

8 ♥♥ **Museum Beelden aan Zee.** This quirky contemporary sculpture museum is built into the sand dunes, steps from Scheveningen's boardwalk. Take time to admire the innovative design, by architect Wim Quist, and the use of natural light that spills into the main hall. Terraces are strewn with sculptures, and indoor galleries look out over the dunes to the sea beyond. Most sculptures are based on the human form; the collection numbers 2,000 pieces and is still growing. On the promenade by the museum, **Fairytale Sculptures by the Sea** ♥ is a permanent installation that's free of charge; the ambivalent cartoonlike figures are by New Yorker Tom Otterness. ⏲ *1½ hr. Hartevelstraat 1. www.beeldenaanzee.nl/en.* ☎ *070/358-5857. Admission 18.50€ adults, 9.25€ kids 13–18. Tues–Sun 10am–5pm. Closed Jan 1, Apr 27, and Dec 25. Tram: 1 to Scheveningseslag/Beelden aan Zee.*

*The cartoonlike figures of Fairytale Sculptures by the Sea, on the promenade of the Museum Beelden aan Zee.*

# The Savvy Traveler

# Before You Go

## Government Tourist Offices

The Netherlands Board of Tourism & Conventions (NBTC) has corporate offices in both New York City and The Hague (Den Haag), Netherlands, but the best place to start for travelers is its informative website, **Holland.com**. For Amsterdam specifically, the top resource is **www.iamsterdam.com/en**, where you will find an extraordinary volume of up-to-date information and inspiration, as well as instructions for buying and using the **I amsterdam City Card** (see p 8).

## The Best Times to Go

"In season" in Amsterdam means mid-April to mid-October, although in truth, the city is rarely empty of visitors. The peak of the tourist season is probably June to August, when the weather is at its finest. The climate in Amsterdam is never really extreme at any time of year, and if you're one of the growing numbers who favor shoulder- or off-season travel, you'll find the city every bit as attractive. Not only are flights and hotels cheaper and restaurants less crowded during the off-season (with more relaxed service), but there are also a number of appealing events going on. You may want to go from late March to mid-May, when the bulb fields west of Amsterdam are bursting with color—it's one of the best times to visit the Netherlands.

## Festivals & Special Events

**SPRING.** Late March to mid-May, catch the **Opening of Keukenhof Gardens,** Lisse (p 17). The greatest flower show on earth blooms with a spectacular display of tulips, narcissi, daffodils, hyacinths, bluebells, crocuses, lilies, amaryllis, and many other flowers at this 32-hectare (79-acre) garden in the heart of bulb country. It's said that some 7 million bulbs have been planted, but who's counting? For more information, see **www.keukenhof.nl**. Daily escorted tours and day trips run from Amsterdam: Speak to your hotel or check www.iamsterdam.com.

On April 27, Amsterdam celebrates **Koningsdag (King's Day)**, a national holiday, with a gigantic dawn-to-dawn street party. The city's canals and central streets are jam-packed with celebrating hordes dressed up in orange clothes, daft hats, and bright orange wigs with Dutch flags waving everywhere. Street music and theater combine with lots of drinking during this good-natured if boisterous affair. ***Tip:*** Wear something orange, even if it's only an orange cap or an orange ribbon in your hair: The Dutch Royal House is the House of Orange, hence the clothes—and Dutch sports teams' orange strips. For more information on Dutch royalty, consult www.royal-house.nl.

The second weekend in May is **National Windmill Day** throughout the Netherlands. Around two-thirds of the country's almost 1,000 remaining working windmills open to the public; among them are Amsterdam's Molen van Sloten, Akersluis 10 (molenvansloten.nl/en; ☎ 020/669-0412), and the windmills at Zaanse Schans (www.dezaanseschans.nl/en; ☎ 075/681-0000).

**SUMMER.** From May through August, catch a performance at the **Vondelpark Open-Air Theater** (p 122). Everything happens here: theater, all kinds of music (including full-scale

*Previous page: Tram in front of Amsterdam Centraal Station.*

classical concerts by the famed Royal Concertgebouw Orchestra), dance, and even operettas. Contact **Vondelpark Openluchttheater** (www.openluchttheater.nl; ☎ 020/673-1499).

In the middle week of June, **Open Garden Days** is your chance to find out what the fancy gardens behind the gables of some of the city's houses-turned-museums look like. A number of the best gardens are open to the public for 3 days. Tickets and an information booklet are available from the **Museum Van Loon** (p 30).

The **Amsterdam Roots Festival,** at the beginning of July at various venues around town, features world music, circus, spoken word performances, and dance, along with theater programs, films, and exhibits. More information is available from **Amsterdam Roots Festival** (amsterdamroots.nl; ☎ 020/244-5736).

One of the world's leading gatherings of top international jazz and blues musicians, the **North Sea Jazz Festival** unfolds over 3 concert-packed mid-July days at Rotterdam's giant Ahoy venue. Last-minute tickets are scarce, so book as far ahead as possible. Visit **www.northseajazz.com/en**.

Europe's most LGBTQ-friendly city hosts **Queer & Pride Amsterdam** events over several days in late July and early August. A crowd of more than 150,000 people turns out to watch the highlight Canal Parade, in which outrageously decorated boats cruise the canals. In addition, there are street parties, open-air theater performances, a sports program, and a film festival. Go to the websites of **Pride Amsterdam** (pride.amsterdam/en) and **Queer Amsterdam** (queer-amsterdam.org/en/) for more information. Electronic music festival **Milkshake** (www.milkshakefestival.com) also takes place in Westerpark around the same time.

The 10-day jazz and classical music **Grachtenfestival (Canals Festival)** plays in mid-August at various intimate and elegant venues along the canals and at the Muziekgebouw aan 't IJ. Closing out the festival is the exuberant Prinsengrachtconcert, which is staged on a pontoon in front of the Hotel Pulitzer (p 136). Contact **Stichting Grachtenfestival** (www.grachtenfestival.nl; ☎ 020/421-4542) for more information.

Amsterdam previews its cultural season with the 3-day **De Opening,** usually held on the last weekend in August. Promotional events run alongside free preview performances of music, opera, dance, theater, and cabaret at theaters, concert halls, and impromptu outdoor venues in the city. Go to the website www.openingcultureleseizoen.nl for more information.

**FALL.** During **Open Monumentendag,** on the second weekend in September, you have a chance to see historical buildings and monuments that are usually not open to the public—and to get in free as well. Contact **Stichting Open Monumentendag** (www.openmonumentendag.nl; ☎ 033/209-1000) for more information. There's more in English on highlights all over the Netherlands at **www.europeanheritagedays.com**.

On the third Sunday in September, participants in the popular **Dam tot Damloop (Dam to Dam Run),** start at the Dam in the center of Amsterdam, head out of town through the IJ Tunnel and Amsterdam-Noord, to the center of Zaandam, an official distance of "10 English miles." There's also a 5-mile night run around Zaandam, with DJs and live bands. Registration for runners opens in mid-April.

For more information, visit **www.nndamloop.com**.

The third Tuesday in September is **Prinsjesdag (Prince's Day),** when the monarch rides in a splendid gold coach to the Ridderzaal (Hall of the Knights) in The Hague for the **State Opening of Parliament,** which opens the legislative session. For more on the Netherlands' royal traditions, visit **www.royal-house.nl**.

During **National Museum Week** in mid-October, most museums in Amsterdam and throughout the Netherlands offer free or reduced admission and have special exhibits. For details, see **www.museum.nl/museumweek**.

WINTER. **Sinterklaas,** Holland's equivalent of Santa Claus (St. Nicholas), launches the Christmas season on the third Saturday of November, when he arrives in the city by boat at Centraal Station pier. His controversial—and to many, deeply offensive—blackface assistant *Zwarte Piet* (Black Peter), has been expunged from all official parades, replaced by festive helpers who resemble chimney sweeps. See **www.sintinamsterdam.nl** for details on city festivities. The departure of Sinterklaas on December 5, the feast day of St. Nicholas, is the signal for Dutch homes to put up their tree.

The city's **New Year's** celebrations—in fact, in the Netherlands, a goodbye to the *Oudjaar* (Old Year)—take place throughout the city center on the night of December 31 to January 1, but mostly at the Dam and Nieuwmarkt. Things can get wild and not always wonderful: Many of Amsterdam's youthful spirits celebrate the New Year with firecrackers, which keeps hospital emergency rooms busy.

From late January to early February, more than 300 indie films are screened during the **International Film Festival Rotterdam.** See iffr.com/en for more information.

## The Weather

Summers are largely sunny, warm, and pleasant, with only a few oppressively hot days. Rain is common throughout the year, including in winter, when winds from the north or east can be very chilly. However, it's now quite rare to experience a big freeze like you see in many a Dutch Old Master painting. Take a warm coat and you'll be fine.

## Useful Websites

- **www.iamsterdam.com**, the city tourist office's outstanding website, is a virtually inexhaustible resource of information and ideas, including the latest arts and nightlife listings.
- **www.holland.com** offers comprehensive coverage beyond Amsterdam's city limits, covering hotels, sightseeing, and notices of special events.
- **www.amsterdamnow.com** is a handy bookmark for temporary art exhibits and new restaurant openings.
- **www.9292.nl/en** helps you navigate from anywhere to anywhere else in the Netherlands, including Amsterdam, with e-ticket functionality in its app.
- **www.dutchnews.nl** keeps you up to speed with mainstream current affairs in the Netherlands.

## Cellphones (Mobile Phones)

Most cellphones now have GSM (Global System for Mobiles) capability, and you should be able to make and receive calls in the Netherlands. Mobile coverage is good all over the city. You can buy prepaid SIM cards or eSIMs from stores all over the center.

Your domestic mobile will likely work in the Netherlands, but roaming charges can be high.

**AMSTERDAM'S AVERAGE DAILY HIGH TEMPERATURES**

| | JAN | FEB | MAR | APR | MAY | JUNE |
|---|---|---|---|---|---|---|
| Temp. (°F) | 43 | 45 | 50 | 57 | 64 | 68 |
| Temp. (°C) | 6 | 7 | 10 | 14 | 18 | 20 |
| | **JULY** | **AUG** | **SEPT** | **OCT** | **NOV** | **DEC** |
| Temp. (°F) | 72 | 72 | 66 | 59 | 50 | 45 |
| Temp. (°C) | 22 | 22 | 19 | 15 | 10 | 7 |

### Car Rentals

There's no point in renting a car in Amsterdam because the public transport system works efficiently, and most attractions are within walking distance of each other. The roads are tiny, often one-way, some pedestrianized, and all are crowded with mad cyclists. Even if you're traveling outside the city, the rail network can likely give you a much more relaxing ride. If you decide on a car, it's usually cheapest to book one online before you leave home. Try **Hertz** (www.hertz.com), **Avis** (www.avis.com), **Budget** (www.budget.com), **Europcar** (www.europcar.com), or a price comparison site such as **Rentalcars.com**.

# Getting There

### By Plane

**Arriving: Amsterdam Airport Schiphol** (**AMS;** www.schiphol.nl), 14km (9 miles) southwest of the city center, is the main airport in the Netherlands, handling the country's international arrivals and departures. Frequent travelers regularly vote Schiphol (pronounced *Skhip-ol*) one of the world's best airports for its ease of use and convenience of connections. It's a major European hub for KLM/Air France.

After you deplane at one of the halls (Schiphol is a single-terminal airport), moving walkways take you to Arrivals, where you pass through Passport Control, Baggage Reclaim, and Customs. Conveniences such as free luggage carts (baggage trolleys), free Wi-Fi, ATMs, restaurants, bars, shops, baby rooms, spa, baggage lockers, device charging stations, and showers are available. There are also two airside hotels, for late arrivals or early departures.

Beyond these is Schiphol Plaza, the main transport hub for getting into the city (or elsewhere in the Netherlands—trains stop at the airport en route to many other Dutch cities). Bus and shuttle stops and a taxi stand are just outside.

**Getting into Amsterdam: Netherlands Railways (NS) trains** (www.ns.nl/en; ☎ 030/751-5155) depart from Schiphol Plaza to Amsterdam Centraal Station; trains stop at Lelylaan and Sloterdijk stations in west Amsterdam on the way. Frequency is 8 trains per hour most of the day; from around 1:30am to 5:30am you must take a bus (N97; see below) instead. The train fare is 5.20€ one-way if you use Tap-to-Pay or OVpay (see "Getting Around," below); a paper ticket costs 1.50€ extra. Tap-to-Pay readers are situated just before the escalators down to the platforms; there are no physical barriers. Tap in here and then tap out at the barriers in your destination station. The ride takes between 13 and 22 minutes.

An alternative rail route serves Amsterdam Zuid and RAI stations. If you're staying at a hotel near Leidseplein, in De Pijp or Oost, in the Museum District, or around Amsterdam South, this route will likely be a better bet than Centraal Station. The fare to Zuid is 3.50€ one-way via Tap-to-Pay; the ride takes around 7 minutes. From Zuid, take tram no. 5 for Leidseplein and the Museum District; Metro 52 for De Pijp or the southern canal ring (the stop is Vijzelgracht); and Metro 51 for Oost and the Jewish Quarter.

**Bus no. 397**, aka the **Amsterdam Airport Express,** departs every 10 minutes from stop B17 in front of Schiphol Plaza. It's a better option than the train for hotels around Museumplein, the Rijksmuseum, and Leidseplein. The equivalent nighttime service, N97, departs hourly. The fare is 6.50€ one-way (11.75€ round-trip). There is no need to prepurchase tickets: Buy from the driver (debit or credit card only, cash not accepted) or tap in when you board. An **Amsterdam Travel Ticket** (see below) includes the airport bus. The journey usually takes about 25 minutes.

The airport-run service **Schiphol Travel Taxi** (www.schipholtraveltaxi.nl) operates private and shared taxis between the airport and anywhere in Amsterdam. It drives you directly to your hotel. The fare varies by exact destination and time of day. A typical fare from the airport to a central hotel is around 60€ for a private taxi with four passengers and two pieces of hold luggage. Vans for up to eight people cost around 10€ more. Book online in advance, entering your flight number and hotel. Hotel shuttles depart stops with A-prefixes.

You'll find **taxis** waiting at the stand in front of Schiphol Plaza. Taxis from the airport are metered. Expect to pay 50€ to 80€ to the center of Amsterdam; the ride takes 25 to 45 minutes, depending on traffic. Rideshare services Uber and Bolt use a dedicated pickup area; follow the signs to "App pick-up."

## By Boat from Britain

**DFDS Seaways** (www.dfds.com; ☎ +44/344-848-6090) has a regular car-ferry service between Newcastle in northeast England and IJmuiden on the North Sea coast west of Amsterdam. The overnight travel time is 15½ hours. From IJmuiden, you can go by DFDS Transfer Bus to De Ruijterkade, behind Amsterdam Centraal Station.

**P&O Ferries** (www.poferries.com; ☎ +44/1304/448-88) operates a regular car-ferry service between Hull in northeast England and Rotterdam Europoort. The overnight travel time is 12 hours. Ferry-company buses shuttle passengers between the Europoort terminal and Rotterdam Centraal Station, from where there are frequent trains to Amsterdam.

**Stena Line** (www.stenaline.co.uk; ☎ 08447/707070 in Britain) has a car-ferry service between Harwich in southeast England and Hoek van Holland (Hook of Holland) near Rotterdam. The travel time is 6½ hours for the daytime crossing and 8 hours for the overnight. Frequent trains depart from Hoek van Holland to Amsterdam, a 5-minute walk from the port.

## By Cruise Ship

Cruise ship passengers arrive in Amsterdam at the **Passenger Terminal Amsterdam**, Piet Heinkade 27 (www.ptamsterdam.com; ☎ 020/509-1000; tram 26), on the IJ waterway within easy walking distance of Centraal Station.

### By Train

Rail services to Amsterdam from other cities in the Netherlands and elsewhere in Europe are frequent and fast. International trains arrive at Centraal Station from Brussels, Paris, London, Berlin and other German cities, Copenhagen, and Vienna and Innsbruck in Austria: See **www.nsinternational.com/en** for a route map. **Nederlandse Spoorwegen** (Netherlands Railways; www.ns.nl) trains arrive in Amsterdam from towns and cities all over the Netherlands. Service is frequent to many places around the country, and trains are modern, clean, and punctual. Schedule and fare information on travel by train is best found by visiting **www.ns.nl/en**; alternatively, call ☎ 030/300-1111. The simplest way to travel is by buying e-tickets in the NS app. Tickets are also sold at railway stations and travel agents.

With a hub in Brussels, the **Eurostar** (www.eurostar.com) high-speed train (top speed 300kmph/186 mph) connects Amsterdam with London, Paris, and Cologne. Travel time between London St. Pancras International Station and Brussels Bruxelles-Midi Station (the most common connecting point for Amsterdam) is around 2 hours. Departures from London to Brussels are approximately every 2 hours at peak times. Two or three trains per day go direct from London to Amsterdam Centraal Station (4–4½ hr.) Travel time from Paris to Amsterdam is 3 hours, 25 minutes. For Eurostar reservations, it is cheapest to book online at www.eurostar.com; buying or amending tickets by phone at ☎ 646/934-6454 incurs a $20 charge.

**Arriving at Centraal Station:** Regardless of where they originate, most visitors traveling to Amsterdam by train find themselves deposited at Amsterdam's Centraal Station, built from 1884 to 1889 on an artificial island in the IJ channel. The building, an ornate architectural wonder on its own (p 30), is the focus of much activity. It's at the hub of the city's concentric rings of canals and connecting main streets, and is the originating point for many of the city's trams, Metro trains, and buses.

You'll find an I amsterdam Store and Information Center inside the station. Other station facilities include a GWK Travelex currency-exchange office, ATMs, an agency for tour tickets, luggage lockers, fast food outlets, convenience store, and a pharmacy, among much more.

***Warning:*** Centraal Station is home to a pickpocket convention that's in full swing at all times. Digital signage warns people to be on their guard. Avoid becoming a victim by keeping your money and other valuables under wraps, especially among crowds.

An array of **tram** stops are on either side of the main station exit—virtually all of Amsterdam's hotels are within a 15-minute tram ride from Centraal Station. Lines 2, 4, 12, 13, 14, and 17 originate at Centraal Station. The **Metro** station is downstairs and well-signposted with a large white "M" on a blue background. Lines M50, M52, M53, and M54 stop here. City **bus** stops are overhead, and a **taxi** stand is outside the main exit. At the public transportation GVB Tickets & Info office, you can buy tickets from teller windows or automatic machines (see "Getting Around," below, for more information). The station is also a departure point for all kinds of water transportation, including the free passenger ferries across the IJ waterway, which depart from behind the station (facing the IJ rather than the center), and canal-boat tours.

### By Bus

International coaches—and in particular those of **Flixbus** (www.flixbus.com)—are often the cheapest way to travel long distances within Europe. Flixbus services arrive at Sloterdijk Rail Station in the west of the city and just one train stop from Centraal Station. Flixbus operates a direct service between London Victoria Coach Station and Amsterdam, with up to four departures daily in the summer. Travel time is between 11 and 14½ hours. From Sloterdijk Station, you travel by train to Centraal Station or take tram no. 19 to the Leidseplein area.

### By Car

A network of major international highways crisscrosses the Netherlands. Three so-called "International E-roads," E19, E35, and E231, converge on Amsterdam from France and Belgium to the south and from Germany to the north and east. These roads also have Dutch designations; as you approach the city they are, respectively, A4, A2, and A1. Amsterdam's ring road is A10. Distances between destinations are relatively short. Traffic is invariably heavy, but road conditions are otherwise excellent, service stations are plentiful, and highways are plainly signposted.

# Getting Around

### By Public Transportation

Most public transportation in the Netherlands uses an electronic system called **OVpay.** Ticket machines at tram stops are being decommissioned and it's likely all public transport payments will soon be digital. For most visitors, the simplest way to travel is using **Tap-to-Pay** with a valid credit or debit card. In our experience, this is more reliable than a smartphone, which sometimes gets confused between payment cards and other travel passes in your wallet; it's worth noting that the Netherlands is constantly improving public transportation technology, so it's very possible these issues will be ironed out by the time you get there. Electronic barriers to Metro and train station platforms, and onboard trams and buses, deduct the correct fare; just hold your card up against the reader and wait for the beep. **You must tap at both the start and the end of the ride.**

Fares are calculated individually based on a number of factors including distance and method of travel. For example, to ride the 2 tram from Centraal Station to Leidseplein costs 1.65€ each way. A one-way journey between Centraal and Zuid on Metro 52 costs 2.40€. For travel within Amsterdam, your daily spend will automatically be capped at 10€, no matter how many trips you take. You don't need to do anything. Children ages 4 to 11 and adults 65 and over are entitled to a 34% discount on all transport fares. To add this discount to your Tap-to-Pay card, download the OVpay app and follow the simple instructions.

Another option for short-term visitors who plan to use public transportation a lot is the **GVB Multi-day Ticket,** 2–4 days. These have the advantage of calculating days by the hour. A 2-day ticket (15.50€) is validated at the time you first use it and lasts for 48 hours exactly. So, with smart planning it can be almost like a 3-day ticket. Likewise for 3 days (actually 72 hr.; 21.50€) and 4 days (96 hr.; 27€). Buy in the GVB app in advance and then activate it when you need to use it for the first time: Your ticket is a

QR-code stored in the app. You can also buy a 1-day child ticket for 5€.

The pre-purchasable **Amsterdam Travel Ticket** (www.discoverholland.com/amsterdam-travel-ticket) costs 18€ for one day's unlimited city travel, including a ride from the airport by bus 397/N97 or NS train. Two days costs 24€, 3 days 30€. However, unlike the GVB tickets (above), these are active by the day. You can't activate it on a Tuesday afternoon and travel through Friday lunchtime. In that scenario, your ticket would be valid Tuesday, Wednesday, and Thursday, expiring at 4am on Friday. You'll need to weigh that against the benefit of the free ride from the airport.

The central information and ticket sales point for GVB Amsterdam, the city's public transportation company, is **GVB Service & Tickets,** Stationsplein (www.gvb.nl/en; ☎ 0900/8011; Mon–Sat 8am–7pm only; ☎ 06/8309-9189 WhatsApp only, same hours), opposite the middle entrance to Centraal Station, open daily from 8:30am to 7pm. Transportation maps are free to download in PDF format at the excellent GVB website: **www.gvb.nl/en/gvb-maps**.

**By Tram:** Half the fun of Amsterdam is walking along the canals. The other half is riding the trams that roll through many major streets. The city has 15 tram routes, many of which begin and end at Centraal Station. You'll likely spend most time riding trams 2, 4, 12, 13, 14, and 17 through the old center; 7 and 14 in the Jewish Quarter; 1, 2, 7, 12, and 19 through Leidseplein; and 3, 5, and 12 through the Museum Quarter. Line 3 sweeps a huge arc from Oost, through De Pijp, the Museum Quarter, and Vondelpark, to Westerpark in the northwest of the center. Trams are frequent (usually) and efficient but can be busy at rush hour. Digital boards at most stops inform you of the wait time. ***Tip:*** Familiarize yourself with the two terminal stops for each relevant line, so you travel in the correct direction, or download the excellent GVB smartphone app for help directing you from just about everywhere to anywhere else in the city.

Getting on and off, most trams operate a one-way system; you usually board toward the front and middle of the tram and disembark at the rear and other middle door. Signs on board are self-explanatory. To board, push the button on the outside of the car beside the door. To get off, you may need to push another button, or better still, loiter behind a local while you learn the ropes. Tram doors close automatically, and quite quickly, so don't hang around. Always remember to hold your card against the reader as you get **on and off** the tram. If you are using an e-ticket with a QR code, note that you need to hold it below the reader (follow the red light), rather than tap. On trams fitted with exit gates, you will not be able to disembark until you have scanned or tapped, pushed the button, and pushed the gate. It sounds more complicated than it is, we promise.

**By Bus:** An extensive bus network complements the trams. Many bus routes begin and end at Centraal Station, departing from an elevated section above the concourse, reached by escalator (follow signs). It's generally faster to go by tram if you have the option, but some points in the city are served only by bus. One useful line is no. 20, which follows the IJ from just north of Westerpark, through Centraal Station, and on to the eastern docks, stopping outside the **National Maritime Museum** (p 59).

**By Metro:** The Metro can't compare to the labyrinthine systems of Paris, London, and New York, but Amsterdam does have its own, with five lines—50, 51, 52, 53, and 54—that run partly overground and bring people in from the suburbs and take them home again, running between 6am and midnight daily. Lines 51, 53, and 54 are the fastest way from Centraal Station through Nieuwmarkt to Waterlooplein on the edge of the Jewish Quarter and the Amstel side of the Oost neighborhood, including a stop outside one of our favorite lodgings, **Volkshotel** (p 138).

The newest Metro line 52 is the quickest for longer north–south journeys. It links Amsterdam-Zuid with Amsterdam-Noord, traveling under the IJ, with convenient stops at De Pijp, Rokin, and Centraal Station.

**By Ferry:** Free and frequent **GVB ferries** (gvb.nl) for passengers and two-wheel transportation connect the city center with Amsterdam-Noord (North), across the IJ waterway. These short crossings are completely free, which makes them ideal micro-cruises as they afford fine views. Ferries depart from Waterplein West behind Centraal Station. The F3 route goes to Buiksloterweg on the north shore, by the **A'DAM Tower** (p 35), with ferries every few minutes round-the-clock. F2 goes to IJplein, a more easterly point on the north shore, with ferries every 6 to 12 minutes from 6:30am to around midnight. Both of these crossings take a couple of minutes. A third useful ferry (F4) goes west to NDSM-Werf, a 14-minute trip that affords a memorable view of the IJ docklands and architecture. This service departs every 15 minutes through the day, half-hourly in the early morning and after 7pm. The last ferry departs NDSM at 2am.

## By Taxi

Hail a cab from the street or find one of the taxi stands sprinkled around the city, including at Dam Square, Museumplein, Rembrandtplein, Nieuwmarkt, and Leidseplein; plus of course at Centraal Station. Taxis have rooftop signs and blue license plates, and are metered. Hotel reception staff can easily order a cab for you, too.

Fares are regulated citywide and all cabs are metered; the meter starts at 3.60€–4.15€, depending on the day and time, and there is a charge of up to 3.05€ per kilometer. A generally reliable service is **Taxi Centrale Amsterdam (TCA;** www.tcataxi.nl; ☎ 020/777-7777). The fare includes a tip, but you may round up or give something for an extra service, like help with your luggage or for a helpful chat. Rideshare services **Bolt** and **Uber** operate in the Netherlands.

## By Water Taxi

Since you're in the city of canals, you might like to splurge on a water taxi. These launches do more or less the same thing as landlubber taxis, except that they do it on the canals and the Amstel River and in the harbor. You get your own private canal cruise. To preorder one—which is compulsory—call **Watertaxi Amsterdam** (www.bookawatertaxi.com; ☎ 020/422-9222) or book on its website using the widget. For up to eight people, a guideline fare for a 30-minute journey in the center is between 140€ and 210€. Water taxis operate daily from 9am to 11pm.

## By Bike

Instead of renting a car, follow the Dutch example and ride a bicycle. Sunday, when the roads are quieter, is a good day to pedal through Vondelpark and along off-the-beaten-path canals, or to practice riding on cobblestones and in bike lanes, crossing bridges, and dodging trams before venturing forth into the fray of an Amsterdam rush hour. There are more than 600,000 bikes in the city, so you'll have plenty of company.

Navigating the city on two wheels is mostly safe—or at any rate not as suicidal as it looks—thanks to a vast network of dedicated bike lanes. Bikes even have their own traffic lights. Amsterdam's battle-scarred bike-borne veterans make it almost a point of principle to ignore every safety rule ever written. Although they mostly live to tell the tale, don't think the same will necessarily apply to you.

Bike rental rates start at 17.50€ a day at **MacBike** (www.macbike.nl/en; ☎ 020/511-5300), which rents a range of bikes, including tandems, eBikes, and seven-speed touring bikes and has convenient rental outlets near Centraal Station at Oosterdoksstraat 106 and Nieuwe Nieuwstraat 19D; by Vondelpark at Tesselschadestraat 1E; and Amstel 140; near Waterlooplein 199. Each is open daily 9am to 6pm. They also operate guided cycle tours around the city and into the surrounding countryside (35€–79€).

***Warning:*** Always lock both your bike frame and one of the wheels to something solid and fixed; theft is common.

### By Car

To say driving in Amsterdam is "not recommended" is an understatement. Don't drive here. Parking is expensive; traffic is dense; trams and bikes cross your path frequently and from all angles; lanes are confusing; and networks of one-way streets make navigation, even with the best map, a problem. You are much better advised to make use of the city's excellent public transportation, or to walk.

### On Foot

The best way to take in the city is to walk. The city center is pedestrian-friendly and, where possible, wheelchair accessible. Carry a smartphone or a good paper map, and watch out for the ubiquitous trams and speeding bikes. It is not unusual to see cyclists deep in conversation, lost in music, or holding hands with a loved one, all at high speed.

# Fast Facts

**ATMS** The first thing to note is that an increasing number of retail outlets and shops—including transportation ticket outlets—**will not accept cash.** It is entirely possible to spend several days here and use only contactless (tap) or other card payment methods. Should you need it, the easiest and best way to get cash is through an ATM. Most North American banks charge a fee for international withdrawals—check with your bank before you leave home and find out your daily limit. There are multiple ATMs in Amsterdam. Many are open 24/7, although you'll want to be a bit cautious about withdrawing cash in quiet areas after dark.

**BABYSITTERS** The best way to arrange trusted babysitting is through your hotel. Many mid- and upper-range Amsterdam hotels can arrange babysitting services. You will normally need to give them plenty of notice.

**BANKS** Among the leading Dutch banks, **ABN AMRO** (www.abnamro.nl), **ING** (www.ing.nl), **Rabobank** (www.rabobank.nl), and **SNS** (www.snsbank.nl) all have branches in central Amsterdam. Most banks are open Monday to Friday from 9:30am to 5:30pm (or 9am–5pm). A few are open for limited hours on Saturday (mornings or 10am–4pm).

**BIKE RENTALS** See "By Bike," under "Getting Around," earlier in this chapter (p 166). The **I amsterdam City Card** (p 8) includes 24 hours' free bike rental.

**BUSINESS HOURS** Shops tend to be open from 9:30am to 6pm Tuesday, Wednesday, Friday, and Saturday. Some stay open until 8 or 9pm on Thursday. Some close on Monday morning, and most stores outside the center will close all day Sunday. Many museums close 1 day a week (often Mon), but may be open during holidays, except Koningsdag (King's Day, April 27), Christmas Day, and New Year's Day.

**CONSULATES & EMBASSIES** **U.S. Consulate:** Museumplein 19 (nl.usembassy.gov; ☎ 070/310-2209; tram 3, 5, or 12).

Embassies are in and around The Hague (Den Haag), capital of the Netherlands: **Australian Embassy,** Carnegielaan 4 (netherlands.embassy.gov.au; ☎ 070/310-8200); **Canadian Embassy,** Sophialaan 7 (www.international.gc.ca; ☎ 070/311-1600); **Irish Embassy,** Scheveningseweg 112 (www.ireland.ie/thenetherlands; ☎ 070/363-0993); **New Zealand Embassy,** Eisenhowerlaan 77N (www.mfat.govt.nz/netherlands; ☎ 070/346-9324); **U.K. Embassy,** Lange Voorhout 10 (www.gov.uk/netherlands; ☎ 070/427-0427); **U.S. Embassy,** John Adams Park 1, Wassenaar (nl.usembassy.gov; ☎ 070/310-2209).

**CREDIT CARDS** In the Netherlands, the card is king (or perhaps only the prince, given that almost everyone pays with their smartphone). Many businesses and transportation services **no longer accept cash.** Instead, payments are taken either via the tap-to-pay system (card or Apple/Google Pay), or by chip-and-PIN, with your 4-digit personal identification number replacing the old-style signature. Keep in mind that when you use your credit card abroad, your bank or card provider assesses a fee. For the latest advice on choosing the best credit card for travel, visit **Frommers.com**.

**CURRENCY EXCHANGE** Currency exchanges are found at Amsterdam's Schiphol Airport and Centraal Station, but airport and walk-in rates tend to be poor. Use an ATM, even if your domestic bank levies a charge. Travelers' checks have gone the way of the Stegosaurus.

**CUSTOMS** Travelers arriving from a **non–European Union country** can bring in, duty-free, 200 cigarettes (or 250g of tobacco), or 100 cigarillos (or 50 cigars); 1 liter of alcohol over 44 proof (22% ABV), or 2 liters under 44 proof; 4 liters of wine; 16 liters of beer; and new goods up to the value of 430€. Travelers arriving from an **E.U. country** can bring any amount of goods into the Netherlands, so long as they are intended for personal use and not for resale; there are generous guideline limits, beyond which the goods may be deemed to be for resale.

**DENTISTS** See "Emergencies," below. Around-the-clock emergency dental care is also available via **Dental365** (dental365.nl; ☎ 085/105-0750). They arrange same-day appointments.

**DOCTORS** See "Emergencies," below. For routine or minor issues, you can also make an appointment via **TouristDoc** (touristdoc.com; ☎ 020/262-4282 [WhatsApp only]).

**DRUGSTORES** In the Netherlands, a pharmacy is called an *apotheek* and sells both prescription and nonprescription medicines. Regular hours are Monday to Saturday from around 8:30am to 5:30pm. A centrally located pharmacy open on Sundays too (afternoon only) is **BENU Dam Apotheek,** Damstraat 2 (www.benu.nl/contact/apotheekzoeker; ☎ 020/624-4331), close to the Nationaal Monument. Inside Centraal Station,

**Amsterdam Central Pharmacy,** De Ruijterkade 24 (amsterdamcentralpharmacy.nl; ☎ 020/235-7822), is open until 7pm or 8pm every day, including Sunday. Pharmacies often post details of nearby all-night services on their doors.

**EMERGENCIES** For any emergency (fire, police, ambulance), the number is ☎ 112 from any landline or cellphone. To report a theft, call ☎ 0900/8844. **Residents of an E.U. country** must have a European Health Insurance Card (EHIC) to receive full reciprocal healthcare benefits in the Netherlands.

**EVENT LISTINGS** The official tourism website **www.iamsterdam.com** is an excellent source for discovering what's on where. It lists and previews exhibitions, concerts, the arts, festivals, and more.

**FAMILY TRAVEL** The **I amsterdam** website (www.iamsterdam.com/en/see-and-do/family-and-kids) has a family travel section that's very helpful.

**HOLIDAYS** National holidays include New Year's Day (Jan 1), Good Friday, Easter Sunday and Easter Monday (Mar or Apr), King's Day (Apr 27), Liberation Day (May 5), Ascension Day (40 days after Easter), Pentecost Sunday (seventh Sun after Easter; also known as Whitsun) and Pentecost Monday, and Christmas (Dec 25 and 26).

**INSURANCE** North Americans with homeowner's or renter's insurance are probably covered for lost luggage. If not, check with **Travel Assistance International** (www.travelassistance.com) or **Travelex** (www.travelexinsurance.com; ☎ 800/228-9792), insurers that can also provide trip-cancellation, medical, and emergency evacuation coverage abroad.

**INTERNET ACCESS** Most hotels in Amsterdam offer free Wi-Fi. Public buildings, museums, and cafes are also good bets for access on the go.

**LGBTQ TRAVEL** **COC Amsterdam,** Rozenstraat 14 (www.cocamsterdam.nl/en; ☎ 020/623-6565), is the local branch of the Dutch LGBTQ+ organization. Their confidential switchboard can listen and answer questions. **Pink Point,** Westermarkt 9 (pinkpoint.nl; ☎ 020/428-1070; tram 13 or 17), is a walk-in information point and store, open every afternoon. It is beside the **Homomonument** (homomonument.nl/en), a memorial to those persecuted for their sexuality.

**LIQUOR LAWS** Supermarkets, grocery stores, and cafes sell alcoholic drinks. The legal age for buying alcohol or drinking it in a public place is 18. Bars in the center, especially around the Red Light District, will often ask for physical I.D.; a photo of your passport may not be enough.

**LOST PROPERTY** Amsterdam's general Lost and Found office is at Korte Leidsedwarsstraat 52, open Monday to Friday 9am to 4pm. It also posts found items fairly quickly at **iLost** (ilost.co). If your luggage is lost by an airline, immediately file a lost-luggage claim at the arrival airport, detailing the contents.

**MAIL & POST OFFICES** Amsterdam no longer has post offices as such; instead, supermarkets, stationers, and convenience stores have postal points run by **PostNL** (www.postnl.nl). Branches of *Gebroeders Winter* (including at Lijnbaansgracht 204) and Albert Heijn (including at Leidseplein 31) have postal points where you can buy stamps or mail a postcard home. There is also a PostNL service point in Centraal Station.

**MONEY** The currency of the Netherlands is the euro, which can also be used in most other E.U. countries. The exchange rate varies, but at press time, 1 euro was equal to around US$1.16 and 0.85£. Credit cards and payments by phone are accepted—indeed, preferred—almost everywhere. In fact, **many businesses will not accept cash, only card or phone payments.** You should probably carry some cash for emergencies or incidentals, however. The best way to get it in Amsterdam is at an ATM (see above).

**NEWSPAPERS & MAGAZINES** Most kiosks sell English-language newspapers, often including *The New York Times International, USA Today*, and the *Guardian*.

**PASSPORTS** If your passport is lost or stolen, contact your country's embassy or consulate immediately (see "Consulates & Embassies," above). Before you travel, you should photocopy and/or photograph the critical pages and keep them separately from your passport.

**POLICE** Call ☎ 112 for emergencies or ☎ 0900/8844 to report a theft. One convenient police station is at Lijnbaansgracht 219 (tram 1, 2, 5, 7, 12, or 19), just off Leidseplein. The police website (www.politie.nl/en) has useful visitor information in English.

**SAFETY** Central Amsterdam is generally safe and walkable. Be aware of pickpockets using various distraction techniques and/or in crowded places such as trams, bars, festivals, the Metro, and Centraal Station. Robbery at gun- or knifepoint is very rare but not unknown. For information on the latest safety or health situation, consult the U.S. State Department's website attravel.state.gov, the U.K. Travel Aware pages (gov.uk/travelaware), or Australia's government travel advisory service, www.smartraveller.gov.au.

**SENIOR TRAVELERS** Mention that you're a senior when you make your travel reservations. People 65 and older may qualify for reduced admission to theaters, museums, and other attractions, as well as discounted fares on public transportation (see "Getting Around," above).

**SMOKING** Smoking is banned in all public enclosed places and on all public transportation. In some places, it is also banned in the streets. Ironically, it's also banned in coffeeshops, although you can still smoke a joint.

**TAXES** Value-added tax (BTW in the Netherlands) is a sales tax set at a standard 21%, with a lower rate of 9% on some essential items. Non-E.U. visitors can get a refund if they spend 50€ or more in any store that participates in the BTW refund program. The shops will give you a form, which you must get stamped at Customs (in Departure Hall 3 at Schiphol; allow extra time). Customs may ask to see your purchase, so don't pack it in checked luggage. Mark the paperwork to request a credit card refund before dropping it with Global Blue or Travelex.

**TELEPHONES** The country code for the Netherlands is +31; for Amsterdam, the city code is either 020 for landlines or 06 for mobiles. To make a **direct international call from the Netherlands,** dial 00, then dial the country code, the area code, and the local number. The country code for the **U.S. and Canada** is 1; **Great Britain,** 44; **Ireland,** 353; **Australia,** 61; and **New Zealand,** 64. Beware of making international calls on your hotel phone—rates can be astronomical.

**TICKETS** The best resource for event, concert, or theater tickets is the "Cultural Agenda" section at the official I amsterdam portal: **www.iamsterdam.com/en/whats-on/calendar**. You can click through to buy tickets prior to your arrival. Hotel concierges or front-desk staff will often book tickets for you, too.

**TIPPING** In cafes and restaurants, waiter service is traditionally included, although it is very much appreciated if you round the total up or leave a small bill. A service charge is included in taxi fares, but a small tip (around 2€) is always welcomed. If you make the driver wait or are going on a long, expensive trip, tip 5%. Tip hotel porters 2€ for each piece of luggage.

**TOILETS** If you use a toilet at a cafe or pub, it's customary to make a small purchase. Museums all have good, clean toilets.

**TOURIST OFFICE** The main resource is online: **www.iamsterdam.com**. It also operates an infopoint and store inside Centraal Station, at De Ruijterkade 28b–d. You can collect a physical **I amsterdam City Card** (p 8) from the store. It is open daily from 9am to 7pm.

**TRAVELERS WITH DISABILITIES** Nearly all modern hotels in Amsterdam have rooms designed for people with disabilities, but many older, townhouse hotels do not even have elevators. Not all trams in Amsterdam are fully accessible for wheelchairs, but all new trams have low central doors, automated ramps, and dedicated wheelchair spaces. Amsterdam's Metro system is fully accessible, as are the ferries across to Amsterdam-Noord. For a full guide to accessible public transportation, visit **www.gvb.nl/en/accessible-public-transport**. Many museums have touch exhibits designed for blind and visually impaired visitors. For much more information, see the dedicated section at the city's official website: www.iamsterdam.com/en/travel-stay/accessibility. **Accessible Travel Netherlands** (accessibletravel.nl; ☎ 06/1520-4812) organizes accessible holidays and experiences.

# Amsterdam: A Brief History

**1200** Fishermen establish a settlement at the mouth of the Amstel River, which is subsequently dammed to control flooding; the settlement takes the name "Aemstelledamme."

**1300** The bishop of Utrecht grants Amsterdam its first town charter.

**1323** Amsterdam's economy receives a boost when it is declared a toll center for beer.

**1350** The city becomes a transit point for imported grain, growing in importance as a trade center.

**1568–1648** The Dutch Wars of Independence ultimately free the Netherlands from colonial rule by Spain. The Dutch Republic is first proclaimed in 1579.

**1602** The Dutch United East India Company (V.O.C.) is founded. It is destined to become a powerful force in Holland's Golden Age of discovery, exploration, and trade, including in human beings.

**1611** First Amsterdam Stock Exchange opens.

**1613** Construction begins on the Grachtengordel (Canal Ring), comprising the Herengracht, Keizersgracht, and Prinsengracht canals.

**1631** Rembrandt, at age 25, moves to Amsterdam from his native Leiden.

**1795** French troops occupy Holland with the aid of Dutch revolutionaries and establish the Batavian Republic; William V flees to England.

**1806–10** Louis Bonaparte, Napoleon's brother, reigns as king of Holland.

**1813** The Netherlands regains independence from the French. When the Battle of Waterloo (1815) ends the bloody Napoleonic Wars, the Netherlands becomes a constitutional monarchy

**1839** Holland's first rail line, connecting Amsterdam and Haarlem, opens.

**1910** A flushable water system for the city's canals is introduced.

**1920** Dutch airline KLM launches the world's first scheduled air service, between Amsterdam and London.

**1928** The Olympics are held in Amsterdam.

**1932** Afsluitdijk (Enclosure Dike) at the head of the Zuiderzee is completed, transforming the sea on which Amsterdam stands into the freshwater IJsselmeer lake.

**1940** On May 10, Nazi Germany invades the Netherlands, which surrenders 4 days later. Three-quarters of the Jewish population—102,000 people—are murdered before the war ends, most of them from Amsterdam.

**1944–45** Thousands die during the Hunger Winter, when Nazi occupation forces blockade western Holland.

**1945** On May 5, German forces in the Netherlands surrender.

**1960S** Amsterdam takes on the mantle of Europe's hippie capital.

**1973** The Van Gogh Museum opens.

**1975** Amsterdam's 700th anniversary. Cannabis use is decriminalized and Surinam gains its independence from the Netherlands.

**1987** The *Homomonument*, the world's first public memorial to people persecuted for their sexuality, is unveiled.

**2001** The world's first same-sex marriage with a legal status identical to heterosexual matrimony takes place in Amsterdam.

**2002** Euro bank notes and coins replace the guilder.

**2004** Controversial film director Theo van Gogh is murdered by an Islamist extremist on the streets of Amsterdam.

**2005** Homophobic assailants in Amsterdam beat up the editor of the *Washington Blade* LGBT newspaper.

**2008** Smoking in restaurants, cafes, bars, and nightclubs is banned.

**2010** The new Dutch coalition government announces plans to prevent foreign visitors from frequenting cannabis-selling coffee shops. This comes to nothing.

**2013** Queen Beatrix abdicates and her son Willem-Alexander is inaugurated as king on April 30.

**2020** Release of Steve McQueen's epic film *Occupied City*, which chronicles Amsterdam's experience of Nazi occupation and documents the city during COVID lockdown.

**2025** Amsterdam celebrates its 750th birthday with events and exhibitions citywide.

# Golden Age Art

**Although there were earlier prominent Dutch artists,** Dutch art really came into its own during the 17th-century Golden Age. Artists were blessed with wealthy patrons whose support allowed them to give free rein to their talents. The primary art patrons were Protestant merchants who commissioned portraits, genre scenes, and still lifes, not the kind of religious works commissioned by the church in Catholic countries. The Dutch were particularly fond of pictures that depicted their world: landscapes, seascapes, domestic scenes, and portraits.

### Gerrit van Honthorst (1590–1656)

A Utrecht artist who had studied in Rome with Caravaggio, Van Honthorst brought the new "realism of light and dark," or *chiaroscuro* technique, to Holland, where he influenced Dutch artists such as the young Rembrandt. Van Honthorst is best known for lively company scenes such as *The Supper Party* (ca. 1620; Uffizi, Florence), which depicted ordinary people against a plain background and set a style that continued in Dutch art for many years. He often used multiple hidden light sources to heighten the dramatic contrast of lights and darks.

### Jacob van Ruisdael (1628–82)

Among the great landscape artists of this period, Van Ruisdael stands out. In his paintings, human figures either do not appear at all or are shown almost insignificantly small; vast skies filled with moody clouds often cover two-thirds of the canvas. His *Windmill at Wijk bij Duurstede* (ca. 1665; Rijksmuseum, Amsterdam) combines many characteristic elements of his style. The windmill stands in a somber landscape, containing a few small human figures, with a cloud-laden sky and a foreground of agitated water and reeds.

### Frans Hals (ca. 1580–1666)

Antwerp-born Hals, the undisputed leader of the Haarlem School (schools differed from city to city), was a great portrait painter whose relaxed, informal, and naturalistic portraits contrast strikingly with the traditional formal masks of Renaissance portraits. His light brushstrokes help convey immediacy and intimacy, making his works perceptive psychological portraits. He had a genius for comic characters, showing men and women as they are and a little less than they are, as in *Malle Babbe* (ca. 1635; Gemäldegalerie, Berlin). As a stage designer of group portraits, Hals's skill is almost unmatched—only Rembrandt is usually judged to be superior. Although he carefully arranged and posed each group, balancing the directions of gesture and glance, his *alla prima* brushwork (direct laying down of pigment) makes these public images seem spontaneous. It's worth taking a day trip to Haarlem just to visit the **Frans Hals Museum** (p 142) and view such works as his *A Banquet of the Officers of the St George Civic Guard* (ca. 1627) and *Officers and Sergeants of the St Hadrian Civic Guard* (ca. 1633).

### Rembrandt (1606–69)

The great genius of the period was Rembrandt Harmenszoon van Rijn, one of few artists of any period to be known simply by his first name. This painter, whose works hang in places of honor in the world's great galleries, may be *the* most famous Amsterdammer, both to outsiders and to today's city residents.

Rembrandt pushed the art of *chiaroscuro* to unprecedented heights. In his paintings, the values of light and dark gradually and softly blend together; this may have diffused some of the drama of *chiaroscuro*, but it achieved a more truthful appearance. His art seems capable of revealing the soul and inner life of his subjects, and to view his series of 60 self-portraits is to see a remarkable documentation of his own psychological and physical evolution. The etching *Self-Portrait with Saskia* (1636; Rijksmuseum, Amsterdam) shows him with his wife at a prosperous time when he was being commissioned to paint portraits of wealthy merchants. Later self-portraits are psychologically complex, often depicting a careworn old man whose gaze is nonetheless sharp, compassionate, and wise.

In group portraits like *The Night Watch* (1642) and *The Syndics of the Cloth Guild* (1662), both in the Rijksmuseum, each individual portrait is done with care. The unrivaled harmony of light, color, and movement of these works is a marvel to be appreciated. Compare, too, these robust, masculine works with the tender *The Jewish Bride* (ca. 1665), also in the Rijksmuseum.

In later years, Rembrandt was at the height of his artistic powers, but his contemporaries judged his work to be too personal and eccentric. Some considered him a tasteless painter who was obsessed with the ugly and ignorant of color; this opinion prevailed until the 19th century, when Rembrandt's genius was reevaluated.

### Jan Vermeer (1632–75)

Perhaps the best known of the "little Dutch masters" who specialized in one genre of painting, such as portraiture, is Jan Vermeer of Delft. Although they confined their artistry within a narrow scope, these painters rendered their subjects with an exquisite care and faithfulness to their actual appearances.

Vermeer's work centers on the simple pleasures and activities of domestic life—a woman pouring milk or reading a letter, for example—and all of his simple figures positively glow with color and light. Vermeer placed the figure (usually just one, but sometimes two or more) at the center of his paintings against a background in which furnishings often provided the horizontal and vertical balance, giving the composition a feeling of stability and serenity. Art historians have determined that Vermeer used mirrors and the *camera obscura*, an optical projection device, as compositional aids. A master at lighting interior scenes and rendering true colors, Vermeer was able to create an illusion of three-dimensionality in works such as *The Love Letter* (ca. 1670; Rijksmuseum, Amsterdam). As light—usually afternoon sunshine pouring in from an open window—moves across the picture plane, it caresses and modifies all the colors.

### Jan Steen (ca. 1626–79)

Born in Leiden, Steen painted marvelous interior scenes, often satirical and didactic in their intent. The allusions on which much of the satire depends may escape most of us today, but any viewer can appreciate the fine drawing, subtle color shading, and warm light that pervades such paintings as *Woman at Her Toilet* (1663) and *The Feast of St. Nicholas* (ca. 1665), both in the Rijksmuseum, Amsterdam. Many of his pictures revel in bawdy tavern scenes fueled by overindulgence in beer and gin.

# Useful Phrases & Menu Terms

## Useful Words & Phrases

| ENGLISH | DUTCH | PRONUNCIATION |
|---|---|---|
| Hello | Dag/Hallo | *dakh*/ha-*loh* |
| Good morning | Goedenmorgen | khoo-*yuh*-mor-*khun* |
| Good afternoon/evening | Goedenavond | khoo-*yuhn*-af-*ond* |
| How are you? | Hoe gaat het met u? | *hoo* khaht *et met oo?* |
| Very well | Uitstekend | *out*-stayk-*end* |
| Thank you | Dank u wel | dahnk *oo wel* |
| Goodbye | Dag/Tot ziens | *dakh/tot zeenss* |
| Good night | Goedenacht | khoo-*duh*-*nakht* |
| See you later | Tot straks | *Tot strahkss* |
| Please | Alstublieft | ahl-*stoo*-*bleeft* |
| Yes | Ja | *yah* |
| No | Neen/nee | *nay* |
| Excuse me | Pardon | *par*-dawn |
| Sorry | Sorry | so-*ree* |
| Do you speak English? | Spreekt u Engels? | *spraykt oo* eng-*els* |
| Can you help me? | Kunt u mij helpen? | *koont oo* may-ee hel-*pen?* |
| Give me . . . | Geeft u mij . . . | khayft *oo may* . . . |
| Where is . . . ? | Waar is . . . ? | vahr *iz* . . . ? |
| a bank | een bank | *ayn bank* |
| a hotel | een hotel | *ayn* ho-*tel* |
| a restaurant | een restaurant | *ayn res-to*-rahng |
| a pharmacy/chemist | een apotheek | *ayn a*-po-tayk |
| the post office | het postkantoor | *het* post-*kan-tohr* |
| the station | het station | *het* stah-ssyonh |
| the toilet | het toilet | *het* twah-*let* |
| To the right | Rechts | *rekhts* |
| To the left | Links | *links* |
| Straight ahead | Rechtdoor | *rekht*-doar |
| I would like . . . | Ik zou graag . . . | *ik zow khrakh* . . . |
| to eat | eten | ay-*ten* |
| a room for one night | een kamer voor een nacht willen | *ayn kah-mer voor* ayn nakht wi-*llen* |
| How much is it? | Hoe veel kost het? | *hoo fayl kawst het* |
| the check | de rekening | *duh* ray-*ken-ing* |
| When? | Wanneer? | *vah*-neer |
| yesterday | gisteren | khis-*ter-en* |
| today | vandaag | *van*-dahkh |
| tomorrow | morgen | mor-*khen* |
| breakfast | ontbijt | ohnt-*bayt* |
| lunch | lunch | *lunch* |
| dinner | diner | dee-*nay* |

## Numbers

| ENGLISH | DUTCH | PRONUNCIATION |
| --- | --- | --- |
| one | een | *ayn* |
| two | twee | *tway* |
| three | drie | *dree* |
| four | vier | *veer* |
| five | vijf | *vayf* |
| six | zes | *zes* |
| seven | zeven | zay-*vun* |
| eight | acht | *akht* |
| nine | negen | nay-*khen* |
| ten | tien | *teen* |
| eleven | elf | *elf* |
| twelve | twaalf | *tvahlf* |
| thirteen | dertien | dayr-*teen* |
| fourteen | veertien | vayr-*teen* |
| fifteen | vijftien | vayf-*teen* |
| sixteen | zestien | zes-*teen* |
| seventeen | zeventien | zay-*vun-teen* |
| eighteen | achttien | akh-*teen* |
| nineteen | negentien | nay-*khun-teen* |
| twenty | twintig | twin-*tikh* |

## Dutch Menu Savvy

**BASICS**

| DUTCH | ENGLISH |
| --- | --- |
| ontbijt | breakfast |
| lunch | lunch |
| diner | dinner |
| voorgerechten | starters |
| hoofdgerechten | main courses |
| nagerechten | desserts |
| boter | butter |
| boterham | sandwich |
| brood | bread |
| stokbrood | French bread |
| honing | honey |
| hutspot | mashed potatoes and carrots, with onions |
| jam | jam |
| kaas | cheese |
| mosterd | mustard |
| pannenkoeken | pancakes |
| peper | pepper |
| zout | salt |
| suiker | sugar |
| saus | sauce |

**FISH (VIS)**

| DUTCH | ENGLISH |
| --- | --- |
| forel | trout |
| garnalen | prawns |

| DUTCH | ENGLISH |
|---|---|
| gerookte zalm | smoked salmon |
| haring | herring |
| kabeljauw | cod |
| kreeft | lobster |
| makreel | mackerel |
| mosselen | mussels |
| oesters | oysters |
| paling | eel |
| sardientjes | sardines |
| schelvis | haddock |
| schol | plaice |
| tong | sole |
| zalm | salmon |

**MEATS (VLEES)**

| DUTCH | ENGLISH |
|---|---|
| rundvlees | beef |
| biefstuk | steak |
| eend | duck |
| fricandeau | roast pork |
| gans | goose |
| gehakt | minced meat |
| haasbiefstuk | filet steak |
| ham | ham |
| kalfsvlees | veal |
| kalkoen | turkey |
| kip | chicken |
| konijn | rabbit |
| lamsvlees | lamb |
| lamskotelet | lamb chops |
| ragout | beef stew |
| rookvlees | smoked meat |
| lever | liver |
| spek | bacon |
| vleeswaren | cold cuts |
| worst | sausage |

**VEGETABLES & SALADS (GROENTEN/SLA)**

| DUTCH | ENGLISH |
|---|---|
| groenten | vegetables |
| asperges | asparagus |
| augurken | pickles |
| bieten | beets |
| bloemkool | cauliflower |
| bonen | beans |
| champignons | mushrooms |
| erwten | peas |
| aardappelen | potatoes |
| knoflook | garlic |

| DUTCH | ENGLISH |
|---|---|
| komkommer | cucumber |
| komkommersla | cucumber salad |
| kool | cabbage |
| patates frites | French fries |
| prei | leek |
| prinsesseboonen | green beans |
| purée | mashed potatoes |
| radijsjes | radishes |
| rapen | turnips |
| rijst | rice |
| sla | lettuce, salad |
| spinazie | spinach |
| tomaten | tomatoes |
| uien | onions |
| wortelen | carrots |
| zuurkool | sauerkraut |

**DESSERTS (NAGERECHTEN)**

| DUTCH | ENGLISH |
|---|---|
| appelgebak | apple pie |
| appelmoes | applesauce |
| cake | cake |
| compote | stewed fruits |
| gebak | pastry/cake |
| ijs | ice cream |
| oliebollen | doughnuts |
| koekjes | cookies |
| jonge kaas | young cheese (mild) |
| oude kaas | mature cheese (strong) |
| room | cream |
| slagroom | whipped cream |
| smeerkaas | cheese spread |
| speculaas | spiced cookies |

**BEVERAGES (DRANKEN)**

| DUTCH | ENGLISH |
|---|---|
| bier (or pils) | beer |
| cognac | brandy |
| fles | bottle |
| glas | glass |
| jenever | gin |
| koffie | coffee |
| melk | milk |
| rode wijn | red wine |
| thee | tea |
| water | water |
| mineraal water | sparkling water |
| witte wijn | white wine |

# Index

*See also* Accommodations and Restaurant indexes, below.

## Accommodations

## Restaurants





# Photo Credits

Title page: Yasonya/Shutterstock; p ii, top: Taiga/Shutterstock; p ii, second from top: Courtesy of Rijksmuseum/Erik Smits; p ii, middle: Courtesy of amsterdam&partners/Mirte VreemannMirte Vreemann; p ii, second from bottom: Harry Beugelink/Shutterstock; p ii, bottom: ColorMaker/Shutterstock.com; p iii, top: Taiga/Shutterstock; p iii, second from top: Courtesy of Café de Ceuvel/Vincent Kuyvenhoven; p iii, middle: Courtesy of Zum Barbarossa/Joep Hijwegen; p iii, second from bottom: Courtesy of Dutch National Opera & Ballet/Marco Borggreve; p iii, bottom: Courtesy of De L'Europe; p viii–p 1: Taiga/Shutterstock; p 3, top: Tanvi Nautiyal/Shutterstock.com; p 3, bottom: M. Vinuesa/Shutterstock.com; p 4, top: Cat Biggar; p 4, bottom: Courtesy of Volkshotel; p 5: Courtesy of Rijksmuseum/Erik Smits; p 7: Courtesy of Rijksmuseum/John Lewis Marshall ; p 9, top: Courtesy of amsterdam&partners/Bryony Rijks; p 9, bottom: Wolf-photography/Shutterstock.com; p 10: Courtesy of Our Lord in the Attic Museum/Rebekka Mell; p 13: © Anne Frank House/Photographer: Rosa Krastel; p 14: Stefan Bernsmann/Shutterstock.com; p 15, top: Courtesy of amsterdam&partners/Richard de Bruijn; p 15, bottom: Pachiska Sririn/Shutterstock.com; p 16: Anton_Ivanov/Shutterstock; p 19: Courtesy of National Holocaust Museum/Mike Bink; p 20: Courtesy of Museum Rembrandthuis/Jaap Vliegenthart; p 21, top: FooTToo/Shutterstock.com/Shutterstock; p 21, bottom: Courtesy of Stedelijk/John Lewis Marshall; p 22: Tina Modotti - Artist and Activist, 2023 © Foam. Photo: Christian van der Kooy; p 23: Courtesy of amsterdam&partners/Mirte VreemannMirte Vreemann; p 25: Courtesy of Moco Museum; p 26: Dutchmen Photography/Shutterstock.com; p 27: Emzzi/Shutterstock.com; p 29: Ivica Drusany/Shutterstock.com ; p 30, top: Dutchmen Photography/Shutterstock.com; p 30, bottom: Wolf-photography/Shutterstock.com; p 31: Kiev.Victor/Shutterstock.com; p 32: Alexander Demyanenko/Shutterstock; p 33: www.hollandfoto.net/Shutterstock.com; p 35: Courtesy of A'DAM Lookout/Dennis Bouman; p 36, top: Sergii Figurnyi/Shutterstock.com; p 36, bottom: Courtesy of amsterdam&partners/Ronald van Weeren; p 37: Courtesy of ARTIS Micropia/Samuel van Leeuwen; p 39, top: Konstantin Tronin/Shutterstock; p 39, bottom: Tatiana Popova/Shutterstock; p 41: Michael Gordon/Shutterstock; p 42: 4kclips/Shutterstock.com; p 43: www.hollandfoto.net/Shutterstock.com; p 44: Kosma Yvar/Shutterstock; p 45: Harry Beugelink/Shutterstock; p 47: Vladislav Gajic/Shutterstock; p 48: JetCamp.com/Flickr; p 49: Nick N A/Shutterstock; p 51: Kiev.Victor/Shutterstock; p 52: Wolf-photography/Shutterstock; p 53: Kiev.Victor/Shutterstock; p 55: Goncharovaia/Shutterstock; p 56: Protasov AN/Shutterstock; p 57: Hanneke Wetzer/Shutterstock; p 59: Melanie Lemahieu/Shutterstock; p 60: Henk van Dijk/Shutterstock; p 63: Todamo/Shutterstoc; p 65, top: Bert e Boer/Shutterstock; p 65, bottom: Bert e Boer/Shutterstock; p 67, top: Barbara Ash/Shutterstock; p 67, bottom: Courtesy of Nationaal Holocaust Museum/Mike Bink; p 68: Dutchmen Photography/Shutterstock; p 69: ColorMaker/Shutterstock.com; p 70: Courtesy of Kramer Kunst & Antiek; p 71: ColorMaker/Shutterstock.com; p 74, top: Eliazar Parra Cardenas/Flickr; p 74, bottom: Courtesy of Book Exchange ; p 75, top: Courtesy of Amsterdam Cheese Museum/Vivian Raubenheimer; p 75, bottom: Courtesy of PGC Hajenhuis/Maikel Thijssen Photography; p 76: Gabriela Beres/Shutterstock.com; p 77: Courtesy of Polspotten/Kasia Gatkowska; p 78: Courtesy of Gerda's Bloemen & Planten ; p 79, top: Michael Gordon/Shutterstock.com; p 79, bottom: Pachiska Sririn/Shutterstock.com; p 80, top: Protasov AN/Shutterstock.com; p 80, bottom: Courtesy of Wijnhandel De Ware Jacob; p 81: Taiga/Shutterstock; p 83, top: Kavalenkau/Shutterstock; p 83, bottom: Wolf-photography/Shutterstock.com; p 84: Wolf-photography/Shutterstock.com; p 85: Melanie Lemahieu/Shutterstock.com; p 87, top: Mary Doggett/Shutterstock.com ; p 87, bottom: Courtesy of amsterdam&partners/Merijn Roubroeks; p 88, top: 365 Focus Photography/Shutterstock.com; p 88, bottom: Marc de Boer/Shutterstock; p 89: Jeff Whyte/Shutterstock; p 91, top: Irisphoto1/Shutterstock; p 91, bottom: Meghan Lamb; p 92: Bert e Boer/Shutterstock; p 93: Courtesy of Café de Ceuvel/Vincent Kuyvenhoven; p 94: Courtesy of Blauw; p 98: Courtesy of Café de Ceuvel; p 99: Donald Strachan; p 100: Meghan Lamb; p 101: Courtesy of The Pancake Bakery ; p 102: Courtesy of Pelusa; p 103: Courtesy of The Seafood Bar; p 104: Courtesy of Tujuh Maret; p 105: Courtesy of Zum Barbarossa/Joep Hijwegen; p 106: Courtesy of Bubbles & Wines; p 111: Courtesy of Proeflokaal Arendsnest/Nathalie Hennis; p 112: Courtesy of Troost Westergas; p 113: Courtesy of Zum Barbarossa/Joep Hijwegen; p 114: Courtesy of Saarein; p 115: Courtesy of Dutch National Opera & Ballet/Marco Borggreve; p 116: Courtesy of The Royal Concertgebouw Amsterdam/Hans Roggen; p 117, top: Courtesy of Eye Filmmuseum/Corinne de Korver; p 117, bottom: Courtesy of Paradiso/Ben Houdijk; p 120: Ben Houdijk/Shutterstock; p 121: Courtesy of Muziekgebouw aan t'IJ/Foppe Schut; p 122: Courtesy of Dutch National Opera & Ballet/Altin Kaftira; p 123: Courtesy of Eye Filmmuseum/ Corinne de Korver; p 124: Ben Houdijk/Shutterstock; p 125: Courtesy of De L'Europe; p 126: Courtesy of Ambassade; p 130: Courtesy of Anantara Grand Hotel Krasnapolsky; p 131: Courtesy of The Arcade Hotel Amsterdam; p 132, top: Courtesy of BUNK Amsterdam Noord; p 132, bottom: Courtesy of CitizenM Amsterdam South/Jeroen C. van Zijp; p 133, top: Courtesy of The College Hotel Amsterdam/JFilipeWiens; p 133, bottom: Courtesy of De L'Europe/James Stokes; p 134: Courtesy of The Dylan/Roel Ruijs; p 135: Courtesy of Hotel 717; p 136: Courtesy of Mr. Jordaan/Wyatt Kong; p 137: Courtesy of The Pulitzer; p 138: Courtesy of SWEETS Hotel ; p 139: Cat Biggar; p 141, top: Wolf-photography/Shutterstock; p 141, bottom: Cat Biggar; p 142: Cat Biggar; p 143: Cat Biggar; p 145, top: Trabantos/Shutterstock; p 145, bottom: Henk Vrieselaar/Shutterstock; p 147, top: Sergii Figurnyi/Shutterstock; p 147, bottom: Emily Marie Wilson/Shutterstock; p 149: Dmitry Morgan/Shutterstock; p 150, top: Peter de Kievith/Shutterstock.com; p 150, bottom: Dmitry Rukhlenko/Shutterstock; p 151: YASEMIN OZDEMIR/Shutterstock; p 153: Nancy Pauwels/Shutterstock; p 154: Ververidis Vasilis/Shutterstock; p 155, top: Ankor Light/Shutterstock; p 155, bottom: Patrick Herzberg/Shutterstock; p 156, top: Vladimir Zhoga/Shutterstock.com; p 156, bottom: Kiev.Victor/Shutterstock; p 157: Kavalenkava/Shutterstock.com; back cover: Anton Havelaar/Shutterstock.